BEYOND
THEODICY

SUNY series in Theology and Continental Thought
—Douglas L. Donkel, editor

BEYOND THEODICY

Jewish and Christian
Continental Thinkers
Respond to the Holocaust

SARAH KATHERINE PINNOCK

STATE UNIVERSITY OF NEW YORK PRESS

Published by
State University of New York Press, Albany

For information, address State University of New York Press,
90 State Street, Suite 700, Albany, NY 12207

Production by Kelli Williams
Marketing by Anne M. Valentine

Library of Congress Cataloging-in-Publication Data

Pinnock, Sarah Katherine.
    Beyond theodicy: Jewish and Christian continental thinkers respond to
the Holocaust/ by Sarah Katherine Pinnock.
        p. cm.—(SUNY series in theology and continental thought)
    Includes bibliographical references and index.
    ISBN 0–7914–5523–8 (alk. paper)—ISBN 0–7914–5524–6 (pbk.: alk. paper)
    1. Holocaust (Jewish theology) 2. Holocaust (Christian theology) 3. Theodicy.
4. Political science—Philosophy. 5. Existentialism. I. Title. II. Series.

BM645.H6 P56 2002
296.3'118—dc21

                                                                    2002017611

10 9 8 7 6 5 4 3 2 1

CONTENTS

Abbreviations

Note: The date of initial publication is placed in parentheses after the title.

GABRIEL MARCEL

BH	*Being and Having: An Existentialist Diary* (1926–1953)
CF	*Creative Fidelity* (1940)
DW	*The Decline of Wisdom* (1955)
EBHD	*The Existential Background of Human Dignity*, William James Lectures (1961–1962)
HV	*Homo Viator* (1941–1944)
FHW	*Fresh Hope for the World* (1960)
MAH	*Men Against Humanity* (1952)
MJ	*Metaphysical Journal* (1914–1923)
MB I	*Mystery of Being*, Volume I, Gifford Lectures (1949)
MB II	*Mystery of Being*, Volume II (1950)
PE	*Philosophy of Existentialism* (1933–1947)
TWB	*Tragic Wisdom and Beyond* (1973)

MARTIN BUBER

BHT	*A Believing Humanism: My Testament* (1965)
BMM	*Between Man and Man* (1965)
EG	*Eclipse of God* (1952)
FSH	*For the Sake of Heaven* (1945)
GE	*Good and Evil* (1952)
HMM	*Hasidism and Modern Man* (1958)
IT	*I and Thou* (1923)
IW	*Israel and the World* (1948)

LBS	*The Legend of the Baal Shem* (1907)
OJ	*On Judaism* (1967)
OMH	*Origin and Meaning of Hasidism* (1960)
PF	*Prophetic Faith* (1949)
PW	*Pointing the Way: Collected Essays* (1957)
PU	*Paths in Utopia* (1949)
TTF	*Two Types of Faith* (1951)

ERNST BLOCH

AC	*Atheism in Christianity* (1972)
MOHO	*Man on His Own. Essays in the Philosophy of Religion* (1970)
PhF	*A Philosophy of the Future* (1970)
PH	*The Principle of Hope*, Volumes I–III (1959)

JOHANN BAPTIST METZ

AA	*Augen für die Anderen: Lateinamerika, eine Theologische Erfahrung* (1991)
EC	*The Emergent Church* (1980)
FHS	*Faith in History and Society* (1977)
LS	*Landschaft aus Schreien* (1995)
PTE	*Plädoyer für mehr Theodizee-Empfindlichkeit in der Theologie* (1992)
SAN	*A Short Apology of Narrative* (1973)
TT	*Theology as Theodicy?* (1990)
TW	*Theology of the World* (1968)

Preface

Dissatisfaction with theodicy is the passion driving the production of this book. In contemporary Jewish and Christian thought, the rejection of theodicy and the development of post-Holocaust theology are closely intertwined. The image of Auschwitz represents a drastic rupture in historical consciousness and philosophical methodology in response to evil. After Auschwitz, theodicy is exposed as perpetrating amoral justifications of evil and rationalistic caricatures of practical faith struggles.

In charting objections to theodicy, the discussions of major authors have been streamlined for the sake of my argument and that of my intended audience, which includes religion students and nonspecialists as well as colleagues in the fields of religious studies, philosophy, and theology. The broad scope of the book makes it inevitable that the relevant figures, issues, and implications cannot be exhaustively explored or developed. I look forward to future conversations and correspondences about these matters with my readers, and to further publications on the subject.

During work on the manuscript, I was privileged to live the writing life while in residence at Yale University, the University of Hamburg, California State University at Chico, and Trinity University in San Antonio. For four years of generous financial support, I would like to thank the Social Sciences and Humanities Research Council of Canada (SSHRC) doctoral fellowship program. I am grateful to the German Academic Exchange (DAAD) for offering me a fellowship for a full academic year spent in Hamburg, 1997–1998. In addition, I appreciate the summer research stipend that I received from Trinity University during the completion of the manuscript.

This book began as a dissertation in the Department of Religious Studies at Yale University under the direction of Marilyn McCord Adams. For his help and encouragement, Cyril O'Regan deserves special mention. I also wish to acknowledge the Yale faculty members, past and present, who were variously involved in the development and completion of this project: Serene Jones, Kathryn Tanner, Louis Dupré, Jim Dittes, and David Kelsey. While living in Hamburg, I benefited from conversations with Helmut

Peukert, Dorothee Soelle, and Jörg Dierken on existentialist, political, and feminist theology. I extend gratitude to Gérard Vallée, John Robertson, Eileen Schuler, and Travis Kroeker of McMaster University who have encouraged my academic pursuits since my undergraduate days in Canada. Warm thanks go to my parents, Dorothy and Clark, who kindled my interest in religious reflection and have always provided unconditional support.

I dedicate this book to my husband, Nial Eastman. It is hard to avoid clichés in so doing, but I cannot resist publishing the fact that he is of infinite value to me. His intelligence, creativity, patience, and loyalty have contributed very directly and substantially to the completion of the book and the fulfillment of its author.

1 Types of Approaches
to Holocaust Suffering
Practical Responses
as Alternatives to Theodicy

THE TOPIC OF EVIL has been widely discussed in academic as well as popular venues in North America and Europe over the course of the twentieth century. One reason for sustained attention to evil lies in the social and political circumstances of recent history. Contemporary consciousness of evil centers around actual events of massive death and destruction that are seared into the collective cultural memory. In particular, World War I (1914–1918) and World War II (1939–1945) are historic landmarks that are influential in shaping reflection on evil and suffering. The First World War represents massive death and destruction, impacting millions of individuals and many nations. It displayed the inhumanity of purportedly "civilized" persons in the indiscriminate slaughter of artillery bombardment, trench warfare, and the gruesome deaths caused by chemical gas. The Great War was a catalyst for widespread loss of confidence in the modern philosophical and scientific ideas of progress, as well as the moral fiber of political institutions and individuals. The Second World War served to confirm and further intensify awareness of the potential of Western nations for horrendous destructiveness and inhumanity. The name "Auschwitz" has become a symbol for memories of mass-death, the dark side of technological progress, moral failure to help victims of Nazi prejudice, and the misuse of bureaucratic efficiency as a tool of genocide. The testimonies of those who have suffered, particularly victims of the Holocaust, have played a prominent role in contemporary Jewish and Christian reflection on evil.[1] But the horrors of war and genocide are not the only focal points for such reflection. Attention is also given to issues of economic justice and the suffering of citizens of poor nations,

and to cases of social oppression, based on racial, ethnic, or gender prejudice, that occur in both affluent and underdeveloped countries. Another
category of suffering that deserves mention is suffering randomly distributed
among all population groups and classes, where individuals are victims of
disease, crime, abusive treatment, natural disasters, or accidents of various
kinds.

Depending on a person's national, social, geographical, and political situation, different instances of suffering are attended to as paradigmatic horrors. For example, during the last few decades many European and North
American scholars, mainly Jewish and Christian thinkers, have focused on
the Holocaust as a pivotal example of the extreme depth of evil and suffering. For persons living in Latin America, on the other hand, social problems
caused by economic dependency and the legacy of colonization are of major
interest. For African Americans, it is the legacy of slavery and racial prejudice that takes center stage. For a white middle-class American, the threat of
violent gun crimes or incurable diseases, such as malignant cancer, may be
the most pressing issues. It is my thesis that there is a correlation between
the kinds of suffering that are given prominence of place and different types
of intellectual response to evil. In other words, the decision about how to
appropriately respond to evil and suffering, whether in practical or theoretical philosophical mode, is context-dependent.

Within the sociohistorical context of this project, the varieties of response to evil and suffering among philosophers and religious writers are numerous, and the strategies of approach are complex. However, four issues
recur repeatedly and figure prominently in contemporary reflection. The
first two issues are "theoretical" ones concerning: (1) the explanation of the
origin of evil, as a cosmological or anthropological question and (2) the justification of suffering, exposing God's reasons for allowing suffering. In contrast, evil and suffering also raise difficult "practical" issues, namely: (3) how
a person can cope and even find meaning in the face of suffering and (4)
how to alleviate or resist suffering by means of individual or collective action.[2] The dominant academic approaches to evil and suffering primarily address theoretical issues of explanation and justification.

THEORETICAL THEODICY

From classical to contemporary times, theists have investigated the theoretical and conceptual questions raised by evil and suffering. Typically, such discussions are categorized under the subject heading "theodicy," a term whose
etymological roots are the Greek words "God" (*theos*) and "justice" (*dike*).

Among contemporary philosophers, it is widely agreed that the core logical problem of theodicy concerns the apparent incompatibility of the following triad of propositions: (1) God is perfectly good, (2) God is omnipotent, and (3) evil exists.[3] According to common, pre-analytic understandings of God's attributes, it would seem that a perfectly good God would want to eliminate evil as much as possible, while an omnipotent God would have the power to prevent some, or perhaps all, evil occurrences. Within the variety of contemporary approaches, some authors focus on the rebuttal of specific objections to theism, taking a strategy of defense. A "defense" proposes logically possible reasons why God might permit evil. Other thinkers shoulder the explanatory task of developing theories concerning God's policy in permitting evil and seeking God's actual justifying reasons for permitting evil.[4] For the purposes of this project, I propose an inclusive definition of "theodicy" as any approach to the issues of evil and suffering that attempts to explain or justify the relationship between God and evil. Theodicy is a discourse that promotes the rational plausibility of theism, whether in a defensive or explanatory mode.

Although theodicy has generated energetic debate in recent times, the logical conundrum raised by the previous triad of propositions is by no means a recent discovery. It was articulated in ancient Greek philosophy by Epicurus, in Roman times by Platonist philosophers Philo and Plotinus, and again in the fourth century by Saint Augustine. Prominent medieval philosophers such as Anselm and Aquinas advanced theistic discussion of evil with sophisticated proposals for understanding God's goodness and power. What is distinctive in the modern era, from the seventeenth century to the present, is that theodicy discussions of God and evil are increasingly formulated in response to the critical attack of skeptics and atheists. An indicator of this heightened interest in problems of evil is the fact that the term "theodicy" is a neologism, coined by German philosopher G. W. Leibniz in the eighteenth century.[5] Leibniz's *Theodicy* is a key reference point for modern discussions of evil and suffering, especially among contemporary analytic, Anglo-American philosophers, as is Hegel's theodicy among continental philosophers. Leibniz is notorious for making the claim that the universe we live in is the "best possible world" that God could have actualized. He neutralizes the badness of evil by claiming that evil is a necessary component in the overall aesthetic goodness, harmony, and plenitude of the universe as a whole. Already during his lifetime, the optimism of Leibniz's best possible world argument was ridiculed. Notable among his critics is the French writer Voltaire who expressed scathing objections to Leibniz's view in his satirical novel of misfortune *Candide* through the character of the priest Pangloss, and also in response to the cataclysmic Lisbon earthquake of 1755. For

Voltaire and modern philosophers such as David Hume, the issue of evil is a lightning rod for attacks on the rationality of theism.[6]

The theoretical approach of Leibniz, although not without its critics, has influenced recent discussion of theodicy. For example, Leibniz's "best possible world" approach to theodicy is reworked by American analytic philosopher Roderick Chisolm. What interests Chisolm is how evil, which is valued negatively, can contribute to the greater positive value of the universe as a whole.[7] He reasons that a world containing evil may be valued as good as a whole, if good elements in the world can include, within themselves, evil subelements. Just as a painting that contains certain ugly blotches can be judged good because of the way that the blotches contribute to the positive value of the design, so can God's creation be judged as requiring some evil as necessary for its positive value. If this is the case, then the good of the whole can "defeat" evil subelements present in the world, for evil is an inherent part of what is good.

More recently, philosopher Marilyn McCord Adams has criticized Chisolm's best possible world theodicy for justifying evil on a global level because such an approach neglects how God's goodness is actualized for each person. But Adams looks favorably on Chisolm's notion of "defeat" as a way to explain how God can overcome evils experienced by individuals. She asserts that God ensures within the organic unity of each person's life that evils are integrated into an overwhelmingly good whole, which has positive personal meaning. According to Adams, God is able to defeat horrendous evils through numerous means, including direct divine contact with persons and divine participation in suffering. Even the mass killings of Holocaust concentration camps are (purportedly) unable to destroy the positive value of life for any individual, since the process of defeat is accomplished by divine intervention during life and also after death. Adam's theodicy does not explain the reasons why God permits evil, but hinges on the divine guarantee that each person's life is of great good to him or her on the whole.[8]

A different angle on theodicy issues is taken by thinkers who consider human free will as a key justification for evil. Many philosophers consider free will as highly valuable, despite the fact that it opens the possibility of evil deeds committed by human beings. An important contribution to this line of thought, among analytic philosophers, is the "free will defense" proposed by American thinker Alvin Plantinga. Plantinga's defense is intended as a rebuttal to atheist critics who argue that it is impossible that God and evil can coexist in any possible world. These critics suppose that a good, omnipotent, omniscient God would want to prevent evil and be able to do so. To counter this objection to theism, Plantinga's defense aims to show that the existence of evil and the existence of God are logically compossible.[9]

Plantinga proposes that a perfectly good God might have created a world containing evils in order to obtain a good result not attainable in any other way. Plantinga's position hinges on the assumption that human free will and freely chosen good actions are of high value, even though free will opens up the possibility of evil. According to his definition of freedom, a "free act" is an act that is not determined causally in any way by one's genetic makeup, by one's environment, or even by God.[10] Moreover, he holds that every free person is possibly sinful and, therefore, free to choose evil. Given the independence of human freedom from divine control, it is clearly impossible for God to guarantee that persons will always freely choose moral good.[11] Plantinga defends God's permission of evils on the grounds that a world containing a favorable balance of moral good over evil might require the existence of free creatures, hence, the possibility of evil. Nevertheless, such a world would be, arguably, more valuable than a world without free creatures at all.

His defense successfully combats the atheistic accusation that theism is positively irrational on an abstract level. But Plantinga does not give a substantive explanatory account of God's justifying reasons and purposes for creation. He distinguishes his defense from "theodicy" because, according to his definition, theodicy seeks to know the actual reasons why God permits evil, whereas a defense seeks only logically possible reasons. Nevertheless, according to my broader definition of the term, Plantinga's approach is categorized under the rubric of theodicy.

Among recent proposals taking a constructive, explanatory approach, *Evil and the God of Love*, by John Hick, is one of the most influential contributions to theodicy debate.[12] Hick's theodicy offers a teleological explanation for evil that prioritizes the moral and spiritual development of human beings. According to Hick, the world is an environment designed to be conducive to the "soul-making" process: a process of development that builds moral and spiritual maturity.[13] In a world suitable for soul-making, persons are not coerced into moral action or recognition of God, nor are the consequences of evil choices prevented by God. Qualities such as courage, persistence, generosity, compassion, and faith can be developed by individuals, often in the face of suffering and adversity. The world contains numerous evils. Some evils result from deliberate human choices to cause others harm; others are accidents, attributed to human actions or natural forces. In some cases, evils can serve as a means to moral and spiritual growth—for the perpetrator, victim, or bystander—although not all evils advance moral and spiritual development.

A major challenge to Hick's theodicy is the existence of dysteleological evil: evil ruthlessly destructive and damaging to persons, evil that seems disproportionate as punishment for wrongdoing and that obstructs the soul-making process. Accounts of the inmates in Nazi concentration camps illustrate how physical and psychological suffering can debilitate individuals. Hick admits the horror of dysteleological evils. However, he explains it as playing a positive role in an environment that is suitable for soul-making. Such evil serves the function of evoking sympathy for those who suffer, according to Hick, because the purpose of such suffering is a mystery. If we knew that God had created the world so that suffering always serves either to foster spiritual development or as fair punishment for one's actions, we would not have compassion for those who suffer or be motivated to help.[14] Hick's response to dysteleological suffering is an eschatology that posits post-mortem existence. He holds that, in the end, the soul-making process of each individual will reach completion and evil will be totally overcome.

On the whole, philosophers engaged in theodicy debate rework the concept of God, building on the contributions of medieval philosophers in order to propose more subtle analyses of the divine attributes. In particular, attention has centered on the notion of divine omnipotence. For example, in his defense, Plantinga proposes that divine omnipotence does not entail that God can make free human beings choose what is good.[15] Hick takes divine omnipotence to mean that God has the power to guarantee universal fulfillment of each individual's soul-making career, continuing into a post-mortem realm, but not that God can predetermine free choices.

An alternative approach to divine power is formulated by process philosophers, inspired by the metaphysics of twentieth-century American philosopher Alfred North Whitehead. Process thinker Charles Hartshorne ridicules the doctrine of omnipotence as a theological mistake because it implies that God is an absolute monarch or tyrant who is unworthy of worship. He holds that it is metaphysically impossible for God to have a monopoly on power because all creatures have partial self-determining power in cooperation with God. His proposal is that God has persuasive power, which lures creatures toward actualizing what is good, but God does not have the power to prevent evil.[16] Divine omnipotence is also rejected by feminist thinkers, such as Dorothee Soelle and Rosemary Radford Ruether, as a patriarchal ideal that is incongruous with divine love. They prefer to conceive of divine power as cooperative and relational power, immanent in the world.[17] The promise of God's future "Kingdom" or "Reign" represents the redemptive ideal of partnership in community, overcoming the social evils of violence and suffering. Divine power is the power of cooperation, while evil power lies in domination. Evil may be described using biblical imagery as the operation of "fallen powers" that are sociopolitical forces in the material world causing violence and oppression. These powers may be represented as spiritual or demonic forces, as well as collective human forces gone awry.[18]

In the intellectual space of twentieth-century thought, the term "theodicy" has accumulated pejorative connotations among some analytic and continental philosophers. Objections are made to the claims of theodicies to discover the actual or possible justifying reasons why God allows evil. Given the epistemic distance between God and God's finite and comparatively puny creatures, it appears questionable whether these reasons can be comprehended or whether language even represents divine reality.[19] Many thinkers find theodicy distasteful because it appears to connote that God plans or permits horrible suffering for our good. They would prefer to say that we cannot know God's reasons, rather than base their case on an instrumental justification of evil, as Hick does. Other thinkers object to theodicy because it seems that the crucial questions of meaning sparked by apparently meaningless suffering are ignored by global justifying reasons or because theodicy effaces the social causes of suffering and moral resistance. In particular, post-Holocaust thinkers widely reject theodicy as morally scandalous.[20] Questioning the religious appropriateness of theodicy, the following chapters are dedicated to the discussion of objections and alternative practical responses.

CONTINENTAL ALTERNATIVES TO THEODICY

This project takes a distinctive approach to the topic of God and suffering by focusing on continental thinkers who eschew theodicy.[21] Their objections to theodicy target the type of comprehensive philosophical account of God and history offered by G.W.F. Hegel, although these objections also apply to Leibniz and contemporary analytic approaches. The Jewish and Christian thinkers examined in this book belong to the twentieth-century intellectual movements of existentialist and Marxian philosophy. The four central figures studied are existentialist religious thinkers Gabriel Marcel (1889–1973) and Martin Buber (1878–1963) and Marxian-influenced political religious thinkers Ernst Bloch (1885–1977) and Johann Baptist Metz (b. 1928). Buber and Bloch are Jewish, while Marcel and Metz are Roman Catholic. In choosing these authors, I do not intend to imply that they provide a representative cross section of Jewish or Christian responses to evil and suffering. Nor do I claim that they somehow typify existentialist or Marxian schools of thought, which are movements dominated by nonreligious exponents. On the contrary, it must be emphasized that these authors are innovators who forge distinctive philosophical perspectives. In developing a typology of approaches, this project accentuates similarities that extend across the boundaries of Jewish and Christian intellectual traditions. For the authors studied, religious tradition is self-consciously refracted through the prism of philosophical assumptions; thus, there is no simple binary distinction between "Jewish" and "Christian" responses to the Holocaust, which would assume an essentialist reading of each tradition. Rather than focus primarily on the differences between Jewish and Christian responses to evil, as is often the case in comparative studies, I capitalize on strategic points of similarity between the two pairs of Jewish and Christian thinkers with common intellectual influences.[22]

Indeed, it is striking that the differences between the authors from the same religious tradition are so pronounced and far-reaching. Although Jewish thinkers Buber and Bloch both have deep intellectual roots in German philosophy and literature, they portray faith in God very differently. Buber is a scriptural Jewish thinker who turns to the Hebrew Bible and Hasidic Judaism as sources of revelation and models of faith. Bloch identifies himself as an atheist, and his universal vision of utopian hope is inspired by a panorama of literary and philosophical writings. Both Marcel and Metz are Roman Catholic thinkers who appeal to divine mystery to account for the persistence of faith and the absence of theodicy answers. However, Marcel's philosophy concentrates on how individual persons find meaning in suffering through acceptance, and hope in God and immortality. Emphasizing resistance rather than acceptance, Metz analyzes faith "praxis" in response to suffering that centers around memory, solidarity, and political protest. Parallels emerge between the existentialist and political pairs of Jewish and Christian thinkers that reveal shared philosophical perspectives on faith across the boundaries of tradition.

An interreligious approach is particularly apt for discussing responses to the Holocaust that reject theodicy because Jewish-Christian dialogue is a hallmark of post-Holocaust thought. For many Jewish and Christian thinkers, the Holocaust has prompted the rethinking of basic questions concerning God's goodness and redemption. Christian thinkers have confronted theological and historical anti-Semitism and reconsidered the supersessionist connotations of the new covenant in Christ, while Jewish thinkers have re-examined the meaning of the covenant with God, the historical role of the Jewish people, and relations with the Christian churches. On both sides, writers have sought to identify how the Holocaust poses a distinctive challenge to theology. Over the span of the twentieth century, interest in Jewish thought among Christian theologians has increased. A case in point is the sizable impact of Martin Buber and Ernst Bloch on existentialist and political Christian theology, respectively.

The major authors studied in this book are "post-Holocaust" thinkers because they all respond to the Holocaust in their writings. For them, the Holocaust serves as a test case for reflection on evil and suffering. However, they are "early" post-Holocaust thinkers, in the sense that they were formulating their ideas before the bourgeoning publication of memoirs, novels, and historical materials made "Holocaust studies" an academic discipline in its own right. Theological responses centering on the Holocaust as a unique and decisive historical event did not develop widely until the 1970s, in response to broad cultural awareness of the Holocaust and the availability of survivors' writings articulating the scope of Holocaust trauma for faith.[23]

As a project spanning the disciplines of philosophy of religion and theology, this book identifies and analyzes the distinctive features of existentialist and political responses to suffering. My aims are both critical and constructive. I analyze the philosophical assumptions and motivations of each author in rejecting theodicy, while, constructively, I expose and profile two types of "practical" approaches that seek productive engagement with evil and suffering in response to Auschwitz. Further, I examine the legacy of these two practical approaches in the writings of more recent authors who take a "contextual" approach to theology and theodicy issues, employing post-Holocaust, feminist, and liberation perspectives. In moving beyond the four major authors, my reflections will center particularly on practical alternatives to theodicy in the Christian tradition, where the influence of these approaches is apparent.

My work calls attention to practice, although the method of approach taken is more formal than practical. The book traces key currents in the recent intellectual history of continental and contextual Jewish and Christian thought. It explores descriptive and phenomenological accounts of faith postures, such as hope, using selected narrative illustrations to study the application of these postures to the Holocaust and other situations of suffering. Centrally, the aim of my comparative analysis is to create space for practical approaches to grow. The exploration of the pragmatic resources of faith in coping with suffering is a neglected task, especially among many contemporary philosophers of religion. Yet, in my view, the discovery of practical religious meaning is more significant than exploring the logical coherence of theodicy in response to testimonies of persons facing actual evil and suffering. This conclusion is supported by contemporary post-Holocaust thinkers who view theodicy as neither productive nor necessary for a faith response to suffering.[24]

In the academy, whether practical or theodicy approaches are the focus of intellectual labor is a decision that reflects the scholar's interests and social location, as well as the interests of readers who make such publications viable.[25] My scholarly work on the problem of evil exhibits special interest in post-Holocaust, feminist, and liberation thought where issues of responsibility and justice converge. I promote a practical focus motivated by concern for those who suffer, particularly due to social causes, and also by the desire to explore the ethical potential of faith to respond to suffering. My engagement with evil and suffering is spurred by historical and political consciousness more than by personal struggle with evil and suffering. As an American and Canadian dual citizen who grew up in a white middle-class Protestant family, I recognize that I have been protected from the impact of evil and suffering in numerous ways by my social location.

Reflecting on my response to the Holocaust, I have often pondered the expression *"die Gnade der späten Geburt"* [the mercy of late birth] and its moral significance in relation to my own birth. This issue came to the fore especially during the year I spent in Hamburg, where I studied German responses to Auschwitz and visited many historic sites connected with the Nazi era. This popular catchphrase, coined by former Chancellor of Germany Helmut Kohl, appears in the media in reference to more recent generations of Germans who bear no responsibility for the Holocaust on account of their youth. In a political context, the phrase implies the desire to let go of the Nazi past and rejuvenate German national consciousness.[26] However, I find myself unable to identify with the sense that it is by "grace" or "mercy" that I am not morally implicated in the events of the Holocaust, even though I am not German. In my case, it is not only my age, but also my nationality and religion that protect me merely by chance from responsibility as a Christian bystander to genocide. If I had lived in Germany during the Third Reich, statistically speaking, I likely would not have resisted the persecution and deportation of Jews. Moreover, in the present, I am also protected by "grace" or chance on a local and global level. My social position has enabled me to benefit from a broad and tangled web of situational factors, such as white privilege, Christian hegemony, higher education, economic comfort, the struggles of the women's movement, international sweatshop labor, and American dominance in global affairs.

Yet my luck of birth does not remove me from the Holocaust or other social and historical injustices. Although I am "late-born," I recognize a strong sense of continuity with Holocaust-era Christians that troubles me very much. I am appalled when I reflect on Christian anti-Semitism throughout the first two millennia of Christendom. I want to think that Christian faith would motivate widespread resistance against suffering and evil perpetrated against the Jews and others, but it often does not. In fact, the opposite is true; faith often justifies exclusion and prejudice. I would also like to think that faith in God helps persons who suffer to survive and combat the causes of suffering, whether during the Holocaust or today. Sometimes it does help, although not always. Drawing on Jewish and Christian writers, this book explores how faith helps victims respond constructively to suffering. Contrary to what many philosophers assume, coping with suffering does not require discovering answers that explain why God allows evil. The widespread rejection of theodicy among post-Holocaust Jewish and Christian thinkers, extending far beyond the group of authors studied in this book, convinces me that there is need for attention to alternative practical faith responses.

It is intriguing to me that Jewish and Christian existentialist and political approaches reject theodicy, despite major differences in their philosophical assumptions. But despite this opposition, it is important to recognize a formal similarity between theodicy and its alternatives. As religious discourses in response to suffering and evil, theodicy and practical approaches perform the same basic function: the task of making faith plausible, although not necessarily in theoretical, propositional, or doctrinal terms. Sociologist of religion Peter Berger observes that theoretical theodicy functions as a support for religious faith against the disruption of suffering that tears the "sacred canopy" of Jewish and Christian belief in a good Creator God.[27] This canopy is the articulation of a world-order affirming God as the good, loving, and just ruler of history. Theodicy is "theocentric" in orientation, in the sense that it attempts to stop the gaps in knowledge of God and God's acts, making it plausible that theistic beliefs are true. According to my definition, "theodicy" is any discourse that attempts to explain or justify God's reasons for permitting evil and suffering.

Alongside the logical conundrums it raises, evil may also provoke a crisis of identity and meaning for the person who believes in God.[28] It is possible to reject theodicy and yet affirm that suffering can be made meaningful without explanation of God's ways. On an individual and a social level, religious attitudes and patterns of action can be resources for constructive engagement in the struggle with suffering. In contrast with theodicy, practice-oriented approaches to evil, such as those offered by existentialist and political philosophers, are "anthropocentric" because they display how faith is a plausible response to coping with evil by showing the pragmatic resources of belief in God.

Existentialist and political thinkers propose two types of practical response to suffering, and to the Holocaust in particular.[29] The term "practical" is not meant to imply that existentialist and political thinkers do not make any theoretical or philosophical claims whatsoever. They indeed do so in developing original philosophical methods to discuss intersubjectivity, morality, evil, and faith in God. However, they do not develop detailed theoretical-conceptual positions about God's attributes or God's activity, nor do they attempt to explain or justify evil globally by proposing actual or possible reasons. The Holocaust is not rationalized as instrumental for God's purposes, but is approached practically from the position of survivors who seek to find productive responses to suffering.[30] They tackle the topic of God and evil by focusing on concrete evil: evil experienced as suffering affecting persons.

The meaning of "suffering" is, most basically, to endure harm. Suffering extends beyond bodily pain to include psychological, social, and spiritual symptoms of distress, such as grief, trauma, depression, isolation, or despair. In response to the Holocaust, practical alternatives to theodicy focus principally on suffering rather than evil. As a result, they tend to assume the perspective of victims rather than perpetrators, although the study of perpetrators' faith attitudes is also a potential avenue for practical investigation.

Existentialist and political approaches have different philosophical assumptions about the main features of faith, and from these models of faith follow distinctive accounts of how faith responds to suffering. Their philosophical assumptions also influence what kinds of suffering are given primary attention. It is my thesis that there are correlations between philosophical method, models of faith practice, and the examples of suffering chosen as paradigmatic.

For existentialist and political thinkers, two practices in response to suffering receive the most attention: (1) the religious posture of hope and (2) the posture of "other-regard." It will become clear that there are different versions of Jewish and Christian hope in God, although the thinkers are united in distinguishing hope from sheer optimism. Moreover, for the thinkers studied, attention to others who suffer is alternately individual or collective in focus. More recently, contextual political and liberation theologians have been formulating practical approaches to suffering, calling attention to persons who suffer injustice or oppression.[31] Existentialist and political approaches offer philosophical precedents for these contextual theologies by their methods of situating evil in terms of relational or socioeconomic realities and by their portrayals of faith as alternately accepting and resisting suffering.[32]

KANT'S PRACTICAL TURN

The philosopher who sets a precedent for practical twentieth-century existentialist and political responses to suffering is Immanuel Kant (1724–1804). In particular, three elements of Kant's approach are influential: his rejection of speculative knowledge of God, his view that faith in God is a necessary postulate of morality, and his dismissal of theodicy.

To understand Kant's negative verdict on theodicy, it is important to appreciate the crucial distinction that Kant makes between "pure" and "practical" reason. Kant's philosophy as a whole is motivated by dissatisfaction with two major philosophical options of his time: the skeptical empiricism of David Hume and the rationalist metaphysics of Leibniz and his followers. On the one hand, Kant rejects Hume's empiricist view that ideas are "mental pictures" derived solely from sensory impressions, and he opposes Hume's skeptical denial that scientists can have knowledge of the truth concerning reality.[33] Nevertheless, Kant takes seriously Hume's sharp critique of Leibniz's rationalist metaphysics, which uses logical deduction from *a priori* principles to obtain knowledge of the truth about reality. Kant ridicules this speculative approach as theoretical web spinning that oversteps the limits of human reason and produces illusory knowledge.[34]

Kant responds to the challenge of skepticism using a divide-and-conquer strategy. He defends the truth of scientific knowledge gained through the use of theoretical reason, but he modestly concedes that we have no theoretical knowledge concerning morality and religion, which he assigns to the practical realm. In the first tome of his mature philosophy, the *Critique of Pure Reason*, Kant meticulously delineates the capacities and limitations of pure speculative reason. In his terms, pure reason studies the realm of *phenomena*, which include objects directly perceived by the senses and entities observable only through their effects, such as atoms or distant planets. The employment of pure reason produces theoretical knowledge of *phenomena* investigated in physics, chemistry, biology, empirical psychology, and other sciences. According to Kant, knowledge of *phenomena* is produced by means of *a priori* structuring principles, known as the "categories," that synthesize the raw intuitions gathered by the senses. The categories are principles of order and relation among *phenomena*, for example, space, time, causality, and substance. All human experience of *phenomena* necessarily involves the application of the categories.[35]

By identifying the subject matter of science as *phenomena*, which, by definition, are epistemically accessible because they are the product of the mind's activity in organizing intuitions, Kant protects the truth of scientific knowledge from skeptical objections. However, Kant concedes to the skeptic (contra Leibniz) that reason cannot obtain *a priori* knowledge of the truth of reality as it is independent of human experience. It is impossible to know "things in themselves," which Kant refers to as *noumena*, because scientific reason cannot bypass the mediation of the categories to access reality.[36]

Given that theoretical knowledge is limited to *phenomena*, it is not surprising to discover that the truth about important ultimate questions, such as questions of religion or morality, cannot be discovered. For example, pure reason cannot adjudicate whether the world has a divine First Cause, nor can it know whether human beings have freedom from the causal laws governing nature. Specifically, Kant identifies four antinomies of metaphysics that are insoluble, where the poles of each antinomy are the positions taken by rationalist and skeptical philosophers, respectively. The antinomies run as follows: (1) The world has a beginning, or it is infinite. (2) Substances are composed of simple parts, or they are not. (3) There is dual causality of nature and freedom, or solely natural causality. (4) There is a necessary being (God), or there is none. Although the antinomy of God's existence is insoluble, Kant proposes that the idea of God can serve as a heuristic device to encourage scientists to pursue progress in knowledge of *phenomena*. Scientific investigators operate *as if* there is a God, who is the single, supreme, intelligent Author of the world, when they presume that nature will display regularity and order, but Kant does not consider it strictly necessary for scientists to believe in God. In contrast, Kant holds belief in God (and freedom and immortality) to be a necessity for human beings exercising moral reason, as we will see shortly.[37]

Kant takes pains to expose the illusions of pure reason in claiming to prove God's existence. Kant dismisses the *a priori* proof of speculative ontotheology, put forward by Leibniz and other rationalist philosophers, because it illegitimately deduces from the definition of God as *ens realissimum* (most real being) that God is necessarily existent. Kant responds that existence is not a predicate: to say that a thing "is" does not add to the concept of a thing, hence, God's existence is not entailed by the concept of the most real being. Moreover, Kant condemns the proof of cosmotheology, which traces the sequence of causes in the universe backwards, jumping to the unwarranted conclusion that there is necessarily a First Cause. And third, Kant dismisses the proof of physicotheology, which demonstrates God's existence as Creator based on the appearance of order in the world.

For Kant, there can be no knowledge or proof of God by means of theoretical reason because God is not a *phenomenon* bounded by space, time, and causality. Kant upholds a central intuition of Jewish and Christian faith in affirming that God is immaterial, invisible and spiritual, transcending all objects and finite beings.[38] He concludes that God belongs to a nonphenomenal plane of reality, which he calls the noumenal realm. God's distinctive ontological status accounts for the epistemic impossibility of theoretical knowledge of God.

It is important to note that Kant considers absence of knowledge of God, not as detrimental, but as a positive advantage for morality. In fact, Kant sees fit to boast that "I have found it necessary to deny *knowledge* [of God], in order to make room for *faith*."[39] Proof of God's existence would create intellectual coercion and negate the possibility of rational and autonomous moral choice. Knowledge that God rewards and punishes human actions would make persons unable to freely will the good for its own sake. Instead, motivation to do good would be based on fear or hope for reward, not on the self-legislation of practical reason.

In the *Critique of Practical Reason*, Kant identifies three aspects of the noumenal realm: God, freedom and immortality.[40] We may well wonder how anything can be said about *noumena* if this realm is inaccessible to theoretical knowledge. Kant responds with the assertion that it is legitimate to make conjectures or "practical postulates" concerning *noumena* based on what practical reason discovers to be the necessary conditions for morality.

Concerning the postulate of freedom, Kant holds that freedom is necessary for moral choices. He asserts that the moral question, What should I do? implies that human beings have the capacity to guide their actions in accordance with self-imposed rational principles. In other words, moral agents act as if they can make rational choices. For the moral outlook to be rational, according to Kant, the human agent must postulate freedom of the will: freedom is a condition of the possibility of morality. Freedom is impossible in the realm of *phenomena*, is governed by deterministic laws of cause and effect, such as the laws of Newtonian mechanics. However, Kant asserts that freedom is possible in the noumenal realm. Kant conceives of human persons as belonging to two realms: as moral agents they recognize themselves as free, but as physical beings they exist as *phenomena* in nature.[41]

The idea of immortality is a necessary postulate of practical reason because, Kant argues, it is rational to will the good only if one believes that it is possible to achieve moral virtue and move progressively toward moral perfection (the *summum bonum*). Practical reason demands moral justice, and justice requires faith that, sometime in the future, happiness will be proportioned to moral virtue. Kant does not envision this moral *telos* occurring in history, as utopian Marxian thinkers would insist. Rather, morality necessitates that we posit the immortality of the soul in the noumenal realm. It is clear that moral hope for justice is not supported by knowledge of *phenomena*, for virtue and happiness are not fairly proportioned in this world, as the book of Job illustrates. Instead, hope requires that the laws governing the realm of nature, indifferent to justice, will eventually be overturned.[42]

Faith in God is a third practical postulate necessary for morality.[43] Moral hope looks toward future justice. But only God can complete the teleology of moral hope, rewarding moral virtue with happiness and harmonizing the order of freedom (*noumena*) and the order of nature (*phenomena*). As a practical postulate, Kant holds that the idea of God should be formulated according to the needs of morality, not the needs of scientific reason.[44] Kant depicts the God posited by practical reason as having the following key attributes: holy lawgiver, good provider of happiness, and just judge of moral actions.[45] God's holiness, goodness, and justice account for why God would want to proportion happiness to virtue. Morality also requires that God have knowledge of all human deeds, the wisdom to judge them, and the power to harmonize virtue and happiness. Kant develops the practical postulate of God in a fair amount of detail. Nevertheless, he remarks modestly that "we have only obscure and ambiguous view into the future; the Governor of the world allows us only to conjecture his existence and majesty, not to behold or clearly prove them."[46] We can have no theoretical expectations of God based on scientific prediction, only practical hopes. But although we lack knowledge of God, it is wrong to assume that moral faith is therefore tentative. According to Kant, the requirements of morality are a very firm basis for positing God's reality and God's morally necessary attributes.

FROM THEORETICAL THEODICY TO PRACTICAL FAITH

Kant's polemical essay entitled "On the Miscarriage of All Philosophical Trials in Theodicy" opens up a new vista of religious response to suffering. Kant defines theodicy as "the defense of the wisdom of God against the tribunal of human reason."[47] Given the limits of pure reason, Kant obviously considers "speculative" theodicy impossible. But he acknowledges that the regulative, moral idea of God raises theodicy conundrums, and he thinks that it is worthwhile to articulate them. Kant identifies physical evil (pain) and moral evil (sin or crime) as aspects of reality that appear contrary to divine and human purpose. The main issue of theodicy for Kant is not the question of why human beings do evil, for he is convinced that the human will is prone to weakness and corruption.[48] Rather, the urgent issue for Kant concerns the nonappearance of justice and purposiveness in the world, and the disappointment of hope. Moral faith demands a teleology ending in moral perfection and the just proportioning of virtue and happiness. However, in the natural order there is no correlation between good deeds and reward or between evil deeds and punishment. Kant's major concern is the unfair distribution of suffering, or unhappiness, irrespective of moral virtue. After testing various avenues of accounting for God's reasons for evil, Kant concludes that theodicies based on moral reason's concept of God are inconclusive; they fail to untie the theodicy knot and reconcile evil with the wisdom of the Creator.

After exposing the failure of theodicy, Kant heatedly argues that theodicy is, in fact, an inappropriate type of faith response to evil and suffering. In contrast, he showcases the book of Job as providing an "authentic" religious response to evil. Kant approves of Job's dismissal of the advice of his friends as neither comforting nor intellectually compelling. Job's suffering cannot be explained rationally as fair punishment for sin, as his friends suggest. Nor should Job's protest cease on the basis of his friends' assurance that God will compensate him for his goodness later in his lifetime. According to Kant, Job's frankness makes him the perfect model of an individual with authentic faith in God. Kant points to two features of Job's response as exemplary: honesty in the avowal of the powerlessness of reason, and sincerity in the expression of his thoughts.[49] Honesty indicates recognition of the limitations of knowledge in the face of divine mystery; sincerity involves admitting that the situation of unjust suffering is deeply scandalous to moral consciousness. These practical postures are accompanied by lament for suffering and protest against the world's injustice. Job posits a God who will respond to his prayers and bring justice, thus meeting the demands of Job's moral sensitivity. Job frankly admits that God's goodness and justice are hidden in his own experience of the physical world. As exemplified by Job, Kant shows that faith is compatible with protest—indeed faith *requires* protest concerning the unfair distribution of suffering caused by moral evil or natural forces. Because moral hope is always unfulfilled, faith stands in tension with the reality of human experience. For Job and all persons who suffer, future justice is not an item of knowledge but of faith. In the following chapters, the analysis of existentialist and political responses to suffering reveals that the themes of hope and protest, found in Kant's analysis of Job, are prominent alongside rejection of theodicy.[50]

HEGEL'S HUBRIS: THEODICY REVIVED

Crediting Kant's objections to theodicy would imply both the rejection of Leibniz's theodicy and more recent theodicies such as the one proposed by Georg Wilhelm Friedrich Hegel (1770–1831). Hegel's contribution is important not only because of his prominence in the tradition of German philosophy after Kant, but because he formulates the epitome of a philosophical discourse that is self-consciously offered as a theodicy. A striking feature of Hegel's philosophy is his bold rejection of the limits that Kant places on speculative reason. Eschewing Kantian epistemic modesty, Hegel asserts that reason can comprehend the idea of God and the internal logic of history from beginning to end. In explicit defiance of Kant, Hegel revives speculative metaphysics and speculative theology. He replaces Kantian moral faith in God with knowledge of God, and he substitutes Kantian hope for divine justice with absolute knowledge of future justice.

For the purposes of this project, the crucial feature of Hegel's philosophy of history is the fact that it functions as a theodicy that justifies all human suffering. According to Hegel, history is ordered in progressive stages that build on one other. Every event in history is necessary for progress. Hegel asserts that developments in history follow a logical pattern. Forward movement occurs by means of dialectical cycles involving conflict, contradiction, and the overcoming (*Aufhebung*) of oppositions. He claims that each dialectical cycle improves on former stages, capitalizing on the strengths of the past and overcoming its weaknesses and inadequacies, which Hegel terms moments of "negativity." Hegel locates human suffering on the negative side of the dialectical movement of history.[51]

Hegel identifies the dialectic of history with the self-development of Spirit (*Geist*), where "Spirit" is defined as the sum of human consciousness and its products, including all aspects of culture and civilization. Consciousness, or Spirit, realizes itself in and through matter and human life. Over the course of history, humanity gradually gains knowledge of the world and is able to shape material conditions into increasingly rational social forms. Since all human activities are sites of Spirit's self-development, the dialectical stages of progress in history show parallel advances in all spheres of life: political and social institutions, scientific knowledge, fine art, and religion.[52] However, Spirit is not merely the name for developing collective human consciousness, for Hegel identifies Spirit with the Christian God. History operates according to a rational pattern because history is the self-movement of God. The final *telos* of history is the Absolute: the end of history is the high point of self-conscious rationality manifest in human individuals and groups, and the total manifestation of God in the world.

Although some interpreters sidestep the religious dimension of his philosophy, Hegel clearly considers his dialectic of history to be a theistic teleology and, thus, a theodicy. His theodicy rests on the claim that history is, in fact, the narrative of God's own self-development. Hegel draws on Lutheran theology to elaborate his understanding of history as the Trinitarian, relational movement of God as Father, Son, and Spirit.[53] Creation is understood as the process through which the aseity of God's self-sufficient Being becomes manifest or, to use theological vocabulary, "incarnate" in the physical world. According to Hegel, the second person of the Trinity, God's Son, is the Logos who goes forth from God and becomes actual in the world. Hegel adapts Luther's dramatic depiction of Christ's crucifixion as the "death of God"—a phrase that expresses the estrangement between God manifest in human life as Spirit and God's absolute Being. According to Hegel, creation and incarnation represent the "othering" or "emptying" (*kenosis*) of God and, at the same time, the manifestation of God in human life. Even what is fragile, finite, and weak, the "negative" in history, is a moment of the divine and found within God. Hence, God suffers in history.[54]

In contrast with free will theodicies that circumvent divine responsibility for evil by blaming human freedom for the existence of evil, Hegel boldly affirms that God's self encompasses evil and negativity. God is not responsible for evil in the sense that God decides to allow evil and was free to do otherwise. Hegel rejects a voluntaristic notion of divine freedom. Rather, God is implicated in evil because history itself is God's history.

To overcome divine self-estrangement and the estrangement of the world from God, individual self-consciousness or spirit must become aware of its status as the manifestation of God's Spirit. Spirit's self-consciousness, displayed in human life, unites Father and Son (God and creation) and the whole human community together in mutual love. The climax and *telos* of history (the Absolute) occurs when Spirit becomes fully manifest in creation and global unity and harmony encompass God, nature, and humanity. Theologically speaking, history's path as a whole can be termed "the movement of divine Providence" because history is God's self-realization in the world. The end of history, for Hegel, is equivalent to the Christian ideas of the "Kingdom of God" and "salvation," which indicate the reconciliation of God and creation.[55]

The final goal of Spirit in history is clearly utopian and ideal in character. Hence, it is remarkable to discover that Hegel locates the ultimate self-realization of Spirit not in the future, but in his own era.[56] Hegel praises Protestant Christianity as the highest religion, constitutional monarchy in Prussia as the most rational form of state government, and his own philosophy as the highest stage of Spirit's realization.[57] Indeed, Hegel's warrant for claiming complete knowledge of God and history rests on his claim to have found an Archimedean place of leverage from which to judge the world. Hegel's philosophy can comprehend the whole because it evaluates history from the perspective of its end, an absolute vantage point.

Hegel's justification of suffering in history takes two forms: instrumental and holistic. Instrumental justification makes suffering a necessary means to achieving the Absolute. The value of the end goal confers value on each of the steps required to reach it. It is also important to recognize Hegel's justification of suffering as holistic.[58] Hegel confers value on suffering by his claim that each step in history is the highest manifestation of God's Providence thus far. Each stage has inherent divine worth in itself and not only value as a means to an end. The framework for Hegel's holistic justification is unequivocally theistic and Trinitarian. The weakness of instrumental justification is the fact that the worth of the historical process is conferred retrospectively only if and when the end is achieved, while the victims of history are merely used as instruments of global progress. Moreover, the global sweep of Hegel's holistic justification also fails to address adequately the position of the victim. Hegel's claim that God's history is the justification for human history (and suffering) does not take into account issues of meaning and justice for individuals who are the "debris" left in the wake of progress. However, God's involvement in history opens the possibility that suffering might somehow have value for victims—for example, if persons were to view their suffering as part of God's history or if they could experience God's presence in suffering.[59]

HEGEL AS PROTOTYPICAL TARGET OF CRITIQUE

It is not difficult to perceive how Hegel's philosophy offers a theodicy of ultimate comprehensiveness. Without apparent scruples, he brazenly justifies the suffering of individuals and groups as part of the alienation and frustration necessary for the positive dialectical developmental process of history. Although it may seem that Hegel is insensitive to suffering, it is a misunderstanding to conclude that Hegel underestimates its horror.[60] On the contrary, he speaks of history as a "slaughter bench" where individuals and groups are sacrificed. Clearly, he recognizes the magnitude of suffering. Nevertheless, Hegel's theory of history justifies and valorizes suffering by mapping all events, even the most horrendous, as points on a continuum of progress. For example, war is legitimated retroactively, serving as a "motor" of history, destroying old civilizations to make way for new ones. Large-scale destruction is only apparently meaningless.

Hegel's system serves as a model for what theodicy aims to accomplish. The following general marks or features of theistic theodicy can be extrapolated from his proposal: (1) theodicy claims knowledge of God and God's acts in history, (2) it holds that there is good reason for suffering, and (3) it rationalizes suffering as unavoidable or necessary. With the knowledge that evil is overcome, hope becomes redundant, and protest irrational. Protest is merely a sign of one's ignorance of God's plan in which suffering is necessary to serve a good end. Critics of theodicy, among them existentialist and political religious thinkers, assert that theodicy legitimizes suffering and that it undermines protest and resistance.

In analyzing objections and alternatives to theodicy in the following chapters, I will begin with the consideration of existentialist approaches. Chapter 2 studies French Roman Catholic phenomenologist Gabriel Marcel, focusing on his attention to "evil experienced," or suffering, and the practical religious responses of hope and fidelity to other persons. Chapter 3 examines German Jewish philosopher Martin Buber, who points to a transcendent dimension in I-Thou relations that gives meaning to suffering shared in community. Chapter 4 makes a transition to Marxian approaches with their distinctive approach to suffering as a socioeconomic phenomenon, while the following two chapters are devoted to analysis of political religious approaches. Chapter 5 centers on Jewish Marxian thinker Ernst Bloch and the influence of his utopian interpretation of hope on the political theology of Jürgen Moltmann, and chapter 6 studies Roman Catholic theologian Johann Baptist Metz and his account of how memory and narrative ground hope and solidarity.

The concluding chapters evaluate the two types of practical response to suffering, contrasting their placement of suffering and their depictions of the practices of hope and other-regard. Chapter 7 argues that both approaches are limited in the scope of faith resources they draw on to formulate a religious response to suffering. However, the political approach is judged to be most promising because of its recognition of the social context of suffering and the importance of resistance. I will test the capacity of the political paradigm to take up key existentialist insights by an examination of recent contextual, post-Holocaust, and liberation theologies among (mainly) Christian theologians who have been influenced by continental thinkers. The final chapter assesses the appropriateness of theodicy in light of the philosophical objections raised. Based on my philosophical commitments and instructed by the critiques and proposals offered by existentialist and political thinkers, I propose four guidelines for contemporary philosophical and religious responses to suffering that point the way beyond the inadequacies of theodicy.

2 Existential Encounter with Evil

Gabriel Marcel's Response to Suffering as a Trial

EXISTENTIALIST THOUGHT IS A branch of continental philosophy that rose to prominence in the turbulent decades following World War I. Major representatives of the movement are Karl Jaspers, Martin Heidegger, Gabriel Marcel, Jean-Paul Sartre, Martin Buber, and Albert Camus. Despite the popular characterization of existentialist philosophers as atheists, a number of existentialist thinkers consider religious faith as an indispensable, positive element of human existence.[1] Among existentialists, the divide between atheism and faith reflects the contradictory and independent influences of two nineteenth-century forerunners of existentialism—Soren Kierkegaard and Friedrich Nietzsche. Both are iconoclastic figures noted for their scathing criticisms of all philosophical systems, ancient or modern, that claim a standpoint of truth independent from the contingencies of existence. Taking up Kierkegaard's attack on Hegel's system in particular, existentialist thinkers ridicule Hegel and other philosophers who purport to have discovered an absolute standpoint of objective knowledge on which to build a theory of God, world, and history.

Existentialist thinkers view human history as an arena of risk, where human persons are burdened with the freedom to determine the purpose and meaning of one's individual existence. The existentialist vision gives a sober and even pessimistic portrait of human life. As a response to uncertainty and threat, existentialist thinkers seek constructive responses to life's challenges. They recommend that the individual discover postures of "authentic" existence, defined by self-consciousness of the possibilities and risks of freedom and willingness to take the heroic leap of choosing to actualize certain possibilities.[2] The authentic subject is not a conformist individual, but someone with the courage to accept the burden of responsibility. Literature is used to illustrate existential postures in context, and a number of existentialist thinkers like Sartre, Camus, and Marcel write literary fiction as well as philosophy.

In existentialist thought, the story of Sisyphus, taken from Greek mythology, has become a symbol of human authenticity and fortitude in the face of suffering. As is well known, Sisyphus is condemned by the gods to roll a giant stone up a hill repeatedly. He never reaches the summit, for near the top he loses hold of the rock, which rolls down to the starting-point, where Sisyphus once again resumes his efforts. What is admirable about Sisyphus is that he is lucid about the futility of the quest, but he continues trying. The moral of his story is that courageous persistence is the mark of authentic, satisfying existence. As Camus puts it: "The struggle itself toward the heights is enough to fill a man's heart. One must imagine Sisyphus happy."[3] Camus considers Sisyphus's task as symbolic of the human situation where happiness should not depend on achieving the ultimate goal, but on fierce dedication to striving. Sartre rephrases the message of Sisyphus's story in his well-known statement that the individual is "condemned to freedom." Human freedom involves endless struggle and suffering, which can be chosen with dignity or succumbed to in despair.[4]

Among religious existentialists, there is also an emphasis on struggle, courage, and freedom, but the conditions of authentic existence include recognizing one's relation to God. The ethical anthropology of Protestant thinkers Paul Tillich or Rudolf Bultmann, for example, takes the biblical myth of the Fall as a descent into "inauthentic" existence where humans become estranged from God and from mirroring God's image. Religious existentialists affirm that the individual is free, but they consider God to be the source of the possibility of this freedom. Marcel and Buber are distinctive in defining authentic existence as participation in relation with others.[5] Both of them consider authentic relation implicitly religious as it manifests love for others and explicitly religious as it manifests the reality of God in relation. Marcel's phenomenological approach is a philosophical method that is religious, in the sense that it takes faith in God as a fundamental datum of experience. Marcel is not an apologist for faith in God, nor does he expound upon Christian doctrine as a Roman Catholic theologian.[6] Rather, his philosophy analyzes the existential attitudes and postures taken by persons of faith, found in actual life situations. Marcel wrote many plays for the theater that extend his philosophical reflection. He emphasizes that stories from his dramas are indispensable in giving the central elements of authentic existence concrete bearing. To distinguish himself from atheistic existentialist thinkers, Marcel has termed his method a "philosophy of existence" rather than "existentialist" philosophy because the latter is heavily identified with Marcel's atheist archrival Jean-Paul Sartre (PE 47).

Marcel's approach to the issue of suffering has practical motivations. It is not evil as a global reality that concerns Marcel, but evil manifest as human suffering. His rejection of theodicy is Kantian in two respects: he dismisses theodicy as a speculative metaphysical system-building enterprise, and he moves the religious problem of evil and suffering to the moral ground of action and practice. Marcel takes a tragic view of existence. Suffering is viewed as resulting from pride and weakness, the vulnerability of the human body, the fragility of human relationships, and the risk that love will be shattered by loss. What interests Marcel are two distinct kinds of encounter with suffering: the challenge of coping with my own suffering, and my response to the suffering of others. The myth of Sisyphus addresses how the individual can be strong in the face of one's own suffering. Alternately, the character of Tarrou in Camus' well-known novel *The Plague* provides an existentialist model for responding to others' suffering. Tarrou altruistically devotes himself to helping persons who are sick and dying. However, his choice to do so is framed as arbitrary, undertaken (like the task of Sisyphus) within an absurd and purposeless world.[7] In contrast, Marcel's response to suffering points toward religious meaning found in interpersonal bonds of love, fidelity, and transcendent hope, which manifest God's reality.

PROBLEM AND MYSTERY IN PHILOSOPHY

Marcel sets up a dichotomy between alternatives representing two modes of living and two modes of thinking, designated by the contrast between "having" and "being," and the categories of "problem" and "mystery."[8]

Objective approaches in philosophy, economics, social sciences, laboratory research, and engineering have in common the study of the human subject and human environment from a third-person standpoint. They take a "problem-solving" approach that requires seeing the world with what Marcel calls an attitude of "having," which frames whatever I see or sense as a thing or object apart from the self (BH 158). To investigate what this attitude entails, Marcel analyzes what is meant when I speak the sentence, "I have x." "Having" implies that "x" is subject to my gaze; it is an object that I observe with detachment and appraisal. When a person takes the attitude of "having," they are in a position to enumerate a thing's characteristics and evaluate them. When "I have x," the object is a thing potentially or literally under my control. The object "x" is valued in terms of its function or use in the natural or human world (BH 163). If "x" is a human being, then "to have x" is to depersonalize the other and view the other as my property or my instrument. The attitude of "having" operates within what Kant calls the phenomenal realm made up of objects detected by the senses in space and time, and it is not coincidental that, like Kant, Marcel is keen to show the limited scope and application of knowledge gained by scientific-style observation of phenomena.[9] According to Marcel, the posture of "having" is found in the natural and social sciences, economics, politics, engineering, and research in technology. He does not take into account that certain theoretical branches of the natural sciences do not study objects as things to be manipulated for human "disposal" or use—for example, astrophysical research on sunspots or distant planets. But he would argue that even in such theoretical investigations, researchers presuppose that the knowledge gained may have technological usefulness in the future.

The sciences and certain branches of philosophy use a method Marcel terms the "problem" approach. Problem solving employs the following five assumptions and procedures. (1) The objects, data, or ideas that it treats are viewed as detached (artificially) from the investigator's experience, as objects over and against the subject. (2) Correspondingly, the thinking subject operates as (purportedly) an anonymous and neutral observer—that is, a purely epistemological subject. (3) The material of the problem is broken down into discrete subproblems for study. (4) It is assumed that human rational abilities are commensurate to the problem. (5) A definite solution is expected (MB I 83).[10] Marcel insists that the problem-solving approach should be criticized because it presupposes a paradigm of detached subject-object relations, because of its pervasively nonholistic approach to phenomena, and because of its bold and questionable assumption that human abilities are capable of producing a precise, decisive answer.

It must be noted that, despite this critique, Marcel does not consider the problem-solving approach to be illegitimate. It is unavoidable that, at times, the perspective of "having" does predominate, not only in regard to scientific endeavors, but also in everyday living. He also acknowledges that the individual can take a scientific view of one's self, and not only of other persons. Marcel even accepts the attitude of "having" and the procedures of "problem solving" as appropriate for the fields of technology, business, or social planning. But he vehemently insists that authentic or genuine relation to other persons, which bears moral and religious significance, requires that "having" and "problem solving" be superseded by a new perspective (CF 145).[11]

Marcel's work is intended as a corrective to mainstream modern philosophy that takes up a spectator point of view toward reality. The assumption that the epistemic subject is a solitary thinker, articulated most famously by Descartes, is considered by Marcel a fundamental misreading of the human condition. Marcel rejects the Cartesian view of the world as a composite of material bodies or objects, apart from the thinking immaterial self. Marcel is at odds with Sartre for portraying the human subject in a Cartesian manner as a solitary individual in conflict with other persons, who pose a threat to the self's freedom. Instead of viewing relations to other persons as a necessary evil, as Sartre does, Marcel's existentialist approach views persons as inextricably linked to each other by bonds of love and loyalty, whether or not this reciprocity among subjects is acknowledged or appreciated.

Marcel argues that it is dangerous for the attitudes of having and problem thinking to predominate as they do in twentieth-century European society, a society where, he claims, both persons and nature are valued in a primarily functional and instrumental manner. Overly high esteem and value is conferred on the ideas of progress, efficiency, and control. Marcel laments the emptiness of a culture dominated by impersonal social planning, bureaucracy, and the quest for technological achievement (DW 2). The predominance of a "technical" perspective, he observes leads to a pervasive despair among persons. This despair in the face of the world of the functional and problematical "consists in the recognition of the ultimate inefficacy of all techniques, joined to the inability or the refusal to change over to a new ground—a ground where all techniques are seen to be incompatible with the fundamental nature of being, which itself escapes our grasp which reaches towards an object" (PE 30). What cannot be recognized by "problem thinking" is the fundamental experience of coexistence with other persons, which can only be perceived by a person who takes an attitude of receptivity to other persons as subjects, rather than as objects of observation. The interpersonal aspect of human reality is what Marcel calls the "mystery of being." This mystery inevitably withstands "an exhaustive analysis bearing on the data of experience, aiming to reduce them step by step to elements increasingly devoid of intrinsic or significant value" (PE 14). Authentic existence involves participation in the community of being and the emergence of fidelity and hope.

MARCEL'S OBJECTIONS TO THE THEODICY PROBLEM

The global, objective approach to evil known as "theodicy" is used by Marcel as a prime example of the inappropriate application of the problem-solving method. Marcel is vehement in his criticism of theodicy, which he labels "sacrilegious" and "dogmatic" (PE 44). The targets of his objections are, broadly, all metaphysical theories ambitious enough to attempt to explain or justify evil. Marcel argues that theodicies proffer "only the ghost of reality" because they "deceive us" with their "inevitable, artificial coherence" (BH 169). Marcel declares theodicy "chimerical," a criticism echoing

Kant's famous claim that theodicy is an illusion of speculative reason (BH 19). The philosopher who dares to propose a theodicy purports to have a God's-eye view of the world, a standpoint from which the beginning and end of history and the purposes of God are visible. Theodicy takes a problem-solving approach toward the topic of evil. Leibniz argues that evil in the universe contributes to achieving maximum plenitude and variety of beings with differing degrees of perfection. Hegel justifies evil historically, rather than ontologically, arguing that evil provides the necessary "negative" elements driving the dialectic of history forward to its perfect fulfillment. For both theodicies, evil serves a broad, global good that is untarnished by the horrendous suffering and destruction of many lives. According to Marcel, comprehensive global objectivity concerning evil, as claimed by Leibniz or Hegel, is impossible (PE 20). Taking a problem approach, theodicy defines the problem of evil as the contradiction between God's goodness and the reality of evil in the world. However, Marcel considers theodicy's purview both narrow and wrongheaded.

The global problem approach of theodicy cannot identify the heart of the matter concerning evil and suffering. Marcel insists that evil is properly understood as an issue that impinges on my very existence. To consider evil as a problem detached from me, a problem to be solved logically and conceptually, is to miss the challenge that evil poses to existence and to faith in God (PE 19).[12] He writes that "evil which is only stated or observed is no longer evil which is suffered: in fact, it ceases to be evil. In reality, I can grasp it [evil] only as evil in the measure in which I am involved." (PE 19) Marcel warns that theodicy's global approach to evil overlooks the threatening character of "evil experienced" by individual persons.[13]

Marcel raises epistemological objections to theodicy language about God because it is both inaccurate and impersonal. Theodicy requires conceptual development of the notion of God that tends to reduce God "to our absurd human proportions" (CF 36). The problem approach of theodicy is incapable of accurately representing faith, which centers around interpersonal relation. The objective discourse of theism represents faith in God as belief in propositions about God and the world, missing the existential core of faith—the act of addressing God and discovering God's light in interpersonal experience.[14] For Marcel, appropriate religious language is language addressed to God, namely, the language of invocation or prayer. He writes that for the religious person, "God is the absolute thou who can never become a him [or it]" (MJ 137). "God can only be given to me as Absolute Presence in worship; any idea I form of Him is only an abstract expression or intellectualization of the Presence" (BH 170).[15] According to Marcel, God emerges in human existence indirectly in moments of grace mediated by intersubjective relation, in community, in fidelity, and in love (FHW 8). Therefore, given the existential character of faith, a religious response to evil and suffering must study the postures of faith as they help the individual cope with suffering.

There is a passionate moral dimension to Marcel's rejection of theodicy. He accuses theodicy of moral turpitude because its global explanations and justifications disregard the role of the victim in giving meaning to suffering and fail to consider the proper response of a person to someone else's suffering (HV 34). To illustrate how theodicy is inappropriate on an interpersonal level, he recounts a conversation between a priest and an invalid who suffers from an incurable disease. During a hospital visit, the priest advises the sick person that the genuine Christian response to suffering is to "adore the power and the wisdom of God through the determinism of those natural forces of which this case was really just a simple example" (TWB 139). In telling the invalid to accept suffering with gratitude, the priest takes a spectator attitude toward the suffering of the other. The priest offers a theory of how God works in creation, a theory rejected by Marcel for its inability to satisfy the sufferer with knowledge of God and also for its moral insensitivity. Counter to the global application of theodicy, Marcel insists that the conferral of meaning on suffering is an act that is the responsibility of the person who suffers. But although the discovery of meaning in suffering ultimately depends on the individual's assent, meaning-making is not a solo task. Interpersonal relation aids the suffering person in discovering possibilities for meaning and in maintaining the religious postures of availability, fidelity and hope—the conditions for the possibility of interpersonal relation.

The important distinction between an interpersonal and a problem-solving approach to evil and suffering was impressed on Marcel during World War I (1915–1918) when he worked for the Red Cross. Marcel's assignment was to find out information about missing soldiers and communicate the news to their families. He found himself torn between two different responses to suffering. One the one hand, the missing soldiers were names on a page for him—mere statistics that he collected and recorded on filing cards. However, in personal encounters with family members of missing soldiers, he found himself empathizing with the suffering of others directly. Marcel writes in an autobiographical essay that "whenever possible, I met personally with the unfortunate inquirers come in search of news, striving to the greatest extent possible . . . to give them the feeling that they were not alone, that I was personally involved in this quest, far too often a hopeless one."[16] His insistence that compassion for individuals who suffer is necessary to an authentic moral and religious response to suffering relates back to his Red Cross wartime experience (CF 75).

FAITH AND HOPE: THE DISCOVERY OF MEANING IN SUFFERING

Marcel's philosophy of experience explores the dynamics of intersubjective relations. He defines authentic relation between two persons as meeting the other person as "Thou." The conditions that make intersubjective Thou-relation possible are availability, fidelity, and hope, which are explored in the following pages. Marcel insists that his philosophy be as concretely tied to experience as possible. He uses his own experience and imaginative exploration of the experiences of others, such as his creative work as a playwright, to depict the existential postures characteristic of genuine intersubjectivity and faith in God. The following account of his position focuses on his formal portrayal of the main aspects of coexistence with other persons. This emphasis is in keeping with Marcel's work, which, as a whole, devotes more space to formal phenomenological depiction of existential postures than to extended reflection on narratives or concrete situations, despite his methodological commitment to the latter.

Relation to the Thou: Availability and Fidelity

The attitude of "availability" (*disponibilité*) is the primary precondition for the meeting of the other person as a "Thou." To be available to the other can be explained as perceiving the other person as an individual who has my whole attention, not as an entity among other entities or as part of a collective group (CF 72). The Thou is a "presence" to me that is bodily and spiritual, apprehended by the senses and in communication. The speech of the Thou to me is what Marcel calls the language of "appeal," for in addressing words to me, the other person asks for recognition. The I-Thou relation requires acknowledgment on both sides. The structure of appeal is characterized by freedom, for neither can I solicit an appeal by force nor can the Thou make me respond. In meeting with the Thou, I apprehend the other as free and I collaborate with this freedom. Relation to the Thou is something to be received as a gift. It is not something under my individual control, but relies instead on the initiative of the other who makes the appeal.[17] Yet it requires that I take a deliberate stance of availability or openness. Marcel does not agree with Sartre's definition of freedom as the autonomy to treat persons any way I choose. Rather, Marcel considers my response to the other "free" when I take a posture of openness and accept my responsibility to recognize the other's freedom. Using artistic creation as his model, Marcel suggests that freedom is found when I enter "into the whole of an activity with the whole of myself" like an artist, not when I remain detached like a technician who masters, controls, and uses an object (BH 173). In other words, creative freedom is found in participation and coexistence with others.

Although availability is a precondition for the occurrence of Thou-relation, its extension into the future requires "fidelity." Together, availability and fidelity are the key components of love. Fidelity is a promise to the Thou who is present, a promise of permanency and the resumption of the Thou-relation stretching into the future. Promise differs from constancy, Marcel argues, for constancy is the following of a rule, the exertion of self-control that may be motivated by egocentric pride or fear of punishment (CF 157). In contrast, a promise is a spontaneous commitment made in response to a Thou. It is not loyalty motivated by rational duty, but by empathy and caring. The promise to be faithful made in the present applies to my whole future, even though the future is beyond my control (PE 35). Hence, fidelity has an unconditioned character, juxtaposed with the self-awareness of my insufficiency to guarantee my promise. Marcel claims that fidelity points toward a transcendent dimension of intersubjectivity, namely, the endurance of bonds of fidelity beyond death into immortality. It is thus implicitly religious.

Suffering as a Trial

There is an asymmetry between the appropriate response to my suffering and the suffering of other persons. As Marcel's critical attack on theodicy shows, he opposes the attribution of uses or meaning to the suffering of other persons. To do so is to show lack of genuine empathy and the inability to imagine the situation of the person suffering. Marcel considers the challenge that faces the person who suffers to be the choice between despair and hope, between declaring suffering to be completely meaningless or assigning meaning to it. For Marcel, the appropriate religious response to my own suffering is to take up a posture toward suffering as if it were a "trial" and a challenge to be withstood. To find meaning in suffering as a trial does not involve formulating reasons why God allows suffering or explanations for how God compensates individuals for suffering. It does not entail acceptance of the claim that suffering is justified as a test sent by God for some good purpose. This would be to take up the line of theodicy, which justifies suffering by showing how it is ultimately made good by God. Marcel's response does not offer hypotheses about God's acts or purposes, but explores the creative initiative demanded of the person who suffers in adopting certain religious postures and engaging in meaning-making.

In declaring suffering to be a trial, the individual accepts it as a given in a way that is not passive, fatalistic, or gripped by fear. Marcel writes that the religious person first accepts "the trial as an integral part of the self, but while so doing considers it as destined to be absorbed and transmuted by the inner workings of a certain creative process" (HV 39). Suffering gains meaning as part of a religious journey from isolation toward relation, from fear toward trust in others, from despair to hope. According to Marcel, "to triumph in the trial is to maintain oneself as soul," which means to maintain openness, relation, and hope (MJ 202). If a person retains the capacity for availability despite personal suffering, then one's eyes open "to the suffering of others which I was unable to imagine before" (CF 76). Thus, my own experience of suffering can increase my availability and my sensitivity to the appeal of others.

There is an element of grace in the appropriation of my suffering as trial. The ability to do so takes more than the application of a technique or of problem solving. Marcel does not recommend theodicy arguments as therapy for making this discovery. For the status of suffering as a trial does not apply indiscriminately to all cases of suffering; it is only the individual's affirmation that "I accept my suffering as a trial" that makes it so. The discovery of religious meaning in suffering is a task assisted by conversation and co-presence between I and Thou. But the victim has priority and is entitled to assign meaning to suffering (TWB 140). This is why Marcel expresses outrage at this seemingly pious advice to someone who suffers from a chronic illness: "Thank God for the grace he has bestowed on you. This suffering has been laid on you to give you the opportunity to merit the heavenly beatitude" (CF 74). According to Marcel, to say such a thing shows that the speaker lacks both empathy and imagination for the person who suffers. The victim will naturally respond by exclaiming: "What sort of God is this who tortures me for my own benefit?" and "What right do you have to be the interpreter of such a cruel and hypocritical God?" (CF 74). These are precisely the questions that motivate theodicy, namely, why does God permit suffering and how is it overcome? It is not the questions of theodicy that are inappropriate, but the type of answers it provides.

The language of trial also raises questions about God and whether a good God would put individuals up to such painful tests. What if God gives "tests" that are beyond a person's strength? Are the events that took place in Auschwitz and other Nazi concentration camps properly interpreted as tests? Marcel skirts such questions with an agnostic reply. He states that we have no basis on which to judge whether a test is beyond our strength, and, moreover, we do not know if God "designs" the tests that we face. As Marcel puts it, "we know neither the real extent of our powers nor the ultimate designs of God" (HV 47). Marcel does not engage in a defense of God's goodness or love, although he is aware that belief in a loving God raises difficult questions. He holds that faith lives with these questions that are ultimately unanswered. The lack of answers does not mean that one cannot pose questions about God and evil, as Job does in the Bible, or discuss such questions with other persons. However, God's nature is mysterious, thus, any supposed theodicy answers must be considered tentative. Most important for Marcel, it is the prerogative of the individual who suffers to accept or reject any proposed hypothesis about God and the meaning of suffering.

Marcel's main emphasis is on how faith can and does endure suffering, in practice, by means of intersubjective relation and hope in God. The religious response to suffering advocated by Marcel is characterized by the acceptance of the inscrutability and mystery of God, and rejection of attempted explanations or justifications from God's side. Positively, it is characterized by the posture of availability and empathy for persons who suffer, and personal engagement in the creation of meaning. The individual faced with suffering enacts meaning-making in a unique set of circumstances, with the help of loved ones.[18]

The task of giving meaning to suffering places the subject in the role of an artist. The responsibility lies with each individual to use creative freedom to enter into intersubjective participation, which makes possible the discovery of meaning. What is missing in Marcel's work is the consideration of situations where an individual is crushed by suffering and despair. Marcel's approach to suffering takes for granted a strong, resilient individual. Related to his focus on capable individuals is his very minimal reflection on the connection between I-Thou relation and activity that aims to alleviate or prevent suffering. He does not consider when it is appropriate for the individual to resist personal suffering. Nor does he consider that in the worst situations, intervention is needed to prevent or remove suffering in order for the victim to muster the strength to cope with suffering. Lack of connection between relational postures and opposition to suffering is a blind spot in his philosophical position.

Hope, Transcendence, and Immortality

Marcel treats hope along with availability and fidelity as the three central elements of a religious response to suffering. Like availability and fidelity, hope is an existential disposition or posture. Marcel defines hope as an attitude of relaxation or openness toward future possibility, which adapts with flexibility to changing circumstances or setbacks. To hope is to be open toward the future. Hope does not fix itself on a certain outcome of events, whether negative or positive (EBHD 143). Therefore, it falls into neither the extreme of despair and pessimism, nor of optimism, which both rest on conviction about the future that is beyond human knowledge. Hope is not based on calculated probabilities of success or failure, which would make it an attitude of "having" or objective prediction. Rather, hope affirms that destructive patterns in history are not determinative for the future. The subject who hopes believes in the openness of the future to good changes and the possibility of unexpected positive events.[19] Hope does not demand an ultimate positive outcome—peace, liberation, or the alleviation of suffering—in the near future. Because hope is patient, hope transcends success and defeat in the present. Marcel asserts that "hope is only possible in a world where there is room for miracles" (BH 75). Nevertheless, Marcel does not display the confidence of certain Marxists, for example, in his expectations for history.[20] He advises that "we must forbid ourselves large and vague more or less utopian ambitions" (MAH 75). Marcel's model of hope focuses on positive expectations for the interpersonal dimension of existence, rather than on seismic shifts in international politics and economics.

The person who hopes does not take catastrophes of suffering in history as reason for despair. Marcel asserts, "To hope is to carry within me that private assurance that however black things may seem, my present intolerable situation cannot be final" (MB II 179). The person who hopes possesses a serenity and trust in God and reality. Hope is not the same as blind optimism, according to Marcel, because the person who hopes does not ignore or deny the brokenness of the world and the reality of suffering (PE 28). Hope goes along with the posture of fidelity to other persons and empathy with persons who suffer. Glimpses of God's presence discovered in intersubjective experience are major sources of hope for Marcel.

As a religious attitude, hope places no limiting conditions on trust in God; rather, it extends unconditional credit to God.[21] Fidelity to God is analogous to the trust required to declare fidelity to a person: complete trust that I will not be betrayed. He describes the person who hopes as having a peace that transcends events. He writes that "we can conceive, at least theoretically, of the inner disposition of one who, setting no condition or limit and abandoning himself in absolute confidence, would thus transcend all possible disappointment and would experience a security of his being, or in his being" (HV 46). A person of faith "puts his life at the disposal of that higher reality; he extends to the ultimate [God] that availability which is exemplified in the fact of dedicating oneself to a person, to a cause" (CF 77). Fidelity to human persons accompanies fidelity to God, for the latter is an affirmation of the value of created reality.

Acceptance of Suffering

Hope in God is the antithesis of protest against suffering, according to Marcel. He observes that a common temptation for the person who suffers or witnesses suffering is to accuse God. One might protest that "if God possessed the attributes with which we commonly endow him, he would not have allowed this monstrous happening" (MB II 153). Marcel dismisses such complaint as mistaken. It is a sign that faith is conditional and dependent on protection from suffering or reward. Marcel claims that the more faith is understood as a living relation to God, the more the temptation to accuse God can be resisted. As illustrated by the conclusion of the book of Job, the abandonment of complaint is the result of encounter with God, although without greater understanding of God's attributes or plans. Marcel claims that the experience of grace in the life of the individual is the main factor that sustains faith and quenches complaint.[22]

The voluntary acceptance of suffering is the most radical manifestation of faith and hope. The struggle toward such acceptance is illustrated in the drama, *Rome n'est plus dans Rome*. The main character must decide whether to stay in exile from Nazi-occupied France or return home. If Pascal returns to France from Argentina, he will be leaving his wife and son behind. He will be risking his life as a journalist engaged in the war struggle. Pascal articulates faith in the face of suffering in the following speech: "I don't know what that moment will make of me, perhaps a rag. I'm not presuming on my own strength alone. I'm counting on God, that he will not abandon me, that he will save me from a final disaster. Either he will take me to himself, or he will give me the strength to withstand the torture."[23] Pascal accepts potential suffering as an act of faith in God. It has meaning because it is dedicated to participation in a cause devoted to helping others. For the person of faith who accepts suffering, Marcel writes, "this suffering must be apprehended as the actual participation in an universal brotherhood" (BH 144). Suffering can have meaning when it is accepted voluntarily as a consequence of responding to the appeal of other persons who suffer.

The moments when a person determines how to face suffering can be viewed as turning points marked by divine grace. Grace appears in Thou-relations with others, enabling the individual to recognize participation in a wider communion of Thous. Marcel calls such turning points moments of grace, or epiphanies, which like "liberating flashes of light serve to assure us . . . that no matter how much a proud and blind philosophy claims that there exists only an emptiness, a nothing, there is on the contrary a fullness of life" (TWB 142). These glimpses of grace are like rays of light piercing existence, giving testimony to God's reality. As a component of hope, Marcel affirms the immortality of the soul. He depicts the aim of religious hope as the restoration of the integrity of the living order in the transcendent and eternal order beyond the bounds of the visible world. Hope believes in the endurance of love between I and Thou after death, hope for the immortality of all persons (BH 77).[24] Therefore, for Marcel hope is inherently religious and intersubjective. Hope means that "I hope in God, the absolute Thou, for the indestructibility of the communion between myself and other beings" (HV 60).

THE LIMITATIONS OF MARCEL'S APPROACH AFTER AUSCHWITZ

Instead of aiming to make faith in God plausible by showing the logical compatibility of God and evil, as theodicy does, Marcel makes faith plausible in the face of "evil experienced," or suffering, by explicating the faith postures of availability, fidelity, and hope. He maintains that only concrete examples can reliably represent faith postures, but he extrapolates a universally applicable model of faith. But, in my view, his conclusions should be recognized as narrower in scope and only selectively applicable.

In his philosophy, Marcel has implicitly generalized the experiences of white, Christian, middle-class Europeans confronted with suffering. He deals with a limited range of examples of suffering. Among contemporary thinkers, it is now more common for philosophers and theologians to recognize that religious postures and responses to suffering are contextual, and the social class, gender, and race of the subject who suffers more often credited with having a constitutive role in the individual's religious and moral response. Despite this limitation of Marcel's work, his existentialist approach sets a precedent for the experience-orientation of contemporary contextual religious thinkers who work within a concrete social context, such as feminist, African-American, and Latin American liberation theologians. For example, James Cone, one of the founders of black theology, discusses and commends Marcel's existential approach to evil. Cone accuses the Western theological tradition of taking a "spectator" approach to suffering that justifies an unjust status quo and social oppression, a point made by Marcel in his criticism of theodicy. With approval, Cone quotes Marcel's statement that "I can only grasp evil in the measure in which it touches me."[25] On this basis, Cone argues that his own Christian response to suffering must unavoidably include reflection on the struggle against slavery and racism, even though the need to examine the social and political causes of suffering is not explored by Marcel himself.

Another productive avenue opened by Marcel's approach is the use of literature as it exposes the contextual intricacies of evil experienced. Marcel's promotion of literature and drama as resources for exploring the dynamic of suffering is echoed in the writings of recent feminist thinkers, who have utilized literature to bridge the experiences of different racial and ethnic groups and to communicate experiences of suffering, survival, and faith. Literature complicates phenomenological generalizations about the character of faith faced with suffering.[26]

When examining Marcel in dialogue with post-Holocaust writers, it becomes clear that Marcel does not take account of the dehumanizing and debilitating effects of suffering, depicted in the writings of Holocaust witnesses. Marcel never considers the situation of a desperate victim who cannot find meaning in suffering.[27] He does not consider that a sufferer may be unable to engage in authentic interpersonal relation until his or her suffering is alleviated. Marcel's model of response to suffering rests on the assumption that the self who faces suffering is strong enough to adopt the postures of availability and hope, which enable meaning-making. Concentration camp survivor and existentialist psychiatrist Viktor Frankl shares Marcel's seemingly optimistic tone about finding meaning in one's suffering, at least in part. Frankl insists that even in a concentration camp, spiritual freedom can be exercised. In Auschwitz, where Frankl attempts group psychotherapy among prisoners, he counsels that all suffering is significant and meaningful because each person has the inner freedom to find dignity and meaning no matter what the circumstances.[28] Yet Frankl is soberly realistic in noting that some prisoners become hopeless and unable to use this inner freedom. On the other hand, Marcel simply assumes the voluntaristic capacity to make meaning, and he does not consider such experiences of evil. The existentialist strategy of coping that Marcel proposes is not for the weak or fainthearted. To confront suffering as a "trial" is an act of heroism, which may be impossible in Auschwitz or other cases of most severe suffering.

Further objections to Marcel's position can be raised concerning his portrayal of hope. In particular, hope seems to be partially in contradiction with Marcel's emphasis on the acceptance of suffering as a trial because hope implies the desire to fight against suffering. Although Marcel observes that the posture of hope looks for positive changes in history, he never considers how hope involves discontent that extends as far as political protest and resistance. For Marcel, the core of hope is confidence in the indestructibility of the bonds of relation and love between individuals, a hope that reaches beyond history to a transcendent realm. His counsel that the individual should accept suffering as a trial deflects attention from evaluating and protesting the causes of suffering in history and society. I judge that Marcel's emphasis on the acceptance of suffering is indeed appropriate and helpful in certain contexts, especially where suffering seems unavoidable and where it is not overwhelmingly severe. However, his approach contrasts sharply with that of Marxian and liberation thinkers, who take social class into account and who emphasize how hope motivates political resistance to effect structural change and combat suffering.

3 Dialogical Faith

Martin Buber's I-Thou Response to Suffering and Its Meaning

JEWISH THINKER MARTIN BUBER is well known as an existentialist philosopher, biblical interpreter, and historian of Hasidic Judaism. His impact on contemporary Jewish thought has been significant and enduring. Moreover, Buber's I-Thou philosophy has widely influenced Protestant Christian thinkers, such as Rudolf Bultmann, Karl Barth, Paul Tillich, and Dorothee Soelle.[1] His most famous book, *I and Thou* (1923), defines the dichotomous attitudes of I-Thou and I-It. According to Buber's definition, faith centers on I-Thou encounter with God and other persons. I-Thou relation is not only essential to faith, according to Buber, but also to society as a whole. It provides a corrective to the increasingly one-sided emphasis on technology and science in the modern world.

There are a number of striking similarities between the approaches of Buber and Marcel: both criticize instrumental and technological attitudes pervading society, both oppose theodicy, and both emphasize interpersonal relation as central to faith. As existentialist philosophers, they criticize idealist metaphysics and system building, while they promote philosophical concern with subjectivity and the self's relations to other persons and the nonhuman world.[2] Buber's approach is distinctive in giving interpersonal relation a communal dimension and an ecological sensitivity not found in Marcel's philosophy. Reflecting on the Hebrew Bible in his mature work, Buber engages the Jewish tradition and theological issues more extensively than Marcel deals with Christian texts and sources. This chapter cannot cover the full complexity of Buber's thought nor his wide-ranging corpus. Rather, its focus is on how Buber's dialogical philosophy militates against theodicy and offers a practical faith response to suffering and the Holocaust.

Buber articulates the practical challenge posed by suffering as hinging on the questions: "How can faith survive suffering?" and "Where does religious meaning in suffering lie?" Suffering raises the problem of the "eclipse of God": the apparent absence of God that periodically recurs throughout Jewish history, most recently in connection with the Holocaust. Buber responds to evil and suffering by reflecting on narratives taken from biblical texts and Hasidic Jewish writings, where persons of faith face major challenges.[3] Generalizing from these accounts, the religious postures that he recommends in the face of suffering are dialogue with God in prayer and I-Thou relations with others in community.

THE DICHOTOMY BETWEEN I-IT AND I-THOU ATTITUDES

The cornerstone of Buber's philosophy is his distinction between I-It and I-Thou relation as two stances or attitudes with which human beings face the world. The I-It and I-Thou dichotomy, like the contrast between "problem" and "mystery" in Marcel's work, has its precedent in Kant's distinction between speculative and practical reason.[4] While speculative reason looks scientifically at objects in terms of their spatial, temporal, and causal properties, practical reason is the realm of freedom and faith in God. It reflects on what is the proper moral stance in relation to other beings. Practical reason postulates faith in the existence of God as a necessary condition of moral relation.

Like Marcel's posture of "having," Buber's I-It attitude takes a problem-solving approach toward other beings. I-It theoretical reason studies physical objects and empirical psychology; it is associated with scientific investigation and rationalist metaphysics. In I-It relation, my attitude toward living and nonliving things is detached, objective, analytic, and instrumental. The "other" is conceived as separate from me and as an object under my scrutiny (IT 7).[5] This perspective is manifest both in theoretical reflection and in active postures. I may take the I-It stance passively, as an idle observer, or I may act as a researcher or technician manipulating things for scientific purposes. When I take an I-It stance of relation toward others, I analyze their properties, evaluate their usefulness, and can use them as tools at my disposal. Buber admits that it is necessary and useful to abstract properties or attributes from an object (EG 45). The scientific study of persons and objects can be productive for humanity, as the advances of technology demonstrate.

Nevertheless, Buber warns that I-It attitudes are overly dominant in twentieth-century society, and neglect of the realm of I-Thou relation is common. The main factors responsible for this trend are advances in science, instrumentalized labor, and institutional bureaucracy (IT 48).[6] The loss of I-Thou relation in contemporary life threatens the human subject. As

Buber puts it aphoristically: "Without It, man cannot live. But he who lives with It alone is not a man" (IT 34). Human life without I-Thou relation is sorely impoverished, even inhuman.[7] The I-Thou attitude is central to morality, religion, and art. It reveals the beauty of the world and the meaning that arises from relations with others as Thou.

For Buber, like Marcel, I-Thou relation is defined as authentic meeting or encounter with the other. To turn toward the Thou is an act of freedom, which requires that I maintain an attitude of openness and respect toward the other.[8] I-Thou relation is characterized by total involvement, exclusivity, mutuality, and directness. When I meet the Thou face-to-face, the Thou "fills the heavens" for me, gaining my complete attention (IT 8).[9] I-Thou relation is a moral attitude because it values the Thou as an end, not as a means. Buber differs from Marcel in extending I-Thou relation beyond persons to art and nature. I-Thou encounter betrays an aesthetic quality, displayed in the intensity of attention to and appreciation for the Thou. Aesthetic appreciation is moral because it marks respect, and even awe, for the other met as Thou. The person who lives in authentic dialogical existence with reality wills the good of both natural and human Thous. Since even a tree can be met as a Thou, I-Thou relation supports ecological concern for protecting the environment.[10]

Buber is also distinctive in the attention he gives to philosophical reflection on society, whereas Marcel's focus is mainly on interpersonal relationships. Early on in his career, Buber associated himself with socialist political thought and was close friends with the prominent mystical socialist-activist Gustav Landauer.[11] His allegiance to what he called "religious socialism" continued through his immigration from Germany to Palestine in 1938. In Buber's terms, socialism is religious when faith serves as the basis and foundation for socialist political institutions. He holds that a socialist society should be a place where, ideally, people discover fellowship and mutuality, where they share "a common relation to the divine center, even if this [center] be nameless" (PW 112). Buber identifies an existentialist I-Thou precondition for the fulfillment of socialist aims of political and economic justice. He decisively dismisses Marx's science of economic materialism that disregards the personal and religious dimensions of social change.[12] He also rejects the Marxian assertion that collective class forces will deterministically bring about a workers' revolution. Buber accentuates the importance of I-Thou faith and the responsibility of individuals in relation as agents shaping society.

For Buber, community (or the "we") does not require that persons are always engaged in I-Thou relations with each other; however, mutual dialogue must be pervasive. Exemplary communities are those small enough for I-Thou relations to potentially occur among all members. Buber particularly admires the Hasidic Jewish community life that he describes in *The Legend of the Baal Shem* and other works. He also endorses the kibbutz style of cooperative work and ownership developed by Jewish communities in Palestine. On the other hand, he criticizes the nations of modern Europe for their bureaucracy, diplomacy, and fixation on technology and efficiency. According to Buber, the modern state exhibits the institutionalization of the I-It attitude.[13] If I-Thou relation becomes extinguished, he warns, there is no possibility for authentic communal life or political peace (PU 135).

Buber does not use religious terminology in the first two parts of *I and Thou*. In this way, he makes clear that I-Thou relation is an activity that does not require explicit religious affiliation or conventional religious belief. Yet, I-Thou is not only an aesthetic and moral posture, but also a religious one that reveals the sacred in everyday encounters. Buber goes so far as to state that the "extended lines of relation meet" in God (IT 100). He rejects the popular assumption that turning to God involves turning away from things of the world. Faith is not otherworldly but this-worldly because God is immanent in human relations and all of creation. To put it another way, in all relations with a non-eternal Thou, I implicitly address the "Eternal Thou" who is God (IT 75). According to Buber, all things in creation mediate God when they are approached as Thou. He states that "genuine religious comprehending of the world includes: proceeding from the present concrete being and situation of the person; entering into the present world situation as the speech of God to me; beholding all that is presented to me and its origination, its being created together with me; and the responsible answer of man, the loving hallowing of the things in the everyday" (BHT 133). When I listen for the address of the Thou to me, whatever kind of entity the Thou is, I treat the Thou as holy and recognize the world as God's creation. As Buber puts it, creation itself is God's address to me (BMM 13).[14] I-Thou relation is an implicitly religious attitude that is found beyond the bounds of Judaism in other theistic religions, as well as in Eastern religions and secular humanistic forms of spirituality (EG 49).

GOD-LANGUAGE WITHIN THE LIMITS OF I-THOU RELATION

Buber distinguishes between two types of faith: belief, which involves accepting propositions about God as true, and trust, which affirms God's reality by turning to God as Thou.[15] He disapproves of "belief" because it bases faith on I-It religious claims. In his view, authentic faith is "trust" in God, who is met in I-Thou encounter. What the individual finds in this encounter is a Thou who is "wholly Other" and also intimately close, as Buber puts it, "nearer to me than my 'I'" (IT 79). Buber asserts that this encounter can provoke awe and fear. On this point, he agrees with Rudolph Otto who claims that God, or the Holy, is encountered as the *"mysterium tremendum*."[16] Where Buber departs from Otto's phenomenology of religious experience lies in his stress on human activity needed to enter and continue dialogue with God, and the personal intimacy associated with I-Thou relation. Buber asserts that when God is met as Thou, "unlimited Being becomes, as absolute person, my partner" (EG 61). The encounter with God is a matter of what Buber calls divine grace, over which the individual has no final control. But the precondition for such encounter depends on the openness of the individual to relation. I-Thou relation requires both active seeking and expectant waiting, or grace.

Buber considers God as a mystery, "undemonstrable and unprovable, yet even so, in relationship, knowable Being, from whom all meaning comes" (EG 46). Hence, the person who receives revelation from God in I-Thou relation "receives not a specific content but a Presence" that inspires certitude (IT 110). I-Thou relation does not give theoretical knowledge. Instead, the individual's life becomes heavy with "lived meaning" that binds the person to God, as well as other persons. This kind of religious meaning is not passively received, but it must "be done" by each person uniquely through action in the context of a specific situation. Meaning-making requires an I-Thou posture of commitment and responsibility to others (IT 111).

In *I and Thou*, Buber asserts, like Marcel, that speech addressed directly to God is the most authentic form of religious language. This conclusion follows from the fact that faith in God centers on I-Thou relation. Buber claims that God "may properly only be addressed, not expressed" (IT 81).[17] He approves of the first-order religious language of I-Thou dialogue that takes place in prayer and psalmic poetry. Such God-language is impulsive and dynamic because I-Thou relation with God is itself ever-changing. But, as a philosopher of religion, Buber does not restrict himself to addressing God in poetry or prayer. In *I and Thou*, he uses objective terms to profile the I-Thou posture, although he emphasizes that the experience of I-Thou relation with God has a directness and intensity that philosophical language can evoke or point to, but not fully describe or capture (IT 95). In his later publications, Buber often turns to narrative as a second-order form of religious language that relates I-Thou dialogue with God. The advantage of narrative is that it does not abstract or systematize language addressing God, but retells events of encounter and revelation.[18]

Buber's refusal to elaborate a detailed I-It concept of God betrays the Kantian assumption that I-Thou relation is distinct from knowledge of phenomena. I-Thou relation occurs between subjects who are fully present to each other without objectification. Buber's antagonistic position toward speculative theology can be traced back to his affinity for mystical writers, articulated in his early book on comparative mysticism entitled *Ecstatic Confessions*.[19] Buber is consistent in prioritizing the intersubjective side of religion over objective elements of religion such as institutions, doctrines, or proscribed rituals. However, his early appreciation for mysticism as an ecstatic experience is countered in his mature work. For instance, in the postscript to *I and Thou*, Buber repudiates the emphasis on the "ineffable unity" and "immediate wordless experience" found among mystics as esoteric and escapist (IT 130). Instead, he proposes that what is most profoundly religious is found in everyday experience: I-Thou relation. The interaction between I and Thou is portrayed as a dialogue between subjects, not as a unification. In his mature writings, Buber seems to consider all mysticism as elitist, individualistic, and asocial. He insists vehemently that I-Thou relation is not mystical, but a natural ordinary capacity of every person.

Nonetheless, Buber's work has affinities with mysticism. For one, his emphasis on God's mysteriousness and his reticence to form a concept of God concurs with the *via negativa* mystics, who hold that language cannot express positive truths about God's nature because of God's transcendence.[20] It is Kantian of Buber to describe the I and Thou as free subjects in what seems to be a noumenal realm of spirit. It is also Kantian to presume that God cannot be experienced as a *phenomenon* or It, hence God cannot be known scientifically. Nevertheless, Buber differs from Kant in treating God as a personality in relation with human beings, rather than impersonally as a moral idea.[21] If we reject Buber's narrow and pejorative definition of mysticism as "ineffable unity" and adopt a wider purview, it is plausible to view the revelation of God in everyday I-Thou relation as a mysticism of the ordinary, where things appear as infused with the divine. I-Thou relation allows a mystical sensitivity to God's constant presence.

Despite his negative remarks about the I-It attitude as amoral and even areligious, Buber does not deny the legitimacy of images, ideas, and symbols for God.[22] He recognizes that they are necessary for the continuation of a religious tradition and for communicating revelation (IT 118). Buber defines the "revelation" of God in the Jewish and Christian traditions as occurring in interpersonal encounter. Revelation consists in the I-Thou relation of individuals with God recorded in Scripture, as well as the continuing revelation of God in history. Such encounter names a "God of the moment"— how God appears in relation—rather than who God is. In saying that God relates to persons as a Thou, one is not licensed to assert ontologically that God is a person, for, after all, even a tree can appear as a Thou. Buber names

God as the "Eternal Thou" to indicate that God is always available as Thou in human experience (IT 101). Personal I-Thou encounter cannot establish as a fact that God is eternal.[23]

It is the role of religious traditions to bring together stories of I-Thou encounters and preserve their memory. Buber remarks that within a community of believers, certain symbols or names for God become dominant.[24] Over time, the Jewish and Christian traditions have gathered testimonies to divine encounter that, according to Buber, in their multiplicity complete and confirm one another to form a single divine voice (BMM 15). Buber warns against the temptation for religious persons to fix or secure these symbols. He obeys the ban on idols characteristic of traditional Jewish thought, rooted in the Ten Commandments. Fixed images are wrong not only because they are an insult to God's transcendence, which cannot be represented, but because they are also harmful to religious life. When ideas and images of God harden into an object, they obstruct the vital religious reality that gave rise to them and the transient quality of relation that is their source. Buber calls for opposition to the idolatrous tendency of institutionalized religion with its cult and dogmas.[25] The overcoming of stagnation can be sparked within religion by renewal or revival of I-Thou encounter with God. The spark may also come from outside religion, from the attack of the atheist who rejects divine symbols and the reality of God altogether. Buber argues that the appropriate religious response to such iconoclasm is not the reworking of traditional symbols to make them more conceptually plausible (as undertaken in theodicy), but a renewed religious search for a new meeting with God (IT 111).

Although in *I and Thou* Buber seems to present religious traditions as heuristic pointers to I-Thou relation that are ultimately optional, his later work affirms the importance of tradition as the context for I-Thou relation. Religious traditions, despite their liability to idolatry, can foster the renewal of I-Thou meeting because they protect and promote the "lived concreteness of the meeting-place between the human and the divine" (EG 63). They do so by keeping alive the narratives of Scripture and tradition and by encouraging prayer and daily rituals, which make an opening for God's presence in the world. Buber allows that I-Thou relation can exist outside of established religions.

In responding to suffering, Buber rejects theodicy for reasons similar to Marcel's: (1) because it is hubristic in its claims about God, (2) because it misunderstands faith as belief rather than relational trust, and (3) because it does not consider a religious response to evil and suffering in its experiential and moral dimension.[26] Theodicy presumes that clarifying the logic of God is the main requirement for the plausibility and persistence of faith. But

Buber counters that it is I-Thou relation to God and other persons that sustains faith and gives meaning in the face of suffering.

A   NARRATIVE   FAITH   RESPONSE   TO   SUFFERING

Buber takes a narrative approach by turning to the Hebrew Bible and Hasidic stories to expose how I-Thou faith responds to suffering. I use the term "narrative" broadly to include accounts of I-Thou relation in Scripture and tradition, whether in the genre of poetic verse, dramatic dialogue, or storytelling. Buber finds narrative an appropriate medium for communicating I-Thou relation because it preserves the concrete and immediate character of the I-Thou event (EG 50). Narratives relating I-Thou encounters do not develop I-It language about God's attributes, like speculative theology. They do not give an I-It description of the sort used in scientific observation, but report conversations in which persons address God.[27] Narrative transmits I-Thou dialogue. Despite his emphasis on the value of narrative, Buber does not reject all objectifying and explanatory discourse, although in his earlier work he makes statements that seem dismissive of I-It language. He embraces the particularity of Jewish scripture, but he goes beyond Jewish narrative to encourage dialogue between religious traditions, as well as intratextual discussion within a given tradition.[28] Buber recognizes the need for meta-level commentary on narrative.

Buber selects narratives that display direct I-Thou relation to God. A basic function of narrative, for Buber, is depiction of the concrete variety of individual I-Thou encounters with God. Scripture is particularly important because it captures the spoken word of I-Thou in the founding events of the tradition, such as God's promises to Abraham. Narratives have more than an historical interest for Buber. He retells biblical and Hasidic stories for the purpose of addressing the contemporary situation, for example, the challenge that the Holocaust poses for Jewish faith.[29] Biblical narratives, like the book of Job, show that I-Thou relation with God helps a person face suffering. Narratives can have a pedagogical function for religious persons, stimulating the renewal of I-Thou reality.[30] Buber asserts that through the hearing or reading of Scripture, God's living word engages or addresses me. For narrative to have a transformative impact, I must be open and receptive to it. In other words, I must hear the words of the text as a Thou addressing me. Buber considers the interpretation of texts as an I-Thou dialogue, where the text addresses the reader as Thou.

Texts that are a monument to past dialogue with God, namely biblical writings, have special aptitude for fostering encounter with God.[31] The reader can identify with one or more characters and empathetically take on their role. By projecting myself into the story, God's words in the Bible can become words addressed to me. The plot of the story becomes my own plot. By identifying with Job, for example, I can voice his protest against unjust suffering as my protest, and I can receive God's words to Job as a response to my suffering. When I identify with the person who encounters God, I myself participate in dialogue with God, and I am motivated to address God with prayers and pleas of my own formulation. Identifying myself with characters from the Bible and tradition can give me both a sense of God's reality in encounter and a sense of belonging to a continuous religious community.

Buber and Marcel both use narratives to show how interpersonal relation can, bring meaning to suffering. However, the narratives that they choose are markedly different. Marcel employs stories of contemporary persons—often fictional—who struggle with faith and suffering. He does not use stories from biblical or traditional religious texts as Buber does, nor does he draw connections between relation and religious community or tradition. In contrast, Buber's approach is biblical and historical. His use of narratives belonging to the Jewish tradition gives his response to suffering a strongly communal, theological dimension.

Hasidic Narratives of Suffering and Redemption

Buber finds much to admire in the stories of Hasidism: intimate dialogue with God, I-Thou relations to persons and nature, and recognition of God's presence in the ordinary.[32] The setting for Buber's historical novel *For the Sake of Heaven* (1945) is a group of villages in eighteenth-century Poland, where well-established Hasidic communities are in conflict with each other.[33] In the novel, a disagreement occurs between two groups of Hasidic rabbis over whether destruction and suffering in history is an apocalyptic sign of redemption (*tikkun*). The Hasidic interpretation of redemption has its source in the Jewish mysticism of the Kabbalah. According to Kabbalistic creation mythology, creation is disordered and damaged because the divine light of creation broke the vessels intended to hold it. The repair of creation and the reintegration of divine and human reality is the task of *tikkun*, the restoration of harmony with God.[34]

On one side of the dispute over the means of redemption are a group of rabbis who consider redemption to be a miraculous occurrence that can be predicted by cosmic signs and historical calamities. They consider the destruction wreaked by the Napoleonic Wars as the apocalyptic herald of divine intervention in history. Buber disapproves of their attempts to predict redemption by esoteric divination or to further it by magical practices. He considers their emphasis on cosmic calamity as an erroneous interpretation of the Messiah's return. Buber does not condone a literal interpretation of myths that portray evil as external and metaphysical, giving esoteric knowledge of the universe that explains massive destruction in history. Rather, he interprets such myths as addressing the threat and constraint that evil poses to each individual existentially (GE 4). It is a moral evasion of responsibility to blame cosmic evil powers for disasters in history that should in fact be blamed on human choices. The true location of evil is in the human person. Hence, according to Buber, redemption must focus on the turning, or conversion, of the individual toward relation with God (FSH 231).

The rabbis in the novel whose position Buber clearly favors are led by a charismatic rabbi called the Yehudi. They consider redemption as basically concerned with how the individual acts, specifically, with the decision of the individual to turn to God (FSH 114). Self-examination and a life lived in I-Thou relation are preparation for redemption, whereas the obstacle to redemption is moral evil—the darkness that abides in every human heart (FSH 37, 164). As one follower of the Yehudi puts it, "We here do not believe that we have any duty except to turn to God with our whole being and to seek to establish his kingdom by a communal life of justice, of love, of consecration" (FSH 239). The movement of redemption, or *tikkun*, advances when the duty to meet God and others in I-Thou relation is met.[35] Religious hope lies in this process of moving toward God.

The issue of how my suffering becomes meaningful, in *For the Sake of Heaven*, is answered in existential, I-Thou terms. Despite unanswered theodicy questions, assurance in faith is possible. Buber rejects the explanation for historical suffering as divine punishment. He appreciates the magnitude of sin in the world as responsible for evil and suffering (FSH 47). But he neither defends God's goodness with reasons why God permits evil, nor does he comment on whether God has the power to prevent or eliminate evil. Rather than engage in theodicy, Buber recommends prophetic prayer, which seeks and questions God, as the most fitting faith response. In a prayer of one of the Yehudi's followers, the issue of suffering is posed as an existential question. The prayer runs as follows: "I do not beseech Thee to reveal to me the mysteries of Thy way; I could not endure them. But this I pray Thee to reveal to me, deeply and clearly, what this thing that now happens means to me, what it demands of me, and what Thou, Master of the universe, wouldst communicate to me through it. Ah, I would not know why I suffer, only whether I suffer for Thy sake!" (FSH 239).

In this prayer we find three meanings in suffering: mystical, ethical, and redemptive. First, meaning lies in encounters with the eternal Thou whose presence itself sustains trust. Encounter between the individual and God is a revelation that gives a wordless certitude that I am bound in relation with God, although to know God in this way is not to lessen God's mysteriousness. It gives confirmation of meaning in this life, in the present, which must be proven true by the actions of the individual (IT 111). Sometimes God seems to be absent from a person's experience, or in eclipse, but Buber maintains that the religious person trusts that God will not desert the person who suffers. Second, the content of this meaning emerges as the discovery of my responsibility to others that occurs both through Thou-relation to God and to others. According to Buber, Hasidism is "mysticism become ethos" because encounter with God makes possible the discovery of responsibility (HMM 198). Meeting with others as Thou manifests God indirectly. Third, suffering "for God's sake" takes on significance as the individual sets personal suffering within the narrative of divine redemption. Similar to Marcel's assertion that the persons of faith accepts suffering "as if" it were a trial, Buber advises that an I-Thou response to suffering can be interpreted as part of the redemption process, consisting of the mending of human relations and the reuniting of God and the world.

Although Buber focuses mainly on how a person finds religious meaning in one's own suffering, he considers I-Thou relation as highly attentive to the suffering of other persons. In one of his Hasidic tales, the Baal Shem (the founder of Hasidism) and some disciples meet a suffering person who is begging alongside the road. The Baal Shem responds with compassion for the beggar, but he instructs his disciples that pity alone is insufficient. It must be accompanied by concrete help for the person who suffers. The Baal Shem identifies two aspects of a faith response to suffering: giving material help, such as food or medicine, and bearing the other person's suffering in one's heart. To do the latter requires entering into the reality of the person who suffers in I-Thou relation (LBS 49). Empathy for the sufferer means to share in the burden of suffering.

The Book of Job

Buber considers the book of Job as the most profound articulation of the question of Israel's historic fate, in particular, her suffering and exile.[36] The historical background of the book is the defeat of the Kingdom of Israel and the Babylonian exile of the Jewish people in the sixth century B.C.E. During this period, the justice of God in relation to human sufferings was hotly debated. Job's friends, who tell Job that his suffering is just punishment for his sins, articulate a theological explanation of suffering also represented in the prophetic book of Ezekiel—the position that there is a divine law of cause and effect that proportions individuals' sins with suffering (PF 187).[37]

According to Buber, this response is unsatisfying to the Israelites in exile who ask God: "Why do we suffer what we suffer?"[38] Aside from his epistemological objections to theodicy as an I-It form of discourse about God, Buber rejects theodicy because the attempt to rationalize suffering as divine retribution fails to satisfy sufferers who see no evidence of the just distribution of suffering among individuals or communities.

Job is the biblical character who exemplifies the refusal to be comforted by theodicy. In all his prayers and pleas to God, what Job longs for, according to Buber, is not proof of God's justice by means of reward for his righteousness, but the assurance that God does "not cause suffering gratuitously" (PF 192). Buber claims that the heart of Job's struggle lies in the painful absence or eclipse of God that shakes Job's trust in God's goodness and reality. What Job is looking for is an existential answer. Job wants to be addressed by God and assured of God's presence.

In the end, God does not offer Job a justification for his personal suffering or an understanding of divine justice in history. The response that Job receives to his complaint and protest is I-Thou encounter with God. As Buber puts it, God offers God's self as an answer to Job's protest. But although Job meets God as Thou, paradoxically, the speeches of God to Job do not speak about God's love or justice but about the grandeur of nature.[39] In response to Job, "Nothing is explained, nothing adjusted; wrong has not become right, nor cruelty kindness" (OJ 224). Nevertheless, Buber concludes that God's encounter with Job indicates that God does not cause suffering gratuitously, although God's speeches do not say this explicitly. Job's trust is renewed by the fact that God addresses him directly in answer to his protest (PF 195). God shows love by responding in I-Thou relation; therefore, Job does not abandon faith in God despite the inscrutability of God's justice.[40]

Buber identifies the practical outcome of Job's dialogue with God as prayer for the sake of his friends (Job 42:8). Prayer is a prophetic act pleading for justice on behalf of Israel. According to Buber, prophetic prayer is a transmission of revelation that is rooted in an "overwhelming experience of life" that acts on the recipient "as a mission" motivating one to become involved with those who suffer (PF 198). The effect of meeting God as a Thou is to transform complaint against suffering into concern for others, which expresses longing for redemption. The prayers and faith of prophets, such as Jeremiah, show that relation with God and ethical responsibility for others are inseparable. Buber emphasizes that encounter with God is not a "mystical experience (in a pejorative sense) for it does not lift a person above ordinary concerns to sheltered, private intimacy with God. I-Thou relation with God invests ordinary life and even suffering with meaning" (PF 201).

In the writings of the Hebrew prophets, Buber finds that a consequence of Thou-relation with God is concern for others as Thou, which leads to the willingness to suffer for God and other persons. Job's intercession for his friends comes after he hears God speak from the whirlwind, a revelation that empowers him to take up a prophetic role on behalf of those who suffer (PF 229). Buber points to the prophetic model of voluntary suffering in Isaiah, a text that, like Job, is occupied with the painful contradiction between God's promises and the fall of Israel as a nation. God's prophet is a figure who suffers for others. The righteous, suffering servant emerges as a symbol of suffering dedicated to God and undergone for the sake of the many who suffer undeservedly (TTF 144–152). Such prophetic suffering is undertaken voluntarily. But individual and unchosen suffering, like Job's, can be made meaningful if it is transformed from a self-centered to an other-directed posture. Buber considers both chosen and unchosen voluntarily accepted suffering redemptive if taken on "for God's sake."[41] The task of suffering is especially important for prophets or prominent leaders, but suffering also can be accepted by ordinary persons whose everyday activities reveal God in the world (OMH 203). Suffering gains meaning as part of the redemptive process of *tikkun* that restores creation—including the individual, the community of Israel, nature, and all humanity—to I-Thou relation with God.

The Eclipse of God and the Holocaust

Buber's essay "The Eclipse of God" is a response to a religious problem he perceives among contemporary persons who experience God as absent. The event of the Holocaust presents an enormous challenge to Jewish and Christian faith in God. Writers such as Elie Wiesel describe how survivors and victims of the Holocaust struggle to find God, often wondering whether their cries to God fall on deaf ears. They were victims whose capacity to turn to God and to trust God was destroyed by radical suffering.[42] The Holocaust is seen as raising the problem not of human disobedience and failure on the part of the Jews, but of divine apathy in the face of genocide. The experience of God's eclipse can be a sign of the estrangement between God and persons who have sinned, but in the case of the Holocaust the sins of Jewish victims are not an acceptable explanation for God's hiddenness. The sins of Nazi functionaries explain the Holocaust, but not the seeming cruelty of God who allowed it to occur. According to Buber, the pivotal question that the Holocaust raises is: "How is a life with God still possible in a time in which there is an Auschwitz? Can one still, as an individual and as a people, enter at all into a dialogic relationship with Him?" (OJ 224).

Buber also raises this question in a lecture entitled "Dialogue Between Heaven and Earth" (1951), where he compares the crisis of faith after Auschwitz with Job's protest against God. Job charges God with injustice and indifference in response to his individual suffering, as do contemporary persons in response to the Holocaust or other massive social suffering. Such a response of protest is markedly different from the acceptance of suffering recommended by Marcel. Buber points out that Job's trouble is not unique, but expressed in other parts of Hebrew Bible, as well as in post-Holocaust thought. God has been in eclipse periodically over the course of Jewish history and the lives of individuals. Buber's model of faith in eclipse is utilized in the post-Holocaust theology of Rabbi Irving Greenberg. Greenberg describes a dialectical "moment faith" that wavers between positive trust or worship, and protest "when the flames and smoke of burning children blot out faith."[43] Like Buber, Greenberg is skeptical of absolute conceptual claims about God's nature, and he rejects theodicy formulations that justify God's relationship to Holocaust suffering.

Buber names two poles of faith in response to suffering: affirmation of God's goodness, justice, and love, and experience of God's silence and apparent indifference to suffering. He asserts that fear and love are two "contrasting modes of religious reality" that are complementary and valid (EG 50). Fear is associated with the eclipse of God, where God is experienced as dreadful and incomprehensible, dreadful precisely because God's being is an incomprehensible mystery. Divine love is revealed in Scripture and tradition and perceived in I-Thou relation with God. Buber concludes that in the post-Holocaust era, persons with faith must turn to God and wait for the end of God's eclipse. Buber predicts that "though his coming [may] resemble no earlier one, we shall recognize again our cruel and merciful Lord" (OJ 225). These two facets of God are both revelations of the divine. But Buber points out that in the Bible and the Jewish tradition the reality of God's mercy and love predominate.[44] Buber counsels persons to turn to God trusting in God to reply, based on the traditional teaching that God loves persons and responds to individuals.

As a consequence of I-Thou encounter with God, the person of faith embraces all of reality as God-given, including suffering. Protest changes to acceptance. Buber considers nonacceptance an unethical and inauthentic religious response. The nonacceptance of suffering is the attempt to escape from suffering by any means, either physically by fleeing it, mentally by means of detachment, or spiritually by means of religious consolations. Acceptance centrally means to consider myself "directed and assigned to the concrete, contextual situation" where I find myself and to accept the suffering that may go along with engagement (EG 49). This attitude echoes Marcel's assertion that the acceptance of suffering means treating it as if it were a trial that is my own to overcome. Moreover, acceptance means going so far as loving reality, suffering included. The embrace of reality is part of the lived meaning that is discovered in I-Thou encounter with God.

In I-Thou relation, the mystery of God's hiddenness becomes a human mystery, the mystery of the separation "between heaven and earth" that redemption will remedy. Buber's approach shows how communal suffering among the Jewish people finds its remedy in communal I-Thou religious life.

POST-HOLOCAUST FAITH IN GOD

Buber substitutes the conceptual assurance of theodicy with the existential assurance provided by I-Thou dialogue to show how faith withstands the challenge of suffering. As Buber puts it: "Meeting with God does not come to man in order that he may concern himself with God, but in order that he may confirm that there is meaning in the world" (IT 115). When God is in eclipse during times of suffering, it is the individual's I-Thou relation with persons, and perhaps also with nature, that allow a person to discover traces of God or the sacred in everyday I-Thou encounter.

It is interesting to note that a number of Jewish thinkers have criticized Buber's response to the Holocaust as evasive and insensitive: evasive because he devotes relatively little space explicitly to this topic in his published works and insensitive because he does not stress enough how the Holocaust creates an unprecedented challenge to faith. The first charge can be answered by observing that in writings such as *Prophetic Faith*, "Between Heaven and Earth," and *For the Sake of Heaven*—texts written in the 1940s—Buber indeed responds to the Holocaust. His response may be indirect, but not evasive. The second charge against Buber rests on the assumption that to truly appreciate the magnitude of suffering in the Holocaust one must declare that it provokes a unique religious challenge. Buber does not hold that the atrocities committed by the Nazis were qualitatively different in impact from other instances of massive suffering in the past (PW 57). Moreover, he disagrees with prominent post-Holocaust Jewish thinkers who insist on the Holocaust's unique religious impact.[45] Buber would affirm that it indicates a loss of memory to insist that Jewish faith has never before been "eclipsed" or gravely threatened in previous history. It underestimates the suffering of the past to claim that the questions that Auschwitz raises about God have never been faced before, not even after the destruction of the First Temple in 587 B.C.E. and the Babylonian exile, or after the fall of the Second Temple in 70 C.E. and the Diaspora. Buber takes seriously past suffering and horrors in Jewish history that have challenged faith in the God of the covenant.

According to Buber, Jewish faith has always involved a dynamic movement in history between God's concealment or God's presence, between the appearance of God as merciful or as cruel. His recommendation for post-Holocaust faith is to trust in God's reemergence.[46] He insists that meaning in I-Thou relation does not hinge only on meeting God directly, but that it is "experienced in [all] living action and [even in] suffering itself" (EG 49). Protest is appropriate in the face of suffering, not as a sign of atheism, but as one manner of addressing God as Thou. To affirm that suffering is meaningful involves affirming that it is part of the process of redemption. The religious person interprets turning to God in suffering as a step toward the restoration of the I-Thou nearness between God and persons and finding hope for the future.

Buber's response to suffering addresses history in a way that Marcel's does not. Marcel gives suffering meaning entirely in terms of personal growth and interpersonal relation. In contrast, Buber gives the individual's response to suffering significance within the process of repair, or *tikkun*, brought about by the deeds of persons of faith. For Buber, faith does not only hope in the endurance of I-Thou love, as Marcel emphasizes, but in God's increasing nearness to the world achieved by moral acts of I-Thou relation. It is also distinctive that Buber recommends a posture of prayer that embraces protest as well as acceptance of suffering. Moreover, Buber differs from Marcel in paying more attention to the fact that faith responses to suffering involve relation that is significant in building community. In other words, there is a stronger social component to Buber's philosophy. However, his political outlook is existentialist in that institutional change depends on the self to turn toward the Thou. The fundamental level of coping and responding to socially caused suffering is interpersonal.

As we will see, Buber's appeal to "prophetic" faith foreshadows the emphasis of Marxian thinkers Bloch and Metz. But despite his religious socialism, Buber's perspective is more relational than political. His view of religious hope lacks an eschatological urgency and expectancy that demands revolutionary social change. His communal faith response to suffering does not articulate the importance of collective political action to resist the conditions causing suffering. Perhaps Buber's response to suffering reflects the situation of the post-Holocaust Jewish community where protest to God and lament are prevalent expressions of faith in the face of past suffering, where personal healing and recovery are sought. Despite the strong moral dimension of interpersonal relation for Buber and Marcel, what is missing or underdeveloped is reflection on the sociopolitical causes of suffering, especially the suffering of oppressed groups and the faith imperative of resistance. The shift to analysis of Marxian approaches in the next chapters will explore how faith in God and hope for redemption can be interpreted through a political lens, focusing on collective social suffering and group resistance efforts.

4 Marxist Theory and Practice
Scientific and Humanist Marxism

THE EXISTENTIALIST THINKERS EXAMINED show predominant concern for relations between individuals, although they do attend to the communal dimension of suffering and its solution at least to some degree. However, they do not frame responses to evil and suffering in terms of political protest, reform, and revolution, as do political and liberation theologians under the influence of Marxism. Before proceeding to investigate the thought of Ernst Bloch and Johann Baptist Metz, it will be helpful to examine the legacy of Karl Marx (1818–1883) and the salient features of Marxist thought. Suffering in the form of collective oppression is the driving concern behind Marx's critique of capitalism. His method takes an "I-It" analytical approach to suffering in history, studied as a social class phenomenon caused by economic factors. In contrast to existentialist thinkers who address the class-independent suffering of the "I" and "Thou," Marx's focus is on the suffering of the underclass or proletariat. Among Marxist thinkers, major disagreements exist over issues such as whether Marx holds a deterministic view of history and whether religion is always quietist and oppressive or can be politically revolutionary. Debates between the two main currents of Marxist interpretation are relevant for understanding the positions of political religious thinkers who selectively appropriate Marxist ideas.

Broadly speaking, there are two competing currents of Marxism: humanistic or warm stream, and scientific or cold stream. These two branches of Marxist thought are distinguished by whether they give greater priority to the "early" or the "mature" writings of Marx. The development of scientific Marxism is indebted to Friedrich Engels, Marx's friend and colleague who served as the official interpreter of Marx's writings in the years after Marx's death. Engels promoted Marxism and communism as political options for

Europe. To serve this end, Engels simplified or, as critics put it, vulgarized Marx's ideas. Interestingly, it was the writings of Engels, and not of Marx, that shaped Marxism as a mass movement in the 1890s, and it was Engels who was the definitive influence on Vladimir Lenin and Soviet Marxist theory.[1]

The belated publication of Marx's important early, humanistic writings is a crucial factor in the formation of two distinct branches of Marxist thought. The works of Marx widely circulated and popularized in the nineteenth century were his post-1845 writings from his "mature" period. Not until between 1927 and 1932 were the earlier writings of Marx first published, such as his *Economic and Philosophical Manuscripts* [1844], the *Critique of Hegel's Philosophy of Right* [1845], and *The German Ideology* [1845–1846]. Scholars note a pronounced shift toward a more scientific emphasis in Marx's thought that occurs between 1845 and 1847, although they disagree sharply concerning the abruptness of the transition and the continuity between his early and later writings.[2]

A further explanation for the persistence of this divide between the two schools lies in the inherent ambiguity of Marx's writings as a whole. Ironically, warm stream Marxian philosophy is often critical of Soviet Marxism, yet both claim to represent Marx's thought. This divide cannot be explained simply by distinguishing between the early and mature writings because nowadays contemporary scholars recognize significant points of continuity between different parts of Marx's corpus. There is a critical humanist emphasis in Marx's thought, which is evident even in his mature writings where his analysis turns to scientific dialectical materialism.[3] Nevertheless, the cryptic and sometimes fragmentary character of many texts gives Marx's interpreters sufficient leeway not only to clarify, but also to extend and supplement Marx's ideas in distinctive ways.

MARX'S MATERIALIST METHOD

Both orthodox and humanist streams of Marxist thought accept the basic features of Marx's "materialist" approach to the study of history, society, thought, and culture. This materialist method of approach centers on the analysis of economics, labor, and social class interests over the course of history, focusing on the implications of industrial and technological advancements.

Materialist Analysis of History

Marx introduces his materialist approach in opposition to the idealism of Hegel. Both thinkers develop a philosophy of history that conceives of history as a rule-governed process moving progressively toward ultimate perfection by means of a dialectical pattern. In fact, Marx borrows the conceptual framework of historical progress and dialectics from Hegel. But whereas Hegel sees world history as the unfolding self-development of collective human consciousness, which he calls Absolute Spirit, Marx overturns Hegel's idealism by claiming that material conditions direct the movement of history and shape collective class consciousness. According to Marx, it is the laws of economics, not human free choice, that determine history and the unfolding of historical progress.[4]

Marx's thesis is that the material conditions guiding the development of history are the relations of production. He defines "production" as the act of shaping matter to meet human needs. Marx considers production as the defining characteristic of human activity. He defines humanity not as *homo sapiens*, thinking man, but as *homo laborans*, working man.[5] Production creates a distinctive mode of cooperation among social groups or classes, relations that are not only economic but also social. To engage in the study of material conditions is to examine both conditions of production and their attendant social orders. Marx calls this socioeconomic structure the "material base" of society.[6] Arising from this base is the "superstructure," which includes political, religious, intellectual, and cultural institutions. The study of history reveals eras differing in material conditions, including different modes of production and social class divisions based on the division of labor, with correspondingly different superstructures.[7]

The focus of Marx's analysis of production is the capitalist society of his time, although he also performs economic analysis of ancient Greece, medieval feudal society, and eighteenth-century pre- and postrevolutionary France. The defining feature of capitalist relations of production is class division between persons with two different sources of revenue: those whose production is rewarded with wages (workers) and those whose income rests on ownership of the means of production (owners). Marx calls wage-laborers the "proletariat" class, and owners the "bourgeois" class.[8] Capitalist society is industrial, thus the bourgeois are owners of factory buildings, property, tools, and machines. Owners employ workers for wages and earn revenue or profit from the exchange of the products produced by workers. Profit comes from the "surplus value" between the exchange value of products and the exchange value of wage-labor and materials. Owners set the wages for workers who are supposedly free agents, selling their labor and competing with each other for work. The bourgeois class has supremacy in society because its control over production creates wealth. According to Marx, it is a law of history that "the class which is the ruling material force of society is at the same time its ruling intellectual force."[9] Class interests create and sponsor "ideologies" in academic fields such as philosophy, economics, and political science that shape institutions of government, education, religion, and culture.

Social Class and Suffering

The proletariat class is oppressed under capitalist modes of production. As a class, it suffers physically and socially. Marx observes that physical suffering results from the demands of long hours of repetitive, backbreaking work, and because of poor wages, insufficient food, and medical care. Increasing division of labor in capitalist society means that labor is simplified, special skills become worthless, and workers are ultimately interchangeable and replaceable.[10] Social misery arises because of the conditions of labor, which are dehumanizing. Marx describes the problem in terms of "alienation"—the alienation of workers from the products of their labor and their alienation from each other and the ruling class. The product is alien because it is not an expression of the worker's own directive to produce; it expresses neither the worker's needs nor creative powers but is produced only for the sake of wages and controlled by the owners of production. Social alienation arises from the competition among wage earners and the huge inequality between proletariat and bourgeois classes. In responding to suffering, Marx focuses exclusively on economic factors and their consequences in causing workers' suffering.

Ideology Critique

Marx's studies of material conditions leads him to conclude that because society is ruled by the dominant class, the superstructure of society will bear the imprint of the interests of this class. He adopts a hermeneutic of suspicion toward all elements of culture, known as the critique of ideology. An "ideology" is defined as a body of ideas and views stamped by the interests and assumptions of a certain social class. It claims universality while covertly defending, justifying, and legitimizing the position of the dominant class.[11] Ideologies shape all the organs of culture. Marx's critique of Hegel's idealism labels the latter's theory of history as an ideology that endorses the status quo. Whatever occurs in history, according to Hegel, instantiates the highest level of rationality and the highest realization of Spirit. In fact, Hegel glorifies his century as manifesting the highest possible forms of state government, religion, and philosophy. From the perspective of ideology critique, Hegel's endorsement of the institutions of nineteenth-century Germany uncritically ratifies the ascendancy of the bourgeois class.[12]

Religion is another central target for Marxist critique of ideology. Religion functions as an apolitical ideology for the proletariat or underclass. Persons who suffer are drawn to religion because it articulates human misery and offers comfort for those who suffer. However, Marx condemns religion precisely because it reconciles persons with suffering. In an oft-cited quotation, Marx argues that "religion is the sigh of the oppressed creature, the sentiment of a heartless world . . . it is the opium of the people" and a "halo" that is put on "this vale of tears."[13] The pernicious influence of Religion in capitalist society is a pernicious ideology that serves the ruling classes by quieting protest. The Christian church teaches the virtues of meekness, obedience, patience, and long-suffering, and it promises that persons who suffer virtuously or piously will receive great reward in Heaven. Such institutionalized beliefs function to suppress critical complaint against suffering and resentment of the ruling class. Hence, they effectively suppress the possibility of revolution. Faith diverts attention away from efforts to change history; it thus serves to corroborate suffering due to social oppression.

THE COLD STREAM: SCIENTIFIC MARXISM

Scientific Marxism is also known as orthodox or "cold stream" Marxism. It fits the popular stereotype of Marxism, disseminated largely by Soviet Marxists, that predicts the inevitable fall of capitalism and triumph of communism.[14] Scientific Marxists reduce Marx's complex theory of history to the simple claim that material economic conditions have a unilateral influence on the political and cultural superstructure of society. This deterministic view of history holds that history moves according to "laws" of material dialectics, which determine the development of economic modes of production and material conditions.[15] The argument is not that the lives of individuals on a micro-level are determined, but that the macro-level progress of history follows deterministic scientific laws. History develops by means of dialectical movement, powered by the underlying conflicts within any given mode of production. The main conflict within capitalism, for example, is the conflict between the classes due to the alienation of proletariat wage-laborers in the process of production. The overcoming of the tension between capitalist economic structures and the oppression of workers who suffer will effect the transformation of existing material conditions into new and better material relations of production. According to the logic of dialectical materialism, the succession of eras in history from feudalism to capitalism to communism is a necessary and predictable advancement.[16]

A key role in the material dialectic is played by suffering, which drives social upheaval. In *Capital*, Marx predicts that the suffering of the proletariat will increase at the hands of bourgeois owners to an explosive point of revolution. The proletariat will act collectively in solidarity, Marx contends, to overthrow the means of production and the dominant bourgeois culture. After capitalism is demolished, the proletariat will establish communist society. Although revolution obviously serves the interests of the proletariat class, Marx considers the proletariat the "universal class" because it creates the conditions for reaching a *telos* of history that serves the universal good.[17] Communist society is defined by fair relations of production, which means communal ownership of the modes of production. Class divisions will be abolished in communist society and the suffering of workers caused by alienation and exploitation will cease. Every worker will engage in activities of production that are self-directed and creative. Communist society makes equality and justice a reality for all persons.

Dialectical materialism is a teleological interpretation of history that takes the form of a secular theodicy. This atheistic theodicy declares suffering caused by class conflict and oppressive labor to be necessary. Suffering plays an instrumental role in orthodox Marxist theodicy, as it does in Hegel's theodicy, serving as the means to a perfect society. Scientific Marxism still holds the Hegelian view that history is rational and teleological, but it substitutes the rational logic of material conditions for Hegel's self-development of Spirit. It assumes the rote necessity of economic development in a progressive direction.[18] But one might question whether economic laws make history predictable, ending in the goal of a communist society. Orthodox Marxism also faces a problem in identifying how to achieve a state of universal good for individual persons and society as a whole. It makes the dubious claims that historical development is strictly teleological and that economic conditions will create a perfect society free of injustice and suffering. It also faces a problem in its justification of evil. I argue that the atheistic theodicy of orthodox Marxists, as well as Hegel's theodicy, should be criticized for justifying collective suffering by making it instrumentally necessary. Such justification labels the suffering of oppressed groups as useful and good for history as a whole, whereas for the victims their suffering is horrendous and unjust. Scientific Marxists would insist that material evolution is for the benefit of all humanity, with no bearing on God's self-development. However, Marxist progress benefits only those persons who exist in the ideal future, after the victims are long dead.

THE WARM STREAM: HUMANIST MARXISM

Humanist Marxism is described as "warm stream" Marxism because of its anthropocentric rather than scientific emphasis. It is also known as "Western Marxism" or "Marxian" philosophy in distinction from Soviet orthodox or scientific Marxism.[19] Important figures in this movement are Georg Lukacs,

Ernst Bloch, Antonio Gramsci, and philosophers of the Frankfurt School of Critical Theory, including Walter Benjamin, Theodor W. Adorno, Max Horkheimer, and Herbert Marcuse. These authors highlight the prominent "humanist" impulse in Marx's early writings, arguing that Marx's economic theories are motivated by his humanist quest to discover the conditions of social harmony and fulfillment for all persons. Marx's humanism involves the universal affirmation of the value of the human subject, who is a history-shaping agent.[20] The proletariat revolution is the strategy of collective political action that is the means to advancing these humanist ideals. As the young Marx puts it, the purpose of revolution is the overthrow of "all those conditions in which man is an abased, enslaved, abandoned, contemptible being."[21] Like scientific Marxists, warm stream thinkers identify the economic conditions of capitalism as the major cause of suffering, and they also hold that political protest is necessary to end this oppression. They agree with a material analysis of suffering, but reject deterministic materialism.

Modified Materialism

Humanist Marxists criticize scientific Marxists for reducing the relationship between matter and human activity by making the claim that there is a one-way shaping influence of base on superstructure. Yet humanist Marxists still hold to the basic thesis that material conditions of production have a primary determining influence on society. In other words, they agree that the culture, religion, philosophy, and politics of capitalist society necessarily reflect bourgeois class interests.[22] But more moderate than scientific Marxists, they claim that there are exceptions to this rule and that not all social phenomena are determined by material conditions. Warm stream Marxists hold that it is possible that within the dominant culture there are eruptions of human creativity and critical reflection that go against the current of dominant class attitudes.[23] The critical, creative impulse is the "warm" counterbalance to the "cold" efficiency of economic influences.

Critique of ideology is the programmatic goal that dominates the work of warm stream Marxists. As in scientific Marxism, ideology critique serves as a mode of analysis to uncover bourgeois class bias. For instance, Ernst Bloch studies religion, identifying forms of faith that contain political, revolutionary utopian hope. He contrasts these with other forms of faith that display bourgeois self-satisfaction and apathy toward social change.[24] Frankfurt School thinkers Adorno and Horkheimer analyze how the bourgeois attitude of "exchange value" dominates capitalist culture, a culture where everything—art, music, nature, and labor—is a commodity for trade, measured in terms of monetary value. Bourgeois culture has become an industry ruled by consumer values. Cultural products, whether they supply necessities or entertainment, are made and disseminated by means of technological mass production. Marcuse extends this critique, combining Marxist and Freudian theory to expose the pathology of bourgeois society, fixated on acquisition and competition.

Frankfurt School Marxist thinkers identify the economic status of Western Europe and America since roughly the 1930s as "late capitalism." In late capitalism, bourgeois culture is a mass culture shared by all classes, since the divide between proletariat and bourgeois has become blurred due to the increase in prosperity of most workers in the West.[25] The proletariat is no longer subject to severe oppression, as it was in the nineteenth century during Marx's lifetime, because increases in the wages of workers have been achieved thanks to trade union activity and state intervention, propelled in part by the activities of Marxist socialist groups. Ironically, the influence of Marxist activists has humanized capitalism and helped alleviate under-class suffering, while undercutting the motivation of workers to stage a revolution.

The main role of ideology critique for humanist Marxists is the awakening of critical consciousness. Its aim is summed up in the famous last sentence of Marx's *Theses on Feuerbach*, which reads: "The philosophers have only interpreted the world in various ways; the point is, to change it."[26] Warm stream Marxists object to the effacement of the role of the subject in scientific Marxism, where agency is attributed to classes whose collective actions are determined by the mechanistic imperative of material conditions. The crude materialism of scientific Marxism ignores the dimension of pedagogy and consciousness-raising in class formation. According to humanist Marxists, a class is not merely a group of people who share similar conditions of work and exploitation, but also a collective of persons who self-consciously recognize themselves as a class. The building of class solidarity requires education in critical thinking, and the critique of ideology can serve this function. Its goal is to make the proletariat subject conscious of the connection between suffering and material conditions, and the possibility of change in history.[27] Marx holds that the bourgeois intellectual has a moral and political mandate to provide the proletariat with "weapons for fighting the bourgeoisie" to awaken and educate them. Marx and most Marxist intellectuals are not members of the proletariat, but they take sides with the class suffering oppression.[28] Humanist Marxists consider critique of ideology as relevant not only for the proletariat class but for all persons, irrespective of class. This critique is not tied woodenly to instigating the proletarian revolution, as in Soviet Marxism, but in promoting a critical awareness of economic forces as causing social oppression and sustaining a shallow mass culture that stifles critique and conceals suffering.

The critique of ideology is itself a form of "praxis" defined as the activity of persons as history-making agents. Praxis is activity that has political consequences. Ideology critique is also known as revolutionary praxis. For warm stream Marxist thinkers, praxis covers any critically conscious activity such as solidarity, hope or protest. It involves critical reflection on both the material conditions causing suffering and ideologies condoning these conditions, as well as political activity to expose these conditions and ideologies to the public in the interest of raising consciousness and inciting rebellion. Praxis has a collective dimension, for critical reflection exposes the suffering of groups under the existing system of economics and reveals that history-making activity is group activity.[29]

Hope: The Rejection of Determinist Teleology

In response to evil and suffering in history, it is crucial to emphasize that warm stream Marxists are not determinists. They deny that history can be mapped according to a teleological, progressive pattern as orthodox Marxists attempt. Instead, they claim that history contains sudden reversals and leaps that are not predictable or logically explicable. The future is viewed as open, uncertain, and at risk. Humanist Marxists recognize that there are disastrous events of suffering and destruction in history, events that do not serve any purpose, such as the Holocaust. The scientific certainty of cold stream Marxism is contradicted by the interruptions of collective suffering. Without a dialectical and progressive teleology of history, there is no possibility of Hegelian theodicy. Suffering in history cannot be justified as an instrument for achieving development. In short, suffering is a scandal with no moral justification.

In the absence of a deterministic plot-line to history, the proletarian revolution is no longer viewed as a necessity, but a possibility. The Marxist study of conditions of production is used as a tool for proposing what "real" possibilities for change history holds. Such study is relevant for political planning, but it is not predictive of the future. Some warm stream Marxist thinkers, particularly Frankfurt School thinkers who study the distinctive features of late capitalism, hold at arm's length Marx's claim that the proletariat revolution is the sure means to overcome capitalism. Warm stream Marxists approve of political involvement dedicated to opposition to bourgeois culture and capitalist injustice, although there are many different views on what forms of activism are appropriate. But the critical emphasis of humanist Marxism gives rise to a counterbalancing tendency, which is an attitude of reservation toward political movements, even revolutionary ones. Critique is applied to political resistance movements themselves, exposing their ideological inconsistencies and coercive use of violence.

Unhinged from a teleological scheme, Marx's ideal of the communist society is viewed as a political hope rather than a deterministic prediction concerning the course of history. The gap between the present and the ideal goal of history is recognized as much larger than scientific, determinist Marxists claim.[30] The effectiveness of the ideal of communism, like the faith ideal of redemption, is that it contradicts and exposes the injustices in present reality and past history. Its function is to spur criticism of the inadequacies of the relations of production in the present. The definition of the communist ideal of a classless society must be thought "negatively," according to Adorno, as the absolute opposite of the suffering, oppression, and injustice found in history. The ultimate goal of history is understood in humanist, and not merely economic, terms as the realization of freedom and justice for all persons. Marx's early writings display the holistic character of the communist utopia where economic conditions of common ownership create a classless society, work satisfies human needs for creative production, and human relations are in harmony.[31] The economic conditions that would make this possible are socialist, but detailed knowledge of such a society is not possible as long as it remains an unrealized ideal.

The ultimacy of Marx's aspirations for society leads warm stream Marxists to compare Marxian hope with religious hope. Although humanist Marxists unanimously accept Marx's critique of religion as "opium" for those who suffer, they argue that certain forms of religious faith are an exception to this rule. For instance, the prophetic strand of Judaism is politicized in the work of Ernst Bloch, Walter Benjamin, and Theodor Adorno, where it is praised for its unflinching critical consciousness. A prophetic outlook inspired by Hebrew scriptures is also found among Christian thinkers such as Johann Baptist Metz, Dorothee Soelle, and Gustavo Gutiérrez, who stress the eschatological character of Jesus' teachings that criticize social oppression. Prophetic hope looks toward future redemption where there will be an end to suffering and injustice. The Marxian vision of communism and religious hope for redemption are ideals that share the same function: they act as a standard by which to measure the gravity of suffering in history. But in contrast with Marx's prediction of the triumph of communism, hope in God is not a form of optimism that predicts progress and justifies massive suffering on the slaughter bench of history, as theodicy does.[32] Rather, hope involves faith in scriptural promises of redemption and God's love, alongside recognition of ruptures of suffering and violence in history and the evident absence of redemption. The next two chapters study interpretations of Jewish and Christian faith, in a Marxian vein, that demonstrate how faith exposes and opposes unjust collective suffering under capitalist ruling-class ideologies, and fosters protest and resistance.

5 Faith as Hope in History
Ernst Bloch and Political
Post-Holocaust Theology

ERNST BLOCH IS A SECULAR Jewish philosopher and a major representative of warm stream Marxism. Bloch's most influential work, the three-volume *Principle of Hope*, interprets traditional Jewish and Christian hopes as congruent with Marxist ones. He considers religious faith as centrally concerned with the gravity of suffering and injustice. Faith in God is congruent with "political" hope for the alleviation of suffering in history and is antithetical to the optimism of theodicy. Bloch's affirmation of the political dimensions of faith was influential on German Christian theology in the late 1960s and contributed to the rise of Latin American liberation theology.[1] Congruencies between the positions of Bloch and Metz will be traced in chapter 6, while the impact of Bloch's thought on the political theology of Protestant thinker Jürgen Moltmann is discussed in the last section of this chapter. For both Christian thinkers, Bloch's perspective on history and hope prompts them to seek alternatives to theoretical theodicy.

SUFFERING IN HISTORY: AGAINST TELEOLOGICAL THEODICY

Bloch's rejection of theodicy rests on his objections to what he calls the "crude materialism" of orthodox Marxism and the determinism of Hegel's philosophy of history taken up by scientific Marxists. Bloch does not abandon the Marxian view that there are dialectical contradictions between modes of production and social relations between classes, which erupt in history to create massive political change. But he considers dialectical methodology as a tool for the study of the connections between economic, social, and political factors retrospectively. It does not lead to certainty regarding communism as the real *telos* of history. Bloch limits the scope and application of dialectics to history by asserting that dialectical logic does not encompass the past exhaustively. Hegel holds that all suffering in history has reason because all history is pervaded by dialectical logic. In contrast, Bloch insists that some events in history are "irrational" outbursts. Suffering and contradictions in history are not always resolved in the *Aufhebung* (mediation) of the past, where its inadequacies are overcome and its achievements somehow preserved. Bloch observes that massive collective suffering crashes through the picture of history as having a logical, teleological development. To prove his point, Bloch cites examples of so-called antihistorical events, by definition, events that bear no apparent logical connection to the achievement of an ideal just society. The Holocaust is a primary example; others selected from history are the Peloponnesian Wars, the rule of Nero, and the Thirty Years' War. Bloch declares that "all these apparently satanic outbursts belong to the dragon of the final abyss, not to the furthering of history" (PH I 310). Applied to the Holocaust, Hegelian theodicy is appalling. His passionate rejection of theodicy after Auschwitz is apparent in his statement: "To take the most hideous example, Hitler was by no stretch of the imagination the negation bringing socialism to final victory" (PH I 114). In denying a seamless logic to history, such massive events of suffering are not counted as necessary building blocks.

The claim that "the future is open" is a catchphrase of Bloch's philosophy (PH I 208). Bloch refuses to legitimate knowledge of the end of history. Like Kant, Bloch considers the rational idea of justice in history as an ideal that is an aim of human hope, but is not an item of speculative or scientific knowledge. Theodicy for Bloch is epistemically an impossibility. Bloch rejects both orthodox Marxist and Hegelian theodicies, not only because of their epistemic claims, but because they are insensitive to the moral scandal of suffering. He objects to the instrumental justification of suffering either as the necessary by-product of economic conditions that will lead to Marx's communist utopia, or as necessary for achieving Hegel's Absolute. Bloch also rejects Hegel's holistic, theistic justification of suffering based on God's self-manifestation in every stage of history. However, Bloch does not deny that suffering can have "use" in history in selective cases. Indeed he admits that the proletariat's suffering is one such instance. For Bloch observes that "misery, once it realizes its causes, becomes the revolutionary lever itself" (PH III 1358). Here Bloch appears to agree with scientific Marxists. Even if suffering is not necessary for Bloch in the sense that it is part of a closed, determinist plot-line, it still seems instrumentally justified.

But, in fact, Bloch's statement that suffering can instigate political change is not an instrumental theodicy justification. His point is not that suffering is necessary in the global scheme of things to make the dialectical logic of progress possible. The "use" of suffering is contingent on a response of protest and resistance. It is critical consciousness of the nature and causes of suffering by a group of people that makes suffering useful as a motivating factor for political activity. Bloch's point is not that misery inevitably leads to revolution, which would be to justify suffering, but that misery can possibly lead to revolution if there is critical awareness and agency among those who suffer.[2]

When Bloch observes that positing the certainty of a utopian end of history "in the face of the misery of the world" is "both wicked and feebleminded," his outrage is not only a dispute about historical dialectics but a moral criticism (PH III 1372). Bloch considers it an offense to victims to place their suffering in a dialectical scheme, which is the antithesis of recognizing and lamenting the horrible and wasteful suffering of the past. Bloch does not judge the past by a theistic standard of what is necessary for divine self-development, as Hegel does, but by a moral and anthropocentric standard of justice and freedom for all persons. A moral perspective on history protests the suffering of the poor and oppressed. In this light, suffering is never tolerable or excusable for a higher end or a global scheme of God's history. From the perspective of persons who are under the burden of sociopolitically caused suffering and those who are sensitive to such suffering, theodicy answers are unacceptable.

HOPE AS POLITICAL VISION AND REAL POSSIBILITY: RESISTANCE TO SUFFERING

Bloch defines "hope" as an "anticipatory consciousness" that looks with suspenseful gaze toward positive future possibilities for history.[3] Bloch uses examples drawn from world history, art, philosophy, and religion to support the observation that utopian imaginings are oriented around hopes for the fulfillment of all humanity and the end of socially caused suffering. The anticipatory consciousness offers pointers toward a new direction in history, which Bloch calls the "Novum" (PH I 124). This anticipatory consciousness or hope has two different sides: subjective and objective. On the one hand, hope is the imaginative anticipation or premonition of a utopia. Specifically, Bloch points to the symbols of religion that move beyond the given to offer guiding images of hope's goal. On the other hand, material conditions (social, political, and economic) are a second source for hope, because critical reflection on these conditions provokes the formulation of utopian hopes that can be realized in history. Hope is both creative and grounded in reality.[4]

According to Bloch, hope includes faith in the "real possibility" of utopian wishes. Hope is militant. It refuses "to be outvoted by anything that has already become" (PH I 147). In its anticipation of change in history, hope refuses to compromise or be content with half-measures (PH I 146). However, the militancy of hope is not based on certain knowledge of the future. Bloch insists that hope can be disappointed, for it bears no guarantee of success. Once the orthodox Marxist philosophy of history is rejected, an acute tension arises between history's contingency and hope's militant optimism. Clearly the subjective, imaginative basis of hope is not alone strong enough support for the conviction that large-scale suffering in history can never block the openness of the future to new possibilities (PH I 200). Bloch's answer to this objection is that hope is rooted in the material process of history's movement; it arises from real objective material conditions of history (PH III 1293).[5] Human consciousness is a correlate of the social, economic, and political conditions of life. Bloch reverses the direction of the orthodox Marxist claim about the connection between material infrastructure and human consciousness. He denies that consciousness is totally determined by material conditions; rather, he affirms that it can become aware of these conditions in order to change them. Hope emerges from the material socioeconomic conditions of history, which lie open to positive possibilities of change for the better (PH I 124). Addressing this connection between material conditions and hope, Bloch writes that "history has its timetable, the works that transcend their time often cannot even be intended . . . this barrier is ultimately founded solely in the historical state of the material, above all in its own processive, unfinished state" (PH I 130). The emergence of utopian hope occurs in very different economic and political circumstances, not only in the Marxist reaction to capitalism, but also in more than two thousand years of Jewish and Christian writings.

Within the history of Western culture, Bloch diagnoses the presence of a substratum of progressive utopian thought. Memory allows subjects to claim this inheritance of utopian hope for the present (PH I 156). Key examples of such anticipations cited by Bloch are Moses' hope in the promised land, Jesus' preaching of the Kingdom of God, and Marx's utopia of a classless society, for each is a "prophetic premonition of the adequate" (AC 255). The content of hope in all three cases is the social and individual fulfillment of all persons, which requires resistance to present injustices and ambitions for change (PH III 1367). The affinity of Bloch's thought with German Romanticism of the nineteenth century is apparent in the holistic character of his vision of human fulfillment and also in his admiration for the daring Promethean religious figures who lead the way toward this hope.

Bloch's utopianism appears religious to fellow Marxists, in a derogatory sense, because he dares to posit an ultimate utopia that goes beyond communism.[6] He calls this absolute utopia the "*Ultimum*," which he describes as a "total leap out of everything that previously existed" (PH I 200). The formulation of this final utopian goal reveals the influence of Hegel, for its aim is human fulfillment in society or, as Hegel would put it, the self-realization of humanity or Spirit. The broad humanist aim of the early Marx's writing is to discover the economic and social conditions under which all people can find fulfillment in work within an egalitarian society.[7] For warm stream Marxists, like Bloch, a communist classless society is not an end in itself but "a condition for a life in freedom, life in happiness, life in possible fulfillment" (PH I 131).

Bloch claims that utopian ideals do not have fully elaborated positive content. Instead, they give direction to political thought and action as a "goal determination of the human will" (PH I 202). By his definition, "the essential function of utopia is a critique of what is present."[8] The most radical goal of hope, the *Ultimum*, can only be understood "in a negative sense, namely as the mere non-existence of the characteristics of the class society, or at most in the deeply remote, still completely hovering meaning of a 'naturalization of man, humanization of nature'" (PH I 131). In positive terms, Bloch describes his utopian vision as an unprejudiced and tolerant classless society, which holds an "inter-subjective solidarity, a many-voiced unity of direction of wills which are filled with the same human-concrete goal-content" (PH III 969). His appeal to the *Ultimum* appears religious to most Marxists because it requires "faith" in a miraculous leap to a perfect social condition. Bloch recognizes that this ultimate utopia is a stretch of both the imagination and the real possibilities of history. He writes that even an attained classless society (a distant utopia in itself) is "separated from the religious-utopian kingdom by a leap which the explosive intention of rebirth and transfiguration itself posits" (PH III 1198).[9] But to critics who might consider the *Ultimum* so distant as to be irrelevant to political planning, Bloch defends his utopia, insisting that this distant goal "is involved in every proximate goal, making it a real goal and not just another more or less simple reproduction of past life" (AC 255). The *Ultimum* is a regulative ideal that acts as a critical standard for discerning injustice and socially caused or exacerbated suffering in the past and present. It is also a symbol of a real possibility in history.

Hope in Bloch's view is a political model of religious faith involving revolutionary political activity, which accompanies anticipation of the ultimate future. Hope is not merely an interpretation of history, as Marx derides Hegel's philosophy for being (PH I 266). The practices of hope are criticism of ideologies and oppressive material conditions, and political resistance.[10] On these points Bloch draws approval from liberation theologians, for they affirm his focus on suffering caused by economic material structures and the immediate link he makes between eschatological hope and resistance.

RELIGIOUS FAITH AS THE PRAXIS OF HOPE

Bloch is distinctive among cold and warm stream Marxists for his fascination with the Hebrew and Christian scriptures and his praise of theistic faith. Although Bloch is an atheist, he finds a tradition of prophetic and eschatological faith in the Bible that is not socially and politically conservative, but sharply critical of suffering caused by economic and political oppression. In his book *Atheism in Christianity*, Bloch offers interpretations of Judaism and Christianity that draw out similarities between biblical prophetic hope and Marxist hope. He finds in the Hebrew Bible and the Christian New Testament powerful expression of the murmurings of the poor and the downtrodden. He claims that biblical narratives express the rebellious sentiments of human "suffering that will suffer no longer" (AC 26). Religious symbols can be prescient of utopian possibilities for history, in his view, and religion can have transformative power in history. Unlike Marx who considers religion to function as an opiate always and everywhere, Bloch argues that religion can function critically to promote change.

Apolitical Christianity and Political Faith

Bloch recognizes that his interpretation of the Bible is at odds with the way the Bible has often functioned in religious institutions. Throughout the majority of Christian history in Europe, as Marx originally observed, the Bible has been put to antirevolutionary uses, and faith has served as an ideology that maintains the political status quo. In the twentieth century, Christian existentialist theology is viewed as an example of just such a religious ideology. Existentialist thought takes the form of a supposedly disinterested, universal discourse, while oblivious to class differences and the connections between social suffering and economic conditions. It proposes an otherworldly form of faith, according to Bloch, because faith centers around the salvation of the individual that occurs in the present by means of private decision.[11] Since the center of faith is the relation of God to the individual, the existentialist approach is deficient in historical consciousness, protest, and resistance. This critique applies more to Marcel than to Buber, who does not portray faith as unconcerned with history or society. However, Buber is in accord with Marcel and other existentialists in recommending an interpersonal

I-Thou response to suffering, and neither Buber nor Marcel emphasizes collective resistance motivated by faith to overthrow the existing political and economic system.

Bloch illustrates the difference between a conservative faith ideology and a politically directed faith by contrasting the attitudes of two sixteenth-century Protestant reformers, Martin Luther and Thomas Münzer. Bloch notes how Luther and Münzer each address the collective material conditions of suffering experienced by German peasants bound, at that time by the feudal system dominated by landowners and clergy who had the advantages of wealth, political influence, and social privilege. In response to the Peasants' War, both theologians offer a theological interpretation of the peasants' daily suffering. Luther's response to the peasants' protest against physical and economic deprivation is to preach patience, meekness, and dependence on God for their needs. Luther comforts the oppressed peasants with the promise of compensation in heaven for their sufferings on earth (AC 23). His refusal to endorse political protest is based on his doctrine of two Kingdoms, which separates church and state authority, thereby authorizing current political leaders as God's designated envoys to be obeyed.

Bloch decries Luther's response as a master ideology, which serves the rich and powerful by suppressing not only political rebellion, but any sort of "this-worldly" hope for large-scale change. In contrast, it is Thomas Münzer who provides a model of political faith for Bloch. Münzer views hope for change in history as essential to faith in God. In his theology, a person with faith is directly empowered by God's Spirit, which enables the boldness to attempt to change history. Moreover, faith in God unites human beings in solidarity with each other. Münzer's eschatology of God's Kingdom is immanent and historical. In his own life, hope in God motivates him to rebel against political institutions and leaders, as part of Christian striving to bring God's Kingdom to earth.[12] Because he took up arms and acted as a leader of a peasant rebellion, Münzer met a martyr's death. Contrary to Marx's assumption about religion as an opiate, the example of Münzer demonstrates for Bloch how faith and protest are linked in the practice of hope.

Moses and Job: Heroes of the Hebrew Bible

Bloch observes that the Bible can be enlisted for both utopian and conservative agendas. The Bible's critical potential, which doctrines and institutions do not have, lies in its narratives of religious figures who symbolize hope and the transcendence of ideology. These champions of faith dare to criticize God or the gods, and they advocate for the welfare of all humanity. In doing so, they follow the prototype of Prometheus who opposes the gods for the sake of humankind, taking fire from heaven to give to mortals living on earth (AC 51).[13]

Among Bloch's heroes, Moses is the earliest in the biblical tradition. According to Bloch, Moses founded the first religion of opposition and revolution, destroying idols, or false gods, and resisting oppression. The Exodus out of Egypt is paradigmatic as an event of liberation that is simultaneously religious and political. The journey to Canaan, the land promised by God, involves opposition to the social injustice of slavery in Egypt. The hope of Moses represents the hope of a suffering and enslaved people (PH III 1232). The model of faith represented by Moses is clearly eschatological; it is a political hope that looks toward God's Kingdom as future expectation. Faith in the future reality of God's Kingdom is at the same time the historical consciousness that real change is possible. Bloch contrasts the God of Moses, the "invisible god of righteousness," with the "gods of astral-mythic fate" worshipped by other nations. The God of Moses cannot be made present in visible form, as an idol, nor is this God a god of Fate who dictates the doom of history. The being of the God of Israel encompasses the present, past, and future (Ex. 3:14). Although God's Kingdom lies in the distant future, it is not otherworldly or extrinsic to history. The *Ultimum* is not already finished and eternally in place, to be reached by either ritual mysteries or an act of existential commitment. The faith response to the suffering of the people Israel is to hope and work toward establishing God's Kingdom.

Another emblematic biblical figure is Job. Bloch reads the book of Job as a breakthrough on the level of insight; specifically, it critiques theodicy as an ideology that is the opposite of faith protest and hope for justice. Bloch holds up the figure of Job as the Hebrew Prometheus who dares to rebel and call God to task for God's lack of justice and abandonment of those who suffer. Although many interpreters consider Job as a text focusing only on one individual's suffering, Bloch (like Buber) offers a different interpretation. He groups Job with prophetic biblical literature, viewing prophetic texts together as a response to the collective suffering of Israel. Job's protest is not only on his own behalf as an individual sufferer, but it is a decisive expression of Israel's dissatisfaction with theodicy explanations for suffering as deserved. The defeat of the Northern and Southern Kingdoms in the sixth century B.C.E. and the captivity of the Israelites in Babylon were the crucial events responsible for the turn against theodicy represented in Job (PH III 1283). Bloch agrees with commentators who firmly reject the rationalization by Job's friends that his suffering is a punishment for sin. What sets Bloch's interpretation of Job apart from Buber's is that Bloch casts suspicion on the apparent repentance and humility that Job displays after hearing God's speeches. Buber, along with the majority of interpreters, affirms that direct encounter with God restores and strengthens Job's faith. But Bloch argues that Job is not satisfied by God's speeches but instead questions the moral authenticity of the God who speaks.

Bloch recognizes that in Job there are competing notions of God in play. One is the notion of God as judge who distributes suffering as punishment for sin—the God of Job's friends who believe that his suffering is just retribution. Another figuration of God is found in the whirlwind. The God of the whirlwind boasts of omnipotence and nature's power and grandeur, but not of justice or promises of redemption (PH III 1234). This God shows no apparent moral concern for injustice. The third God is the God to whom Job prays as he protests his suffering. This God of justice is addressed when Job calls out for God to "witness" his suffering (Job 16:18) and to act as an "advocate" for those who suffer (Job 19:25). According to Bloch, this God is the hope of Israel, the God of Moses who leads oppressed people out of captivity. Typically, interpreters of Job agree that the whirlwind God is the advocate that Job sought and the answer to Job's complaint. However, Bloch is unique in driving a wedge between the whirlwind God and the divine witness to whom Job prays (AC 111–115). Bloch views the happy ending of Job's story with suspicion because he considers Job's repentance as complicit in a religious ideology of acceptance and passivity centering on an omnipotent tyrant God who is an oppressor, not a God of hope and protest. Job rebels against this tyrant God, but retains hope in the advocate God, the God of justice. The book of Job offers a model of religious discourse that articulates dilemmas of faith clearly and unrelentingly and exposes the tension between suffering and faith as basic within the Jewish and Christian traditions. The narrative of Job legitimizes protest and opposition to theodicy, but it does not justify God morally. Instead, it offers a model of faith opposition to suffering without explaining or defending God's goodness.

Like Bloch, liberation theologians also commend Job's protest and rejection of theodicy explanations. Gustavo Gutiérrez and Dorothee Soelle note how Job himself takes on the role of advocate for those who suffer; he is aware that poverty and abandonment are a collective problem that calls for solidarity.[14] Job is not concerned only with his own plight, but also with the plight of others who suffer unjustly. Politically, the book of Job shows that it is a moral scandal to silence the voice of someone who suffers, including victims of social oppression. A troubling feature of Job is how it exposes the sadistic connotations of a God who destroys Job's family and property and tortures an innocent person.[15] The God of the prologue and epilogue, who allows the Accuser, or Satan, to test Job, is rejected by both Bloch and liberation thinkers. However, the God of the whirlwind can be a positive image of the divine, even though the whirlwind does not represent moral justice.

Contrary to Bloch's position, politically oriented thinkers do not necessarily reject the God of the whirlwind as a cruel spectator. Indeed, Gutiérrez and Soelle find positive significance in Job's dialogue with God. They hold that this encounter enables Job to accept suffering without theodicy answers. Although in her earlier writings, Soelle joins Bloch in criticizing the whirlwind God as amoral, she has since come to agree with Gutiérrez that political protest should be accompanied by mystical faith that detects God's direct presence in suffering. Job's faith is a wager that God cares for victims of injustice; it is not an instrumental faith, expecting reward. Job encounters God, even though God's being transcends comprehension.[16] In my view, the whirlwind speeches are the key to a practical response to suffering. Direct contact with God does not answer Job's questions, but it makes meaning and the acceptance of suffering possible. As Gutiérrez and Soelle observe, and Buber would agree, the whirlwind God displays a gratuitous love in creating and sustaining the world, although this divine love does not fit narrow human definitions of justice.[17] These liberation theologians advocate political resistance to suffering, as does Bloch, but they take a position analogous to Buber's in claiming that suffering can be accepted and gain meaning through dialogue with God. Political protest and encounter with God are not mutually exclusive responses to suffering, as Bloch assumes.

Jesus and the Immanence of God's Kingdom

Bloch considers Jesus to be the culminating prophetic figure in the Jewish utopian and messianic tradition. Bloch reads the gospels as portraying an historical Jesus who took the side of the poor and oppressed, who rebelled against the temple leaders, moneychangers, and other powerful figures who represent the institutionalization of injustice. Jesus died as a rebel against the religious and political establishment, a troublemaker who loosened the bonds of religious law, tradition, and family obligation (PH III 1262). Bloch describes Jesus as the founder of a community of "love-communism" who preached voluntary poverty as a means to a transformed socialist community where all things are held in common (Acts 4:32). Jesus did not approve of poverty as such; rather, he criticized religious and political institutions for causing or condoning suffering due to poverty and oppression (PH III 1264).

Bloch considers the incarnation of God in Jesus Christ as an eschatological symbol. As both Son of Man and Son of God, Christ's incarnation signifies historical eschatological hope overcoming the spatialized image of a superworldly God and a supernatural kingdom separate from history (AC 164). Bloch resists interpreting the arrival of God's Kingdom as an event that occurs, independent of history, through the inner conversion of the individual, as Protestant theologian Rudolph Bultmann would have it. The Kingdom of

God is at hand, as Jesus teaches, in the sense that it is a historical possibility.[18] His death and resurrection are a prefiguration of the fulfillment of the King-dom. In Jesus Christ, the transcendent symbol of the God "who will be" be-comes an immanent symbol simultaneously related to society (Kingdom) and humanity (Son of God). In Bloch's interpretation, God's Kingdom is a symbol of the total hope content of humanity, which anticipates Marx's vision of a so-ciety without oppression where human beings live in harmony with each other and nature. This religious symbol functions to motivate critique of suffering in the present and to foster political resistance. "In light of the *Ultimum*," writes Bloch, "everything seems like unfinished work" (PH I 221).

The strength of Bloch's response to suffering is that he reunites the po-litical and religious, so often held apart by both Marxists and Christians alike. Using political criteria, he seeks to make faith plausible in the light of massive suffering according to political criteria, showing how faith, hope for history, and protest are linked. But as we will see, theologians such as Metz and Moltmann part ways with Bloch by insisting on the reality of God and the need for God's participation in realizing the *Ultimum*.

HOPE AND SUFFERING IN JÜRGEN MOLTMANN'S POST-HOLOCAUST THEOLOGY

Bloch's *Principle of Hope* has decisively influenced Christian political, post-Holocaust German theology, as represented by Jürgen Moltmann, Dorothee Soelle, and Johann Baptist Metz.[19] They take from Bloch the conviction that hope is situated in the struggles and contingencies of history. Such hope is incompatible with a teleology that neatly resolves the plot-line of suffering in history. Confronted with the Holocaust and other massive cases of suffer-ing, faith should not try to move beyond the rupture it creates. In fact, the historical reality of suffering cannot be reconciled with redemption here and now. Redemption of those who have suffered remains an opaque goal of hope, something anticipated rather than known. Attempts to transcend the Holocaust with salvific claims disregard the interruptive character of suffer-ing in history. A theodicy that proposes explanations and justifications for suffering negates the anticipatory status of faith and hope, minimizes the scandal of suffering, and ignores the importance of protest.

Theology of Hope

The thinker who most explicitly borrows from Bloch's philosophy is Jürgen Moltmann, whose early political theology translates Bloch's insights into Chris-tian theological terms. Moltmann echoes Bloch in advancing an eschatological interpretation of faith. As the title shows, Moltmann's *Theology of Hope* (1967) was inspired by admiration for Bloch's *Principle of Hope*. Like Bloch, Moltmann criticizes Hegel's teleological theodicy for denying the contradiction between suffering and redemption, and thus effacing the reality of persons standing in the midst of history and its suffering.[20] In Moltmann's analysis, Christian faith centers on hope, which is utopian and political. Hope decidedly has this-worldly political aspirations, and it "seeks for opportunities of bringing history into ever better correspondence to the promised future," which consists in God's promises of peace and justice.[21] In history, anticipatory signs of God's future Kingdom exist where love, self-surrender, and hope for justice and freedom are found. Nevertheless, human beings can see only the very partial fulfillment of God's eschatological promises in history.[22]

Biblical accounts of the life of Jesus are decisive for understanding the posture of hope. Moltmann interprets the narratives of the cross and resurrection in an eschatological mode. He argues that the resurrection has the anticipatory character of promise, not an already-accomplished victory. It represents the "not-yet" but "real" possibility of redemption for all those who have suffered and died. As anticipated but not known, redemption cannot be defined explicitly in positive terms. The present lies under the sign of the cross, which symbolizes human suffering throughout history. The memory of Christ's betrayal, torture, and death on the cross represents suffering caused by human cruelty and the feeling of abandonment by God. In sum, the cross indicates the uneasy tension between the reality of history, as a history of suffering, and religious hope in redemption.

Moltmann's political theology has two dimensions — liberationist and Trinitarian—that coexist in methodological tension. The dimension consistent with Bloch's philosophy is the liberation emphasis on faith praxis and hope. In particular, Moltmann proposes that narratives about Jesus Christ reveal faith postures or "praxes" that should be imitated. He places particular emphasis on the cross as the central event in Jesus' life. Divine suffering on the cross is understood as enacting the paradox that love for those who suffer can lead to suffering. Moltmann displays how God and human suffering are related through Jesus' praxis of suffering, which includes solidarity, resistance, hope, and willingness to suffer and even die for others.[23] Religious hope is a practice suspended between suffering and God's Kingdom, between the cross and resurrection. The memory of the cross teaches persons how to suffer in a productive and meaningful manner, with hope for redemption. Moltmann's interpretation of suffering adds an important element to Bloch's proposal. The practice of hope not only resists and protests suffering, but it includes the acceptance of suffering as a political act of solidarity.

Divine Suffering after Auschwitz

The second dimension of Moltmann's political theology, elaborated in his major work, *The Crucified God* (1973) and later volumes, is Trinitarian and systematic. Specifically, it involves the proposal that God's suffering is the only viable answer to theodicy questions and the only effective Christian response to the Holocaust. Moltmann asserts that on the cross, God suffers as a victim. He claims that God's suffering in the event of the crucifixion, as the Father and the Son, encompasses all human suffering. God's suffering in Christ shares the dynamics of human suffering in its physical, psychological, and social aspects, including the wrenching experience of abandonment by God. Christ's cry of dereliction, "My God, why have you forsaken me?" is the focal point of Moltmann's theology of divine suffering. On the cross, Jesus Christ (the second person of the Trinity) experiences abandonment by God the Father (the first person) along with bodily pains and the pain of betrayal by many of his followers. But God the Father also suffers because of love for the Son.[24] To conceive of divine abandonment, Moltmann must allow for distinct experiences between the divine persons of the Father and Son. This unconventional interpretation of divine suffering requires that Moltmann go beyond the strictures of the classical Western Christian notion of the Trinity, departing from the standard interpretation of the Nicene creed statement that there is one divine nature and three divine persons. For the task of reinterpreting the Trinity and the complexity of God's nature, Moltmann borrows from Eastern Orthodox thought. In Orthodox theology, the three persons of the Trinity are given certain independence of experience or feeling. The doctrine that the highest good, God, is unchanging, simple, self-sufficient, and impassible, affirmed in the classical theism of Western Christianity, is rejected.[25] Moltmann asserts not only that God is capable of suffering, but that God experiences various sufferings as Father and Son.

The motivation for Moltmann's Trinitarian innovation is his desire to formulate a Christian response to the Holocaust that faces up to the massive interruptive character of suffering in history. The attribution of suffering to God is Moltmann's alternative to traditional theodicy, predicated on divine omnipotence and impassibility. The significance of the cross in view of horrendous suffering is that "the great abyss of the world's godforsakenness is thus taken within the Trinitarian love between the Father and the Son."[26] In asserting that God suffers, Moltmann intends to draw attention away from the theodicy question: 'Why does God allow human suffering?' The cross is the most effective Christian response to theodicy, in his view, because in Christ's death, "God no longer stands before the forum of the human question of theodicy, but is himself [*sic*] incorporated in it."[27] The participation of God in suffering indicates solidarity between God and victims. The feeling of abandonment, or the "eclipse of God" in Buber's terms, and suffering itself are valorized as essential to faith, rather than rejected as a mark of atheism. Divine suffering confirms that history is unavoidably and thoroughly scarred by suffering. But how does the fact that God suffers help persons withstand suffering? Suffering is not hopeless because of the resurrection of Jesus Christ. Since the crucified God is also the resurrected God, suffering in the present bears the promise of future redemption. Hope rests not only on utopian promises of God's Kingdom, as Bloch would have it, but on the redemption of the world through the suffering of God on the cross.

However, the Trinitarian treatment of suffering in Moltmann's theology neither escapes the problems of traditional theodicy nor avoids triumphalism.[28] The anticipatory "not-yet" character of the resurrection becomes effaced in Moltmann's discussions of the Trinitarian history of God. Despite his criticism of Hegel, Moltmann's theology shares the liability of Hegel's theodicy: both offer a resolution to the plot-line of history. Moltmann embarks on the theoretical project of giving an account of God's inner life from creation to redemption. The dialectical tension between suffering and faith for persons in history becomes lost in conceptual elaboration of the Trinity.[29] Another point of criticism, and another parallel with Hegel, is the fact that Moltmann's identification of God's suffering with all suffering in history makes suffering instrumental for salvation. Moltmann does not intend God's suffering to minimize the scandal of human suffering, but he does so by giving it positive historical usefulness. His Trinitarian theology loses sight of the "not-yet" character of hope in its conceptual elaboration of God's nature and undermines political expectancy and protest in response to the scandal of suffering in history.

A further objection to Moltmann's notion of divine suffering is raised by feminist thinkers who are concerned about the masochistic glorification of suffering, represented by the cross, and the high value placed on suffering as divine. Focus on the crucifixion portrays suffering as the hallmark of faith, as if suffering should be sought to serve God. But, as Delores Williams points out, suffering for the sake of others is a form of surrogacy, or substitution for others' suffering, that has been an abusive phenomenon in African-American women's history. Such suffering is not redemptive. In her view, rather than the cross, the ministerial vision of Jesus' life deserves symbolic priority and imitation. Instead of suffering, why not focus on the incarnation of divine creativity in human action as modeled by Jesus Christ?[30] Life-affirming faith practice should take priority over execution or suffering, as a model for faith. Feminist theologians affirm that to live with faith in

God means to live a life of love, joy, and sharing. It is the memory of Jesus' life and resurrection, not the cross, that is the more positive inspiration for political activism and resistance to suffering.[31] Hope seeks peace and healing found in God's overcoming of suffering.

The idea of divine suffering does not make the logical disjunction between God's goodness and the history of suffering any less problematic. Moreover, divine suffering is not necessarily a helpful concept in response to the Holocaust and other massive suffering. Based on practical considerations, it is inconclusive whether faith in a God who transcends suffering is a stronger motivation for hope and resistance than faith in a suffering God. I reject Moltmann's assumption that a passible God is the most fitting concept of God after Auschwitz. For one, God can be understood as identifying with human suffering without locating suffering directly in God's own being. In Jewish thought, God's suffering and exile are identified with certain facets of God, such as the *Shekinah* in Kabbalistic philosophy, while Christians can affirm suffering in Jesus Christ, God's Son, without extending suffering to God's self. Against Moltmann, Catholic theologian Thomas Weinandy has developed an account of Chalcedonian Christology that shows convincingly how God's nearness to human suffering can be practically helpful to sufferers without denying divine impassibility. Second, the traditional view of a God who does not suffer ontologically holds the advantage of accentuating the fact that divine love transcends suffering.[32] A nonsuffering God provides a stronger basis for hope in the overcoming of suffering in response to the Holocaust. Although inspired by Bloch's philosophy, Moltmann's theology develops a systematic account of God's being and history that contradicts the promissory character of hope and the Marxian emphasis on practice. His theodicy of divine suffering leads to difficulties in justifying divine goodness no less troubling than those of other theoretical theodicies.

Marxian Hope as Eschatology

The political approach is distinguished by its efforts to make the intersection of faith and suffering plausible in terms of the practice of hope. Within the contingencies of history, hope does not possess teleological knowledge, but an eschatological anticipation of redemption. The contradiction between suffering and hope for God's Kingdom is the religious impulse for protest that carries over into political activity.[33] The role that God plays in hope is importantly different for Bloch and Moltmann. Bloch considers God as a symbol of a utopian possibility to be realized by human action. In contrast, Moltmann (and Metz) consider hope as the affirmation of human possibilities along with reliance on God's power to redeem history. It is agreed by political thinkers that Jesus serves as a model of how faith responds to the suffering of others, particularly groups of poor and oppressed persons. But it is not agreed whether divine suffering can diffuse theodicy questions. Placing God on the side of suffering justifies neither the amounts, kinds, and distributions of suffering found in the world, nor the magnitude of suffering. The contradiction between divine omnipotence and human suffering in traditional theodicy is evaded by Moltmann, but the question of why a loving God would allow the suffering of humanity remains vexing. From Bloch's standpoint, there is insufficient knowledge of God to solve such conundrums.

In the next chapter, we will discover that Metz does not find Moltmann's Trinitarian proposal to be an improvement over traditional theodicy or a necessary move in response to the magnitude of the Holocaust. Metz takes the Jewish prohibition against idolatry and Marxist ideology critique as warnings against attempts at theodicy, where knowledge of God is used to justify suffering. He proposes a prophetic model of faith in which contradiction between God's promised justice and suffering in history is never eased. Rather, it is on account of this contradiction that faith fuels protest and resistance. Under the influence of warm stream Marxist thinkers Walter Benjamin and Theodor Adorno, Metz is distinctive in recognizing the mystical character of politically oriented faith and the importance of Holocaust memory for hope and protest.

6 Solidarity and Resistance
Johann Baptist Metz's Theodicy-Sensitive Response to Suffering

BLOCH PRAISES RELIGION FOR its revolutionary potential from the standpoint of humanist Marxist philosophy. Johann Baptist Metz, in contrast, is a Catholic thinker whose work falls under the rubric of political fundamental theology.[1] However, Metz's thought bears strong resemblance to Bloch's method of interpreting Jewish and Christian faith to expose their political dimensions, using the tools of warm stream Marxist thought. Like Bloch, he reads the Bible as centrally concerned with resistance to socially caused suffering and as eschatological in impulse. Metz is intolerant of all theologies, particularly existentialist types, that do not recognize the socially critical character of faith. The political theology developed in Metz's major work *Faith in History and Society* (1977) aims to show how faith responds with critical consciousness to what Marx termed "material" historical conditions, namely, the economic, social, and political conditions that are the causes of suffering. Metz is militant in rejecting theodicy, especially Hegelian theodicy with its attribution of logical progress to history. Metz considers this teleological view of history antithetical to the reality of suffering, which interrupts and fractures history. As an alternative to theodicy, Metz advances a "theodicy-sensitive" religious response to suffering. His response shows how faith and suffering are not in contradiction, as theodicy might assume, even though satisfying answers to theodicy questions cannot be found. The kind of faith that is plausible in the face of suffering, according to Metz, is the prophetic model of faith of the Bible: faith in response to situations of collective suffering. Metz elaborates his model of political faith using the categories of memory, narrative, hope, and solidarity.

81

Reflecting on his major influences, Metz claims that his preoccupation with suffering is shaped by three key crises in his intellectual development: Marxist philosophy, Third World oppression, and the Holocaust.[2] Each crisis has been significant for Metz in exposing the social and political character of suffering in history, and the Eurocentric and bourgeois tendencies in Christian practice and theology.

The first crisis, Marxist philosophy, is a bombshell because of its sharp critique of religion. Metz acknowledges that religion indeed has functioned to suppress protest against suffering. He applies Marxist ideology critique to contemporary Christian faith, which, he observes, shares the bourgeois apathy of Western European society, an apathy evasive of suffering. The warm stream Marxist thinkers who have most influenced Metz's thought are Walter Benjamin and Theodor Adorno. Metz places great importance on Adorno's insight that the religious notion of redemption functions critically as a "negative" ideal, beyond full conceptualization and beyond the reach of historical realization. Redemption is a measure for injustice in history, Metz affirms.[3] The critical function of redemption does not rule out the "real possibility" of redemption anticipated by persons of faith. Metz objects to both Adorno's statement that redemption always remains an unrealized ideal and Bloch's view that the *Ultimum* is a possible human achievement. Humanist Marxism, as represented by Bloch and Adorno, does not find itself resolvable in Jewish and Christian eschatology because it denies God's reality. Metz insists that redemption is really possible precisely because of divine involvement. The Marxist thinker who lends support to this view is Benjamin, who views the messianic moment of redemption as apocalyptic and interruptive of history (FHS 176).[4]

The second crisis that shapes Metz's political theology is awareness of Third World poverty and oppression. His political theology is a Western analogue of Latin American liberation theology. He agrees that liberation from suffering is the guiding theme in Scripture. Metz praises liberation theologians for drawing attention to a type of suffering and injustice Eurocentric theology typically has ignored, specifically, to widespread economic and political problems that cause poverty and suffering in Latin America (AA 49). The failure to reflect on the Western orientation of theology as an academic discipline is, according to Metz, connected with the failure to reflect on the inequalities and injustices between wealthy and poor nations.[5] Like Marxist thinkers Metz draws attention to socioeconomically caused suffering, and he discovers in the Jewish and Christian traditions a critical response to such suffering.

The third formative crisis for Metz is the Holocaust. He is gripped by the memory of suffering symbolized by Auschwitz. From his own experience as a teenager in Germany during World War II, Metz identifies with the feeling expressed by Holocaust survivors of God's absence from history and their protest against God's indifference to suffering. Metz asserts that a Christian response to suffering ought to give Holocaust victims authority with respect to the religious interpretation of this catastrophe.[6] Metz concurs with Holocaust survivor and novelist Elie Wiesel in exposing the lack of answers to the questions that innocent suffering poses, and in rejecting theistic theodicy explanations and justifications as offering neither intellectual nor emotional comfort in the face of Auschwitz.[7]

Chapter 6 is organized in three parts. The first focuses on Metz's critiques of bourgeois forms of subjectivity, existentialist thought, and theodicy—critiques that clear away inadequate cultural and religious options in preparation for Metz's constructive theological intent. The second part studies Metz's theological proposals concerning the role of memory, narrative, and eschatology formulated in *Faith in History and Society* and other works. The third part analyzes Metz's more recent proposal for a theodicy-sensitive theology centering around prayer, mystical experience, and messianic social practice. Against theodicy, Metz argues for the plausibility of faith as a response to suffering, not for its ability to answer questions about God, but because it is clear-eyed in its recognition of the severity of suffering in history and because it responds actively with eschatological hope and protest.

METZ'S CRITIQUES OF BOURGEOIS SUBJECTIVITY AND EXISTENTIALIST THEOLOGY

Metz uses the adjective "bourgeois" as a pejorative term to describe the attitudes, assumptions, and behaviors of middle-class citizens in capitalist, Western Europe.[8] What defines the bourgeois subject is a consumer outlook, an operational attitude toward persons and things, the absence of historical memory, an absence of hope, and the privatization of religion. As we have seen, Marcel and Buber also criticize contemporary society as having a distorted perspective, but they identify technology and its instrumental "having" or "I-It" attitude as the major problem. In comparison, Metz's emphasis on the ills of consumerism, capitalism, and class injustice, rather than science and technology, is a consequence of his Marxian influences.

The bourgeois subject, according to Metz, views land, nature, art, manufactured objects, and human labor as commodities for sale. Conversely, anything lacking monetary exchange value falls outside of this dominant scheme of value and becomes marginal in importance. Aspects of life that are not easily quantified in terms of capital exchange, such as love and loyalty, religion, aesthetic taste, and morality, become pushed into the domain of the private subjective realm.[9] Able to live comfortably based on adequate financial resources, the bourgeois subject does not confront suffering due to economic impoverishment or arising from inadequate nutrition and medical care. Overall, the bourgeois subject tends not to look beyond issues that affect the middle-class consumer.

Metz objects to the adoption of an operational attitude toward objects, nature, and human persons. Typical of technological engineering and social planning are the amoral standards of efficiency, speed, growth, and progress (TW 117). In the same vein as Marcel's and Buber's objections to the I-It relation, Metz displays a deep-seated concern for the apparent dehumanization of persons at the hands of science and bureaucracy. A consequence of this operational thinking with its valorization of productivity is that only effective or useful persons count as subjects. Judged by instrumental criteria, the subject becomes replaceable. Persons no longer able to work become marginalized, and persons who earn low wages are correspondingly of low social value. This economic perspective toward subjects does not involve sympathy or solidarity with those who are devalued in the scheme of productivity. Metz connects instrumentalism with apathy, for this view of the subject suffocates the political identity of the subject as a self-determining agent in history. The notion of freedom becomes trivialized under consumerism as the "freedom to dispose of materials, services, [and] technical processes" (FHS 35). Metz agrees with Marcel and Buber that an important function of religious faith in this society is to "protect the individual against being taken as a number on a human-progress-computer-card" (TW 118). Despite their similar rejection of technological attitudes, Metz considers the positions taken by existentialist thinkers bourgeois and apolitical because they construe the subject as part of an intersubjective realm without accounting for the impact of social conditions.

A factor in bourgeois society that contributes to lack of concern about suffering in history is the devaluing of tradition. This disregard for the past cannot be explained merely as a side effect of the commercial focus in bourgeois society. The bourgeois economist, for example, does not ignore the past, but studies it to formulate strategies for economic success, although this attention to the past is not likely to be sensitive to suffering or the resources of religious traditions. The bourgeois subject Metz has in mind is an ordinary person whose consumer interests do not spur interest in history or economic theory. Neglect of the past and its authority is diagnosed by Metz as a symptom of the modern infatuation with progress.[10] He connects the absence of serious interest in tradition with the loss of religion's importance in society. Metz observes that in contemporary capitalist society the memory of history is pursued for private reasons, as a hobby or a form of entertainment. This disrespect for the past leads to the masking of the gravity of suffering in history and a loss of critical, moral consciousness. Neglect of religious memory deprives subjects of memories of biblical narratives where suffering is connected with hope for historical change, political resistance, and faith in God. Such memories oppose the bourgeois apathy toward history, serving as a lever for critique of and resistance to suffering caused by social and political injustice (FHS 115).

The meaning of "hope" for the bourgeois subject living in a capitalist society is individualistic and monetary, emphasizing an increase of economic prosperity, comfort, and success. Such hope does not require political change of established economic institutions; in fact, it requires only the uninterrupted continuation of existing conditions of capitalism (EC 4). According to Metz, bourgeois citizens do not have political hope for change in society because they already have a secure future. They do not need changes in economic and political structures to achieve prosperity. Meanwhile, there is no hope for the sake of poor workers, whether in Europe, America, or less economically developed countries. Metz contrasts bourgeois hope with religious hope for an end to suffering and oppression. His eschatology is "apocalyptic" in that it emphasizes the non-identity between the broken reality of history and hope for God's Kingdom and history. Hope in God ruptures the illusions of modern progress (FHS 178).

Metz points to the fact that Christianity as an institution and Christian thought have taken on bourgeois characteristics. Metz agrees with Marxian ideology critique that religion more often than not serves to validate the economic status quo and obstruct the critical resistance of persons who suffer. The ideology of religion in contemporary society supports bourgeois apathy and consumer hopes. Faith in God has become privatized in bourgeois society; it is used selectively to meet the spiritual needs of individuals, such as the alleviation of anxiety and the quest for personal happiness or fulfillment. Relegated to the private realm, bourgeois faith has no political impetus (EC 2). Metz concludes that such faith only serves to confirm political passivity.

Metz argues that this critique of religion in society also applies to certain types of academic theology. In particular, he targets existentialist thought, which he accuses of ignoring the historical and political character of faith (PTE 149).[11] His main objection to existentialist approaches is their understanding of the subject and the essence of faith. Existentialist thinkers abstract the notion of the subject from any specific historical context, such that the subject is allegedly void of any particular cultural and social identity.

What is defined as central to faith is the individual's relation to God and love for others. Metz considers this definition of faith as restricted to personal life, reflecting slavishly the bourgeois attitude that religion is a private matter of subjective religious sensibilities. Existentialist religious thought secretly enthrones the middle-class subject because it fails to situate faith in God in terms of social and political awareness of the history of suffering (FHS 27). It misreads the Bible, diluting the eschatological hope shown by Moses, Jesus, and the prophets. Both Metz and Bloch point to the "realized eschatology" of Bultmann as an example of bourgeois theology. Bultmann proposes that God's Kingdom occurs in the present as a spiritual reality, rather than a future hope (TW 95). The urgent expectation of redemption of history, which has political implications, is replaced by the individual's goal of salvation and eternal life.

THEODICY AND THE EFFACEMENT OF SUFFERING IN HISTORY

In presenting his political and narrative paradigm of theology in *Faith in History and Society*, Metz is harsh in his criticism of theodicy, both the teleological theodicy of Hegel and scientific Marxism, and the post-Holocaust "suffering God" response to theodicy formulated by Moltmann and others. Teleological theodicies are criticized for portraying history as an inexorable movement that cannot be interrupted, in which all events are necessary, and where a successful *telos* is guaranteed. Metz agrees with Bloch that, in view of the actual tragedies and horrors of history, the assertion that suffering is justified for the sake of progress is a logical, dialectical systematization that falsifies the reality of history. The gradual, progressive notion of history is counter to the biblical apocalyptic perspective that hopes for the interruption of history for the sake of victims. Benjamin's image of history as a storm that piles wreckage upon wreckage, while the angel of the future looks on in horror, is a powerful metaphor that Metz uses to point to the scandalous character of history, which is far from progressive.[12] According to Metz, Hegelian and Marxist emancipatory freedom "marches forward over the prostrate backs of the dead" and disguises its guilt by the rallying cries of revolution (FHS 129). Teleological accounts of history efface the memories of the victims through success-oriented accounts of progress that instrumentalize suffering.[13] In contradiction, Metz agrees with Benjamin that "the greater freedom of future generations does not justify past sufferings nor does it render them free" (FHS 128). Stringent moral and religious concern for victims, lost in history's rubble, does not step over them or refuse to remember their narratives of suffering. Politically conscious faith looks for future redemption that includes even the dead.

Theodicy and Bourgeois Apathy

Metz argues that teleological theodicy corroborates the mainstream bourgeois view of history, seen as a continuous, impersonal, and inexorable movement. Although this model of history's forward movement is derived from the teleological plot-lines of orthodox Marxism or Hegelian philosophy, the important difference is that the bourgeois perspective does not view history as necessarily moving toward social fulfillment or Bloch's *Ultimum*. For the bourgeois subject, the future is "without grace," which means that no final redemption is envisioned and there is no expectation of apocalyptic interruption in history. There is no hope for radical change, either revolution on a political level or redemption on a religious level (FHS 174). Metz argues that this lack of hope goes hand in hand with bourgeois apathy toward suffering in the past and efforts to change history in the present. With no anticipation of change in history, the bourgeois subject tries to avoid suffering at all costs, for example, by using money to secure comfort and health. Lack of hope in historical interruption and lack of memory of suffering in history are together responsible for a marked absence of political resistance in bourgeois society (FHS 127).

Metz accuses theodicy of corroborating the apathetic bourgeois attitude toward suffering because it does not ignite the consciousness of bourgeois persons to become agents shaping history. Both the inevitability of the teleological perspective and its bourgeois counterpart lack the impetus for protest against suffering. Applying Marxian ideology critique to theodicy, Metz raises the suspicion that theodicy offers alleged knowledge that consoles but has no moral or political force (FHS 129). Theodicy is the antithesis of recognition of the scandal of suffering because it condones the social mechanisms that cause it. Theodicy silences narrative memory with argumentative soteriology that uncritically and falsely reconciles the contradictions of hope and history (FHS 212). By the standard set by Marx in his "Theses on Feuerbach," theodicy is an ideology because it interprets the world but does not seek to change it. A faith response to suffering that takes a critical political posture toward history must involve protest against injustice and immanent expectation of apocalyptic interruption in history (FHS 176).

Auschwitz and Anti-Theodicy

The second major objection Metz raises against theodicy arises from post-Holocaust reflection. Metz argues that victims of horrendous suffering must have the definitive word in response to evil. In his famous essay "Christians and Jews after Auschwitz" Metz announces: "Faced with Auschwitz, I consider as blasphemy every Christian theodicy (i.e., every attempt at a so-called justification of God) and all language about meaning when these are initiated outside this catastrophe or on some level above it." In the same passage, he advises Christian theologians that "meaning, even divine meaning, can be invoked by us only to the extent that such meaning was not abandoned in Auschwitz itself" (EC 19). From the position of the victim, according to Metz, the suffering symbolized by Auschwitz remains surd to theodicy justification.[14] Its horror cannot be made good in terms of moral development, economic progress, or divine self-development. The witness of the victim shows that post-Holocaust theology must articulate protest to God, which refuses comfort. In response to thinkers who claim that the Holocaust marks the triumph of doubt or despair and the end of faith in God, Metz asserts that because there were victims who prayed to God in Auschwitz, prayer and trust in God is not invalidated (EC 18). But he cautions Christians not to impose soteriological meaning on the Holocaust. In his view, dialogue among Jewish and Christian communities is crucial for remembering the past truthfully, reaching reconciliation, and making theological pronouncements.

Objections to Divine Suffering

A third frontier of Metz's objections to theodicy is his critique of the claim that God suffers, a position that has become common in twentieth-century post-Holocaust theology (FHS 130). Protestant theologians Jürgen Moltmann and Eberhart Jüngel, and Catholic theologians Karl Rahner and Hans Urs von Balthasar, are major representatives of this approach. They take the incarnation of God and God's suffering on the cross as a means to reconcile suffering and divine love, thus dissolving the theodicy conundrum of divine omnipotence and evil. Their response to the issues raised by theodicy is that God is not the distant spectator of suffering but a participant in the world's suffering as God incarnate in history. One reason for Metz's criticism of this divine suffering response is that it requires formulating theoretical accounts of God's inner life and God's history based on the narratives of the Bible (LS 95).[15] He objects to Trinitarian theology that narrates God's history beginning to end, like Hegel's philosophy of history. A Trinitarian theory of history's development is criticized for proposing an ambitious understanding of God's development and for theoretically positing redemption as history's finale (TT 70). Metz, in contrast, promotes a narrative theology focusing on the story of Jesus Christ as a source of hope as well as critical memory. He calls for theology to articulate the memory of salvation without foreclosing the "not-yet" future in an idealistic system (SAN 110).

Metz objects to the identification of human suffering with divine suffering. He criticizes Moltmann for assuming that divine suffering is an appropriate universal symbol to encompass all suffering, an assertion called into question in light of Auschwitz (TT 70). Metz observes that the suffering of Jesus does not encompass the often despairing, hopeless, and futile character of the most severe human suffering. It is not comparable to the suffering of a person who is psychologically broken by extended suffering and whose self-identity is shattered. The suffering of Jesus is not comparable with the suffering of a child in Auschwitz because Jesus makes conscious choices that lead to his crucifixion. He accepts the risk of trial and crucifixion voluntarily as a consequence of his mission, whereas children and others are unwilling and immature victims. In Elie Wiesel's book *Night*, there is a memorable episode where public hangings are held in a concentration camp. One adult, who is being hanged on criminal charges, cries out "long live liberty" as the noose is fastened. For this mature individual, suffering and death can become acts of defiance and resistance. The prisoners who are onlookers are far less troubled by this death than by the hanging of a young boy described as a sad-eyed angel. The boy's prolonged death has no positive meaning for himself or for the inmates who are onlookers. The boy is an innocent victim who has committed no crime deserving death and who does not invest his death with rebellious meaning. At the end of this episode, a voice within Eliezer, the book's protagonist, answers the question "Where is God?" with the phrase "He is hanging here on this gallows."[16] In the context of *Night*, it is ambiguous whether this phrase is an expression of atheism or faith. I take it paradoxically as indicating both together. However, I reject Christian interpretations of this passage as a recapitulation of the cross or as confirming divine suffering as a theological doctrine. The boy's death is not redemptive, nor is his death an affirmative symbol of God's presence. The only positive meaning that can potentially be attributed to the boy's suffering on the gallows is for the person who retains the story as a memory that incites moral protest. Ultimately, I agree with Metz that human suffering is more scandalous than the suffering of Jesus Christ or God; thus, the Trinitarian history of God is not adequate for representing the history of suffering (TT 69).

Metz does not consider Moltmann's attribution of suffering to God as successful in deflecting responsibility for human suffering away from God. The divine suffering alternative to theodicy does not put to rest the agonizing question: Why is there innocent suffering? Moltmann acknowledges that there is no explanation for why God permits such a huge burden of suffering to be placed on humanity; he too protests such theodicy answers.

Metz does not oppose Moltmann's position because he fails to answer "why" but because his theology of history offers a myth of quasi-Hegelian completeness to resolve the history of suffering.[17] For Moltmann, the estrangement between Father and Son is supposed to last as long as human suffering in history, which creates a point of solidarity between God and humanity. Metz complains that this soteriology lacks a vital sense of risk and the vast distance between suffering in history and promised resurrection (FHS 132). In Moltmann's Trinitarian account of history, God's love cannot possibly be defeated and God ultimately overcomes suffering. Divine suffering appears as a negative stage in the dialectic of history, to use Hegelian terms. By failing to respect the non-identity of suffering and salvation, Moltmann's response is incongruous in the perspective of the Holocaust where struggle with suffering is unresolved. Refusing theoretical theological accounts of history, Metz holds that theology should fundamentally center on the narrative memory of suffering and hope for redemption (SAN 109).

METZ'S POLITICAL FAITH: DANGEROUS MEMORY AND SOLIDARITY

An understanding of Metz's objections to bourgeois culture, existentialist theology, and theodicy prepares us to investigate his distinctive construal of Christianity. Metz's theology is itself an interruption of other theology discourses, in particular, those that corroborate bourgeois apathy toward history and the bourgeois privatization of religion. This interruption is effected by the memory of histories of suffering in the Bible and by the apocalyptic expectancy of hope.[18] Metz considers the Bible the original embodiment of faith language and hence the source and model for a faith response to suffering. He proposes that narratives of the Bible contain dangerous memories, "dangerous" because, in response to the oppression of the poor, the Bible offers stories of religious persons who dare to protest suffering and anticipate the possibility of political change in history with hope, solidarity, and resistance (TW 88).

Biblical Narrative as Memory

The Hebrew Bible provides numerous remarkable narratives of the hope of God's people in the face of historical adversity. In fact, Metz argues that suffering is the dominant concern within Jewish history, as indicated in the writings of the prophets, in the Psalms, and in Job (FHS 171). The Exodus from Egypt led by Moses is one such story of suffering and hope, and the Babylonian exile of Israel in the sixth century B.C.E., followed by Israel's release and the rebuilding the Temple in Jerusalem, is another. The writings of the Hebrew prophets are models of tenacious hope in God, which is radically critical of innocent suffering and expectant of justice in history.[19] Metz interprets the Gospels as showing the continuation of this Jewish eschatological vision of history and preoccupation with unjust suffering. Metz points out that Jesus' career was marked by an orientation toward the future, symbolized by his proclamation of the Kingdom of God, and also by concern with suffering and injustice. Jesus Christ took up the interests of persons who were poor, weak, economically oppressed, and marginalized by society. He resisted others' suffering but also accepted suffering himself as part of the practice of resistance. Metz asserts that narratives about Jesus Christ model a "way of hope and expectation" that is simultaneously political and mystical in content (FHS 179).

Metz interprets the resurrection as a dangerous memory that signifies the overcoming of injustice, the release from oppression, and the promise of human freedom for all, which is what is hoped for in the realization of God's Kingdom (FHS 111). The resurrection is a symbol of the future fulfillment of God's promises to overcome suffering and death.[20] The past-present-future temporality of Metz's apocalyptic interpretation of eschatology can be considered Eucharistic. In the Eucharist, the narrative of Christ's last days, his crucifixion and resurrection, is remembered and reenacted. It is made present by the sharing of bread and wine in imitation of the Last Supper with the disciples, the solidarity of the church community, and the articulation of shared hope for redemption. Metz considers the narrative of Christ's death and resurrection as a paradigmatic expression of the hope held by "the slaves and damaged people of this world" (EC 12). Memory represents the cross and resurrection as undergirding hope for the fulfillment of God's promises that will interrupt the history of suffering.[21]

The Functions of Religious Memory

The memory of narratives of suffering is critical and political in two senses. First, narratives uncover the truth of the past, which is that history is overbrimming with massive suffering. Suffering is a theme in biblical stories and faith traditions that must not be ignored. Second, narratives must be remembered in order to analyze the causes of suffering, a step necessary for developing political strategies of resistance. Metz is in agreement with Adorno and Benjamin about the radical brokenness of history and how the hope for redemption offers a sharp critique of suffering. As Adorno asserts, redemption provides the truest perspective on history because it reveals to what a large extent the world is "indigent and distorted."[22] Remembering the past in this light is dangerous because the Jewish and Christian hopes for redemption can spark protest against suffering (FHS 195). Memory plays a liberating function.

Religious narratives assist the subject to become conscious of freedom and the potential for human agency and self-determination in history (EC 12).[23] According to Metz, subjects find their identity with reference to the history of suffering of their own tradition. Loss of memory is connected with loss of hope and identity. Metz observes, in reference to African slaves, that it was common practice for slave traders and owners to suppress and oppose slaves' knowledge of their history and indigenous cultures. The destruction of memory under oppressive social conditions "led to the confirmation of their existence as slaves and their systematic deprivation of power in the interest of complete submission" (FHS 66). Conversely, active memory prompts the subject to become aware of collective suffering and its causes, and to realize the power of persons to act as agents in history (FHS 165). This realization is a political mode of recognition of the religious truth that all persons are "subjects in the presence of God" (FHS 68). Metz does not assert, as cold stream Marxists do, that the solidarity sparked by memory requires membership in the oppressed proletariat class. One need not experience collective suffering stemming from material oppression to recognize that it should be protested. Metz and Bloch agree that critical consciousness arising from the memory of suffering is accessible to all persons.

Another significance of religious memory, exemplified in biblical narratives, is that it spurs religious hope. Echoing Bloch, Metz defines Christian hope as a "creative and militant eschatology" that does not wait for an already existing Kingdom of God to be revealed, but anticipates it in history. Hope is not only a matter of remembering God's promises of justice, but acting to assist the realization of transformation in history. God's Kingdom signifies the redemption of history and society, "the achieving of an eschatological order of justice, the humanizing of man and the establishing of a universal peace" (TW 96).

Yet Metz is in accord with Adorno in stating that the content of religious hope, instead of being conceived in positive terms, should be defined as the obverse of present reality where justice, peace, and freedom are threatened (TW 124). The critical ideal of redemption measures the shortcomings of attempts to approximate redemption in history. In keeping with his strategy of negative theology, Metz does not detail the content of hope in resurrection or redemption. Especially in his mature work, he emphasizes the apocalyptic character of eschatology and the cross as the defining memory of Christian faith. Through an apocalyptic lens, memory and hope are less centered on historical change than on the interruption and critique of history, which is viewed as profoundly imbued with suffering.

Metz traces the idea that memory has redemptive and revolutionary significance in the work of Benjamin. Benjamin proposes that redemption involves the mystical uniting of past and present by means of memory. He offers a material-historical interpretation of redemption as the revolutionary moment where the full memory of past oppression propels the overthrow of the causes of oppression. The messianic moment of redemption brings retrospective justice to the victims of suffering, according to Benjamin. It makes victims of the past more than the "debris" of history. Redemption represents the coming of God's Kingdom in history, which unites God and creation.[24] Neither Metz nor Benjamin considers redemption as adequately represented by the Marxist ideal of future emancipation, which is the achievement of a classless society (FHS 114). Rather, Metz reinscribes transcendence on Marxist hope for history by considering redemption as messianic and mystical, transformative of the past as well as the future. Religious hope differs from Marxist hope because it depends on human action in tandem with God's initiative in history. Metz's political faith is mystical in the sense that it affirms human agents as participating in the cross, which is a dangerous memory connected with hope for resurrection.[25]

In conclusion, it is worth noting the multifaceted and pivotal role that narrative plays in Metz's political model of faith. Narratives are essentially histories or biographies of groups of persons. Some narratives focus on persons of faith and others do not, yet both are important for theology. All narratives of suffering can spur moral protest. They can also be used by Marxist analysis to identify and address deformations of social-political reality. Narratives of suffering also provide the basis and motivation for solidarity, catalyzing moral shock and sympathy with victims. Recognition of shared causes of suffering between groups lies in identifying similar material conditions. Certain narratives tell of efforts to fight the causes of suffering and injustice. These narratives of community-building and liberation struggles are positive memories that encourage solidarity and hope. A subcategory of resistance narratives are those with religious content, particularly biblical narratives. These narratives tell about persons who face suffering with faith in God and hope for liberation in history. Biblical narratives incite subjects to recognize their history-making capabilities and become active in resisting suffering's causes for God's sake. Such narratives model and inspire the religious postures of solidarity, hope, and protest toward suffering.[26]

A THEODICY-SENSITIVE RESPONSE TO SUFFERING AFTER AUSCHWITZ

The call for a "theodicy-sensitive" theology is a hallmark of Metz's publications during the 1990s. Metz does not in the least renounce his opposition to theoretical theodicy. Instead, his proposal is to make theology maximally sensitive to suffering by placing theodicy questions front and center. His theodicy-sensitive method focuses on faith practices in response to suffering: memory, protest, and hope. Such theology takes a sober view of history, illustrated particularly well by the title of Metz's important essay on the subject, "*Landshaft aus Schreien*." The title is a phrase borrowed from a poem by the post-Holocaust German Jewish poet Nelly Sachs. The phrase translates cryptically as "a country out of cries/screams." The preposition "*aus*" (out of, from) has no corresponding verb; hence, multiple projected meanings can be applied. The country, Germany after the Holocaust, is constituted or built "out of" the cries of victims. It is also a land "from" which cries ring out and disturbing memories arise (TT 66).[27] With this brokenness of history as a starting point, Metz reflects soberly on the question: What form of God language and faith praxis can meet the theodicy challenge raised by the memory of Auschwitz and by the testimonies of people living under poverty and oppression? The proposal Metz puts forward makes faith practically plausible because it honestly confronts the past and responds with action to alleviate suffering, not because it answers theodicy questions about why there is suffering. According to Metz, the contradiction between suffering in history and anticipated redemption remains insoluble (SAN 107).

The prophetic, eschatological expectation of biblical Israel is Metz's model for a sensitive faith response to suffering. According to this model of faith, the disappointments of history are continually in tension with God's promises and the posture of hope. In examining the religious language used in biblical narratives, Metz points to the importance of prayer as a religious response to suffering. Metz considers prayer as a form of first-order religious language, which is a religious practice situated in a concrete time and place. The prayers found in the Psalms, the Hebrew prophets, and Job are read by Metz as expressions of political protest against the suffering of God's people (TT 66). Prayer is the form of God language that most dramatically embodies the urgency of suffering because it is dynamic and rebellious. Prayer includes rejoicing and complaint, songs and cries, trust and doubt. Metz praises the suppleness of prayer for articulating the ambiguities of faith, particularly the tension between protest against suffering and the confidence of hope in God (LS 98). Metz concludes that the language of prayer displays an artless refusal to be comforted by ideas or myths that are developed in the second-order religious language of theodicy.

Respect for God's transcendence, commanded in the Jewish prohibition against making images or idols of God affirmed by Metz, entails that theodicy attempts to explain God are criticized as forms of idolatry that justify suffering (LS 99). Metz prioritizes narrative theology over argumentative theology or theodicy because it maintains the historically situated character of theology. Like Buber, who also emphasizes the importance of narrative, Metz disapproves of formulating "fixed" or systematic concepts of God. Both thinkers prioritize first-order languages of prayer and narrative as socially situated discourse, responding to specific circumstances of suffering (SAN 110). The key difference is that Metz considers protest and resistance integral to theological discourse, whereas Buber does not address political resistance in discussing the eclipse of God or responses to the Holocaust.

In his writings on theodicy-sensitive theology, Metz applies the adjective "mystical" to describe the political model of faith, which he develops in *Faith in History and Society* and later books.[28] The chief illustrations of mystical faith practice are the gospel narratives of the life of Jesus Christ. Metz calls Jesus a "mystic of open eyes" because Jesus observes suffering in history and its social causes and he acknowledges the nonappearance of promised redemption. Yet Jesus never ceases to pray to God, which is a sign of trust, even in the cry of dereliction from the cross that receives no answer from God (TT 67). Analogous to the prayers of Job and the Hebrew prophets, Christ's prayers show unceasing concern and protest over others' suffering. Hope in God for the redemption of victims in history is mystical because it is directed toward redemption that transcends the pervasive reality of suffering in history. The strength of hope is mystical in its endurance, which is attributed to God's help. This mystical-political model of faith promoted by Metz is also known as "messianic praxis" or the "imitation of Christ" (FHS 235).[29]

A further mystical aspect of faith is the acceptance of suffering in imitation of Christ. Based on the example of Jesus Christ, Metz argues that accepting suffering is not necessarily a betrayal of political protest, but whether acceptance is appropriate depends on the circumstances. For example, Metz opposes political acceptance of suffering on the part of persons who experience collective oppression. But he proposes that there is such a thing as a mysticism of voluntary suffering, which can apply to even oppressed persons. He calls mystical suffering "*die Mystik des Leidens an Gott*," which translates as "the mysticism of suffering unto God" (LS 84).[30] This phrase has different shades of meaning based on the ambiguity of the preposition "*an*." First, it can mean that a person "suffers from God" as one suffers "from" an illness. Metz does not intend to imply that suffering comes from God's agency, but that faith in God intensifies suffering to a heightened degree. Faith increases awareness of the horror of suffering because it views history from the uncompromising standard of universal redemption. The hiddenness of God in times of suffering is a factor that makes suffering more acute. Second, "*Leiden an Gott*" can be translated as "suffering unto God," which is suffering dedicated to God and entered into for God's sake. Suffering becomes meaningful as serving God when it is intentionally accepted in solidarity with others who suffer. To identify one's own suffering with Jesus Christ's suffering lends meaning that is taken on voluntarily in solidarity with victims (LS 101).

The proposal that faith is mystical as well as political provides a bridge to the existentialist approach. Metz's political approach has the scope to substantially acknowledge the role of religious meaning-making in responding to suffering. However, Metz does not go far enough in elaborating the mystical meaning of resistance and how it is compatible with acceptance of suffering, which seems to be the opposite of resistance. Metz's use of narrative memory indicates a methodological commonality with existentialist approaches, which make use of narratives to investigate the dynamics of relation. Narrative can articulate interpersonal encounter, as Marcel and Buber recognize, as well as provide a social context that locates faith in history and society on a material level. Although inspired by Marxian critique, Metz's response to suffering is important for building bridges to areas of faith practice where existentialist reflection can contribute to enriching a political approach to faith.

7 Pragmatics, Existential and Political Comparison, Contrast, and Complementarity

THE EXISTENTIALIST AND POLITICAL methods of approach converge on the insight that a Jewish or Christian response to suffering should include reflection on religious practices. Despite the significant differences in their portrayals of faith, two religious postures emerge as central to both approaches: hope and other-regard, portrayed as I-Thou relation or solidarity. But existentialist and political approaches also offer competing proposals that demonstrate faith to be a plausible practical posture in confrontation with suffering. Existentialists promote faith as facilitating survival, interpersonal bonds, and meaning-making, while political thinkers show faith as promoting awareness of collective suffering and action to alleviate suffering. However, in the end, neither approach offers a comprehensive account of the practical resources of Jewish or Christian faith to meet the challenge of suffering. The previous chapters have shown that religious practices in response to suffering occur on multiple social levels, all of which deserve consideration: individual, interpersonal, small-scale communal, and sociopolitical.

The first part of this chapter probes the contrasts between existentialist and political methods of approach. It analyzes the central examples of suffering used by each author to identify their social and economic interests. Their differing social class orientations motivate them to portray the postures of hope and other-regard in distinct ways. I criticize the one-sided tendencies of existentialist and political approaches, while appreciating that the contrast between them cannot be simply characterized by the dichotomy between responses of acceptance and resistance, or between personal and collective emphases.

The second part pursues the thesis that existentialist and political approaches formulate insights about faith postures that can be viewed as complementary. They both assume the situated character of all faith responses to suffering, a point usually ignored by theodicy approaches. I judge the political response superior given its effective recognition of situation or context as formative. The contemporary analogue of the Marxian political approach is liberation theology, which takes into account contextual factors concerning gender, ethnic, racial, linguistic, and regional identity. These contextual theologies are basically political, but they incorporate existentialist insights into reflection on suffering and resistance. To explore the complementarity and the limitations of the two approaches, I will interrogate existentialist and political conclusions about the religious postures of memory, solidarity, and hope in conversation with recent post-Holocaust, liberation, and feminist thinkers, focusing on Christian authors who bear the legacy of continental approaches. These contemporary thinkers offer correctives and supplements to political perspectives, while melding together insights from both types of approach. To conclude, I will explore the mystical orientation that is implicit in the practices of memory, solidarity, and hope, and explicit in the voices of persons who intentionally confer meaning on suffering. Different levels of meaning can be found, whether suffering is voluntarily undertaken for the sake of resistance or whether it is involuntary, caused by social and political conditions or natural happenings such as diseases or disasters.

CONTRASTING PERSONAL AND POLITICAL APPROACHES

Political thinkers argue that existentialist religious thought is "bourgeois" in character. The weight of this charge is not biographical, because not only Marcel and Buber but also Bloch and Metz belong to the middle class. This ideology critique of the class bias of existentialist thought can be pursued according to either cold stream or warm stream Marxist principles. In its strong form, on the basis of the cold stream Marxist position, the existentialist depiction of faith is viewed as a form of bourgeois ideology determined by the economic conditions of European capitalism in the early twentieth century, lacking critical purchase on social and economic oppression. Evidence to support this charge is the fact that the existentialist model of faith focuses on the private sphere of existence and on subjects who are neither poor nor part of an oppressed group. For the bourgeois middle-class subject, religion has mainly subjective or private importance. Its main role is to help the individual find comfort or reassurance. The existentialist focus on the interpersonal life of the individual condones the bourgeois subject's political apathy toward suffering in history—apathy due to the blinders of bourgeois ideology that render socioeconomic critique of collective suffering impossible. Cold stream Marxists conclude that religion is an ideology that, along with existentialist thought, deserves to be rejected in its entirety. This accusation against existentialist thought exaggerates its allegedly private orientation, at least in the case of Buber who extends the significance of I-Thou relation beyond the interpersonal to the community level.

The more moderate, warm stream Marxist position holds that existentialist religious thought is flawed because it internalizes bourgeois assumptions without recognizing their influence. This explains why the existentialist model of religious faith does not recognize certain economically caused collective suffering and why it lacks political protest. It also explains why existentialist thought focuses on the individual and interpersonal aspects of religion. However, existentialist insights about coping with suffering are not completely invalidated. Existentialist thought is accused of corroborating a bourgeois outlook on suffering and bourgeois assumptions about faith postures, but it is not dismissed as merely a puppet of class interests. Insights of the existentialist position can be salvaged after its shortcomings are made clear. I reject the hard-line critique of cold stream Marxists, but I consider the warm stream version of ideology critique as illuminating for assessing the positions of Marcel and Buber in contrast with those of Bloch and Metz.

Situating Suffering in "Existence" and "History"

The purpose of this section is to examine how each thinker has particular biases toward, or interests in, certain kinds of suffering. It is my thesis that there is a correlation between the model of faith that is proposed and the types of suffering addressed. For instance, the existentialist thinkers studied locate the significance of religion in interpersonal relation: for Marcel, among groups of family and friends, and for Buber, among small communities. These philosophers frame the subject in terms of I-Thou relation, untainted by scientific or objective I-It assessment. Within relation, the "I" does not perceive the social placement of the "Thou," therefore it cannot take account of economic or social conditions or differences between subjects. It is not as if Marcel and Buber ignore social factors, since both authors notice the damaging implications of technology in society and the effects of war. They reflect on how these developments affect the individual as such. But existentialist philosophers study the universal category of existence in a way that is slanted toward the reality of middle-class existence. The existentialist purview is validly labeled as "bourgeois" and "apolitical" in orientation because of its omissions. One thing missing is the insight that certain groups of people suffer more than others due to social, economic, and political oppression or discrimination. Bourgeois or middle-class persons often do not notice this collective aspect of the distribution of suffering because capitalist society is organized for their advantage, relatively speaking.

When existentialist thinkers turn to suffering, they gravitate towards class-independent instances of suffering as their chief examples. Marcel and Buber focus on types of suffering that can affect any class, for example, suffering from physical illness, broken personal relationships, bereavement, or war. They assume that these types of suffering are of the highest importance for all subjects. Such class-independent kinds of suffering indeed raise problems for religious faith and are worthy of attention. But critics claim that these kinds of suffering are of chief concern for the bourgeois middle class (although not exclusively this class) because severe suffering due to class oppression is absent. Although Buber's attention to the plight of Jews in the Holocaust does target collective suffering, it is not systemic suffering caused by the economic structures of capitalism. A flaw in the existentialist response to suffering is the lack of attention to groups who experience systematic oppression due to economic and political institutions, and the resultant failure to commend political resistance.

While existentialists consider the essence of Jewish and Christian faith as participation in relation, political thinkers consider faith as essentially preoccupied with the contrast between suffering and the promise of God's Kingdom. There is a correlation between the political models of faith proposed by Bloch and Metz and their focus on the evils of collective suffering. Political thinkers read Jewish and Christian scriptures as giving numerous examples of a future-oriented, utopian, eschatological outlook on history in response to the injustices of suffering. As portrayed by Marxist-influenced thinkers, prophetic faith remembers the horrendous suffering of the past, protests suffering in solidarity with all victims, and hopes and acts to bring alleviation of suffering in the future. Buber too portrays faith as prophetic, although his focus is on the suffering of the Jews as a group rather than the suffering of oppressed classes in general. However, Buber's type of prophetic faith does not involve revolutionary action to combat the causes of suffering. In contrast, the political approaches are self-consciously oriented toward the suffering of the underclasses and its alleviation. For instance, Bloch considers the plight of the proletariat the major contemporary problem of suffering, although he also draws attention to the suffering of groups of poor and oppressed persons in earlier eras of history before the emergence of capitalism. Metz widens his focus beyond the proletariat by emphasizing non-Eurocentric examples of class suffering, such as poverty in Latin

America. The political approach assumes that oppression can be abolished because it is socially caused, although finding effective strategies to end injustice can prove immensely difficult. It is precisely at this juncture that utopian hope provides the motivation to keep trying.

Stepping outside of Marxist class interests, both Bloch and Metz consider the Holocaust as an important example of suffering in history. Indeed, the Nazi-engineered genocide, committed against Jews, gypsies, homosexuals, political dissidents, and others, did not target one social class. One of their main goals in sending millions of individuals to death camps was the extermination of certain undesirable groups, spanning all social classes, considered detrimental to the racial purity of the Aryan German nation. For the political approach, not only class-based suffering but also collective suffering caused by systemic prejudice based on racial, religious, or ethnic grounds is judged as a negative rupture in history that must be protested. Feminist and liberation thinkers appropriate the political approach and apply it to the socially caused suffering of "liminal" or "marginal" social groups, such as women, racial minorities, and the poor—people who have lacked a political (and theological) voice. In the last analysis, what is Marxian about the religious responses of political thinkers is their emphasis on collective oppression and collective resistance to suffering that aims to bring about drastic and fundamental changes in economic, political, and social structures.

The Religious Posture of Hope

The contrast between existentialist and political forms of hope is highlighted and sharpened by comparing the two authors who discuss hope most extensively: Marcel and Bloch. An important point of agreement in their reflections is the observation that the main feature of hope is "openness" toward the future. They agree that hope is not the same as uncritical, naive optimism and also that hope never gives up in defeat no matter what horrendous things might happen. However, their models of hope diverge sharply concerning future political conditions. Marcel's hopes for history are politically conservative and private in emphasis. The examples that dominate Marcel's reflection on hope are personal ones, for example, a mother's hope that her son has not been killed in war, or a husband's hope that his spouse will recover from a cancer operation. His tragic perspective on existence focuses on the fragility of intimate relationships and the hope that fidelity in relations of love can endure, even beyond death. Compared with Buber's portrayal of faith, Marcel is distinctive in his explicit appeal to immortality as central to hope in God. Marcel does not promote a faith-based hope for the overhaul of the oppressive economic structures of capitalism, something political thinkers consider essential. Marcel's inattention to removing the systemic causes of suffering appears to condone political passivity in the face of socially caused suffering in history.

In Marxian terms, existentialist thinkers operate, at least to a significant degree, with bourgeois assumptions. But, contrary to political accusations, Marcel's response does not condone mere apathy on an interpersonal level. Fidelity to the Thou who suffers means staying with the person in trouble and potentially risking one's safety in doing so. It is even possible that fidelity might motivate one to become politically active and participate in collective resistance against suffering, although Marcel does not develop this conclusion. On the other hand, given Marcel's tragic perspective on history, it is unlikely that he would find the hopes for dramatic change held by political activists realistic. Marcel focuses on the private realm, and he seems to have minimal hope for changing institutions by means of political resistance.[1]

Buber is an existentialist thinker who locates faith both on the interpersonal level and on the level of redemption in history. He considers I-Thou relation as a means to restore creation to harmonious relation with God, part of the process of repair (*tikkun*) and redemption that occurs among individuals and small groups, such as Hasidic communities. For Buber, hope for redemption is not the anticipation of revolution by the oppressed class, as Marxists hold, nor is it accomplished by radical political action. Steps toward redemption are taken when the subject takes an I-Thou attitude toward persons and nature, and enters into dialogue with God. Buber claims that steps toward I-Thou relation form the basis for creating just and peaceful local communities. Buber's hope for redemption in history resembles the Hebrew prophetic ideal of redemption advanced by political thinkers. Overall, the Jewish and Christian thinkers studied operate with compatible notions of redemption as hope for an end to violence and injustice, and reconciliation among persons and God.

Buber recommends large-scale adoption of the I-Thou posture as the means to transform or redeem history. Only if persons make this first step is establishment of socialist forms of community possible (PW 112). To Marxian thinkers, Buber's approach seems apolitical because he thinks that the remedy for problems in society depends on the turning of each individual to an I-Thou posture. The response to suffering framed by Buber has a personal starting-point, whereas Marxist solutions require a shift into an I-It posture that motivates solidarity and makes possible the formulation of political strategies to resist suffering. Buber does not appreciate the critical role of the I-It attitude for a faith response, nor does Marcel, although Buber focuses on history, rather than immortality, as the arena of hope.

I conclude that the approaches of Buber and Marcel corroborate bourgeois political apathy indirectly because they fail to link faith acceptance of
suffering with the need to resist its political causes through collective social
action. However, their positions do not necessarily exclude the subject's involvement in group resistance. A person could take an I-Thou posture toward small-scale community while participating in institutional resistance.
Indeed, Buber's biography shows that he was politically engaged during his
lifetime, both in Germany and after immigrating to Palestine in 1938. He
was involved in political debates over socialism, Zionism, and Arab-Jewish
relations.[2] What distinguishes the existentialist approach is not lack of political concern, but the identification of I-Thou relation as the core means of
social change and the center-point of faith in God.

The political approach considers resistance as a necessary component of
faith, based on a strongly eschatological reading of Jewish and Christian scriptures. Hope in God, it is argued, entails utopian hope in history. What
prophetic hope for God's Kingdom and Marxist hope for a future communist
society have in common are the ideals of freedom and justice for all persons.
Such hope is recognized as crucial, especially by the underclasses because they
are the primary victims of social injustice. This approach maintains that
although it may seem so, attention to the plight of oppressed persons is not
sectarian. Persons of any class ought to be concerned about socially caused
suffering. Moreover, the changes demanded by the oppressed classes do not
benefit the poor alone. These changes will result in a just, egalitarian society
that maximally benefits all persons, even the upper classes who will lose their
cultural dominance, economic control, and political privilege.

The existentialist account that locates the roots of evil and suffering in
the absence of I-Thou relation is contradicted by the analysis of political
thinkers. They argue that it is not the sins or choices of individuals, but the
capitalist division of labor and economic oppression that are the true causes
of suffering. Although they do not accept orthodox Marxist analysis of the
mechanics of revolution, political thinkers still hold that large-scale changes
in socioeconomic conditions are the key to alleviating suffering. Moving
away from the Marxist idea of utopia, Metz and religious liberation thinkers
accept the importance of political resistance without embracing communism
as the means to God's Kingdom. However, in rejecting the anchor of orthodox Marxist determinism, the confidence of hope for achieving utopia based
on theories about progress and dialectical materialism is undermined. If the
future is open and undecided, what makes religious utopian hope a real possibility and not merely wishful thinking? The answer is that, for warm
stream Marxists, like Bloch, Benjamin, Adorno, and Metz, such hope is a
critical stance without scientific knowledge of the future. Hope functions as

a Kantian practical posit. The motivation to pursue justice requires faith in the real possibility of future justice. Faith and hope are practical necessities for moral action—preconditions motivating resistance to the causes of suffering in solidarity with victims. Similarly, the notion of redemption, for the political thinkers studied, functions as a Kantian practical ideal in response to the moral scandal of suffering in history. Redemption serves as an ideal aim for human action. Hope in redemption is practically effective because it motivates a person to participate constructively in history to make things better.

The role of God in the utopian future is contested among the Marxian thinkers studied. Both Metz and Moltmann take a stand against Bloch's secularized eschatology. Bloch equates hope for God's Kingdom with hope for a perfectly just and humane society, and considers the *Ultimum* as a state achieved by collective human action in history. Political theologians join Bloch in affirming that religious hope is intrinsically linked with protest and resistance to suffering in history, but they assert that God's Kingdom cannot be established by human efforts alone. Even though political thinkers emphasize human capability, they recognize that the goal of ending injustice often seems beyond reach, at least within one's lifetime. Moreover, religious hope in redemption aims at justice and fulfillment for the dead victims of suffering, as well as the living. The achievement of an ideal, just society will prevent future suffering, but, lacking God's involvement, it cannot remedy the suffering of the past for individuals who have died. It is faith in God and immortality that allows Jewish and Christian thinkers to hope that even the dead will be redeemed by the achievement of God's Kingdom, although neither existentialist nor political thinkers speculate on how this might happen.

Marcel's existentialist version of religious hope places hope in God alone, rather than human efforts. On the other hand, Buber takes a middle position between Marcel and political thinkers. Like Marxist-influenced thinkers, he holds that redemption requires human efforts to reunite God and creation. Where he differs is in recommending existential I-Thou relation as the basis for changing society and ultimately bringing redemption. Buber's I-Thou remedy for social problems does not address how institutional oppression creates unequal power distribution among subjects that can prevent interpersonal and I-Thou relation.

An atheist Marxist critic would reject both types of theistic hope, arguing that hope in God de-motivates resistance efforts to change history. Such an accusation would apply to Metz and Moltmann, as well as Marcel and Buber. But, as Bloch argues, faith does not necessarily corroborate bourgeois, apolitical indifference because it can be a potent impetus for ethical action. Practical approaches to hope can successfully fend off the charge of political passivity by pointing to the fact that the human contribution to redemption accompanies God's contribution. Since responsibility for history rests on human persons who prepare the way for God to bring ultimate resolution to the scandal of suffering, faith is not antithetical to political involvement.

The Religious Posture toward Other Persons: I-Thou Relation or Solidarity

Attention to the suffering of others or "other-regard" is constructed quite differently with the philosophical tools of existential and political methods. Each model of other-regard, I-Thou relation or solidarity, has distinctive ramifications for faith postures toward the suffering of others.

A strong point of the existentialist approach is that it differentiates between my response to my own suffering and my response to the suffering of other persons. Addressing the first issue, existentialist thinkers conclude that my own suffering raises the key question: How does suffering gain religious meaning for me as a subject? Attention to this question appears to support the bourgeois assumption that religion serves the primary purpose of meeting private needs for security or meaning. To counter this assumption, it is important to recall that the religious postures described by existentialist thinkers centrally concern attitudes toward other persons, not exclusively the needs of the self. When Marcel speaks of accepting my suffering as a "trial," he means that I courageously face suffering while maintaining bonds of fidelity and empathy with others. Likewise, Buber's proposal that I-Thou encounter with God is a source of meaning does not imply that faith is essentially private. I-Thou relation with God impacts not only the individual, but also how the self relates to other persons and community. The task of meaning-making is not a solo affair. It takes place in dialogue between I and Thou. However, only the individual agent can take final responsibility for the crucial decision to confer meaning on suffering and accept it for God's sake. Marxist critics stereotype the existentialist perspective as bourgeois and apolitical because it focuses on how religion meets individual needs for security or meaning. On the contrary, the quest to understand suffering as meaningful does not necessarily contradict or undermine the political impulse to resist the causes of suffering. In addressing the challenge of suffering to the self, existentialist thinkers attend to a dimension of religious practice that receives minimal attention from political thinkers, presumably because, in their view, it is not an issue germane to solving the oppression of the lower classes.

The second main issue for existentialist thinkers, the suffering of the other, raises the basic question: What should my posture be toward the victim of suffering? It is important to note that I must not adjudicate the meaning of the Thou's suffering, although if the other person asks for assistance I can help with such questions. When I meet a person who suffers, the appropriate response is empathy for the Thou and an attempt to understand. An I-Thou perspective does not permit me to propose theodicy explanations or justifications, Marcel argues. Persons should not presume that they know why suffering is distributed as it is, nor attempt to defend God's goodness by giving reasons. It is wrong to prescribe how someone should respond to suffering, but it is constructive to engage in disciplines that teach me how to respond to my suffering and others' suffering.

The limitation of the I-Thou posture toward the suffering of others is the fact that it does not provide the resources to identify causes of suffering or differences between individual's social situations. Existentialist reflection on suffering fails to consider whether or not I-Thou relation can effectively bridge economic and social group divisions. Marcel and Buber assume that I-Thou relation can occur between any two people, regardless of social status. But it is naïve to assume that there are no barriers to I-Thou relation. Since I-Thou relation requires firsthand contact, it may easily become restricted to the bourgeois social environment of the middle-class subject. In fact, it may be easier for a bourgeois individual to regard a tree as a "Thou" than people of other socioeconomic classes. The I-Thou relation brackets the Thou's social location—profession, economic status, gender, ethnic group, and so on—because only an objectifying, impersonal I-It gaze observes such details. Clearly, a negative consequence of identifying I-Thou relation as *the* authentic religious posture toward the other is the fact that it lacks the critical leverage to reveal social barriers that should be recognized and removed.

Solidarity is the term that political thinkers use to describe the religious posture of other-regard. While orthodox Marxists consider solidarity as a proletariat class phenomenon arising from shared economic oppression, warm stream Marxists broaden the frame of reference. According to the warm stream Marxist definition, solidarity involves consciousness of suffering and its causes. Metz defines memory of narratives of suffering and collective resistance as the foundation for solidarity. Memory or narrative, for political thinkers, is I-It discourse that tells about what has happened to others in the past. Following the example of Marx, the guiding interest in recovering the past is to discover the causes of large-scale suffering and oppression. Political thinkers target memories of groups who have suffered from social and economic oppression in the past, for example, groups of slaves, proletariat workers, and European Jews. Since critical consciousness based on memory is not class-dependent, nor is it dependent on I-Thou relation with persons involved, solidarity extends potentially to all victims of history, limited only by one's scope of awareness of the stories of victims. Both political and liberation thinkers broaden the Marxist focus on classes that are economically disadvantaged to include marginal groups in society whose oppression is not necessarily economic, such as racial minorities or women. The posture of solidarity recognizes the scandal of suffering, particularly socially caused suffering; hence, it motivates protest and resistance on behalf of victims. Metz identifies solidarity with the virtue of love, thereby objecting to the bourgeois assumption that the biblical command to love one's neighbor is personal and apolitical. Solidarity is the commitment to bring justice, liberty, and peace to all persons. In other words, it is the commitment to bring about redemption in history. Marcel and Buber articulate a personal framework for attention to the suffering of other persons, in contrast to the political model in which "other-regard" extends to persons beyond my circle of acquaintance.

An advantage of the political approach lies in its application of the resources of the social sciences (political science, economic theory, sociology) to analyze suffering in history. Faith, as Bloch portrays it, assumes a conception of history as dialectical movement toward an ultimate goal. In contrast, Metz and Moltmann are not wedded to a Marxian understanding of history. They take Scripture and Christian doctrine as the basis for their vision of history and eschatology. Their political hopes hinge on an alternative social vision drawn from the biblical prophetic tradition, interpreted in terms of Marxian categories such as protest and solidarity. However, to fulfill their political aims, they need to more thoroughly engage in structural analysis of institutions to understand the interrelatedness of human agency and social systems.[3] If faith praxis liberates people from oppression and injustice, it must use political strategies developed in response to analysis of society. Only then does faith have the critical purchase to identify the appropriateness of resistance to specific social and economic circumstances.

COMPLEMENTARITY BETWEEN POLITICAL AND EXISTENTIALIST APPROACHES: THE PRACTICAL INSIGHTS OF CONTEXTUAL LIBERATION AND POST-HOLOCAUST RESPONSES TO SUFFERING

The preceding analysis shows that both existentialist and political approaches are selective in the types of suffering they consider and in their portrayals of a faith response. Neither approach offers an adequate account of the connection between addressing problems of suffering on the individual level and on the systemic level. Existentialist thinkers do not give sustained consideration to the fact that some individual suffering deserves resistance and demands social change. The main advantage of the political approach is its critical awareness of the socioeconomic causes of suffering for different groups. But political thinkers need to be more critical of the Marxian assumption that economic systemic transformation will relieve the suffering of all humanity. The political approach also needs to deal more adequately and subtly with issues of class, race, and gender as factors that shape faith responses to suffering. The following sections will address these shortcomings through exploration of the perspectives of victims, bystanders, and witnesses to the Holocaust and other cases of horrific suffering.

The postures of solidarity and hope, depicted by political thinkers, effectively display the capacity of faith to resist suffering. They make clear that protest and resistance are pivotal faith responses. On the other hand, a strong point of the existentialist approach is the exploration of how nonchosen, involuntary suffering, such as suffering caused by bereavement or illness, can be accepted as potentially meaningful. Marcel and Buber are perceptive in developing how "other-regard" has subtle relational dynamics and not only collective, social import. I will argue that reflection on interpersonal dialogue and meaning-making, promoted by existentialist thinkers and neglected by political thinkers, is crucial for the elucidation of faith's engagement with suffering.

Existentialist and political types of faith response to evil and suffering flow from different streams of continental philosophy, but these currents have converged in the work of more recent thinkers. The importance of the authors studied is most apparent in contemporary Christian thought, where continental thinkers including Buber and Bloch have been influential, particularly on the many "contextual" theologies developed since the late 1960s.[4] As opposed to the conceptual or propositional approach to religious thought found in theodicy, contextual thinkers operate with the conviction—advanced in a limited way by existentialist as well as political thinkers—that all theological language is situated in particular historical circumstances. Contextual theology effectively enlarges the Marxian-inspired political approach by recognizing that faith discourse incorporates individual and communal identities. By bringing the political and existentialist approaches into conversation with a variety of contextual theologies, represented by post-Holocaust, liberation, feminist, womanist, mujerista, African-American, and Latin American writers, the second part of this chapter explores how the political approach to evil and suffering can be expanded and deepened to include the insights of existentialist thinkers. My analysis focuses on how practical responses to evil and suffering involve four key religious postures, which display existentialist and political dimensions: memory, solidarity, hope, and mystical faith.

Memory

Marxist-influenced political thinkers place high priority on the significance of memory, defined as critical consciousness of suffering. Memory recalls narratives that expose the scars left by suffering on history and the yearnings of victims and their disappointed hopes for change. Narratives are retold in an I-It mode to be analyzed using economic and political theories to determine the causes of suffering and pragmatic solutions to it. In particular, Bloch and Metz demand remembrance to expose the injustices of capitalist society. I propose that the scope and significance of memory can be articulated with greater nuance through reflection on the role of dialogue and the I-Thou and I-It distinction in conjunction with political formulations and perspectives.

For Benjamin, and Metz who follows his lead, the memory of history evidently has a personal, as well as a political, dimension. There is a sharp moral sensitivity behind Benjamin's Marxian reading of history, which retrieves the voices of victims, their complaints against suffering, and their demands for justice. The warm stream Marxist approach toward the past can be described as alternating between an I-It and an I-Thou posture. Memory gives access to the scientific, historical facts of oppression, but also to the struggles and hopes of the oppressed. Memory can be a form of empathy with persons in the past because it revives the victims' stories and their motivation to correct systemic injustices causing oppression. Memory of others' suffering can spur urgent action in the present.

The word that Benjamin uses for "memory" is "*Eingedenken*," a term that connotes that the act of memory involves entering into the past (indicated by the prefix *ein*) and not just mechanically recalling or reproducing the past.[5] I consider this quasi-Marxian view of memory amenable to further development to show how it can encompass both the personal attention and political analysis that motivate resistance to the suffering of others. To elaborate the meaning of *Eingedenken* using Marcel's vocabulary, memory is a posture of availability to hearing the cries of victims. Memory is also an attitude of fidelity, which involves taking up the victims' protests against injustice, a political conclusion that Marcel does not draw.

To use Buber's philosophical framework, memory is a way of listening to past victims as Thou. Through memory, I hear their stories as testimonies that appeal to me for help and that make me a witness to suffering. The act of my witnessing and the other's testifying are political acts of historical urgency. In post-Holocaust literary reflection, the role of the reader is framed as a witness whose moral agenda is to prevent injustices of the past from recurring or being forgotten. For historical records of the Holocaust to effectively "testify," they must be received by the reader, or witness, as addressed to one's self. Memory is not objective but engaged. It is an act of witnessing that includes listening to the Thou, expressing solidarity with sufferers, and resisting on their behalf.[6]

Marxian thinkers use I-It analysis to reveal both causes and solutions to oppression. But, evidently, the political approach to memory is not solely analytical and scientific, taking a spectator attitude, but also passionately concerned and engaged in struggle against suffering. On the contrary, it is the bourgeois view of the past that takes a pervasively I-It perspective toward history. Metz observes that for the typical middle-class subject, history is viewed dispassionately as a bare succession of events, ultimately progressive but devoid of importance for the present. Indifference toward collective suffering in history is an immoral form of memory because it condones the past suffering of victims. Similarly, existentialist thinkers view I-It relation to individual persons as immoral (or amoral) because it dehumanizes other persons.

There are shortcomings in the political understanding of memory where the function of memory is presumably to awaken the satiated bourgeois subject from political complacency. According to Metz, for middle-class subjects the avoidance of suffering can be corrected by means of biblical and other historical memories of suffering that serve a dangerous function. While this moral aim is positive, Metz's reflections on Holocaust victims and the role of dangerous memory remain entrapped in bourgeois assumptions.[7] Metz employs memory to see suffering through the victims' eyes. But his theological approach assumes the gaze of someone who is privileged and not enmeshed in suffering. For the middle-class person who remembers, memory is dangerous because it provokes socioeconomic critique and protest. On the contrary, from a victim's position, the memory of suffering may merely reproduce the painful symptoms of trauma and bear destructive psychological consequences. In extreme cases, it can even endanger survival. Concerning ongoing suffering, memory may reinforce hopelessness and motivate passive acceptance, rather than empowering struggle against the weight of suffering and provoking consciousness of moral agency. With respect to past suffering, concentration camp survivors find that Holocaust memories place them back in the experience, provoking negative reactions such as anguish, humiliation, guilt, disconnection, or terror.[8] Clearly, not all memories serve the productive, dangerous role that Metz intends. Moreover, it is important to distinguish between responding to actual conditions of suffering as needing relief, and remembering and responding to the traumatic memory of past suffering, a subtlety lost on Metz. For bygone suffering, the memory of suffering may provoke resistance, while for the victim who suffers presently, basic coping and survival skills to sustain strength are required before resistance is even an option.

Is the memory of suffering helpful for victims? Metz assumes so, but he does not consider that memories of suffering may discourage or enrage victims, or that an obsession with such memories may block recovery from the trauma of past horrors. The dangers of memory in psychological and spiritual terms are not explored. From the position of victims, there are different kinds of memories that play a role in surviving past suffering. Feminist theologian Flora Keshgegian grapples with the role of memory in faith, applied to reflections on the Holocaust, Armenian genocide, slavery, and child abuse. Responding critically to Metz, she makes a crucial differentiation between three types of memory: memory of suffering, memory of resistance and agency, and memory of connection with life and wholeness. Drawing on psychological trauma theory, she analyzes the function of memory for survivors to show that memories of resistance have greater potential to empower the victim than those of suffering, while memories of wholeness generate hope by inspiring an alternative vision of life not dominated by suffering. In reality, suffering is the most potentially destructive type of memory. Only together do these three modes of remembrance take into account the complex facets of suffering and survival, recovery and resistance.[9]

From the perspective of the middle-class subject, the memory of suffering is potent as a critical lever. Feminist liberation theologian Sharon Welch proposes that memories of suffering act as a "counter-discourse" that challenges the dominant discourses of those in power, which are produced by politicians, corporate leaders, advertisers, and the media. Speaking from the social position of a bourgeois Christian, Welch observes that middle-class people usually avoid memories of social suffering because such memories do not directly involve one's self. Memories of oppression and exclusion can raise awareness among people who are unknowingly, or knowingly, complicit bystanders or perpetrators. Welch cautions that the faith response to these memories should not involve reifying or labeling the victims as "other" or automatically taking responsibility for "them" and proposing solutions to their problems. Narratives of persons who are marginalized or oppressed should function to uncover "the limited appeal of our capitalist economic system, [and] our limited appreciation of the vitality and determination of other peoples to shape their own identities."[10] Such memories are dangerous, in Metz's terms, not only because they interrupt and contradict the discourses of the status quo, but because they interrupt personal ignorance of complicity with structures of oppression.

The assemblage of narratives gathered by contextual theologians, re-membering the Holocaust and other cases of collective suffering, does not give a universal and complete account of the mechanisms of oppression, nor ultimate strategies for preventing historical injustice. The goal of universality is a misguided ambition of modern philosophy, including theodicy. Rather, narratives expose ambiguity and complexity. There is neither one funda-mental explanation for oppression, nor one political faith response to suffer-ing. On the contrary, the memory of suffering is a counterdiscourse that wages a struggle against all purportedly universal discourses. It accentuates the ruptures in history and refutes optimistic belief in modern progress. The liberating function of memory is to enlarge one's perspective to include the viewpoints of other social positions, while admitting that all perspectives are permanently partial.[11] For the middle-class subject like myself, narratives of suffering expose limitations of perspective and the harm caused by naïve or misinformed assumptions on a social scale. Memories of resistance or whole-ness can also spur critique of the past, but their function is more directly to motivate hope for positive developments in the future.

Importantly, memory's political significance does not exclude an inter-personal dimension. Memory is an ongoing process of dialogue between the past and present, with texts and among human beings. Modeled on Buber's I-Thou relation, the dialogue of remembrance involves openness, listening, availability, and trust. However, it must also involve critical awareness and consciousness of social standpoint. It would be purely an I-It process if the purpose of memory were only to develop technical solutions for overcoming suffering. But, primarily, the practical faith posture of memory attends to the voices and testimonies of the oppressed. While the I-It mode is rooted in ex-ertion of power and control, memory is an attitude that opens up space for silenced voices to speak and be heard in the present. Rather than impose an analysis of social problems "from above" in response to suffering, memory validates the agency of the victims, as they describe their situations and their coping strategies.[12] Witnesses amplify the testimonies of victims who articu-late memories of horrors, resistance, and positive moments of well-being.

Memory can give suffering religious meaning of various kinds. If under-taken in solidarity with victims, the memory of others who have suffered can be meaningful. Memory of voluntary suffering for the sake of resistance is meaningful as an expression of agency, courage, moral opposition to injustice, and faith commitment. But, for victims, memory is not always meaningful. Survivors generally refuse to give involuntary, horrific suffering inherent meaning. As Elie Wiesel and other Holocaust writers have articu-lated, concentration camp suffering appears retrospectively as meaningless and useless in itself, rather than purposive. It is entirely unjustified in theodicy terms.[13] However, the memory of suffering (not the suffering itself) may be meaningful for victims when shared as a witness to the terrible scars and ruptures found throughout history. Memory is a form of truth-telling and a pathway toward recovery. Moreover, memory can build solidarity between victims and nonvictims.

Solidarity

Memory can foster mutually transformative solidarity among diverse subjects. The political notion of "solidarity"—identification with oppressed persons and persons who suffer due to social injustice—is illuminated by means of existentialist insights. Liberation thinkers hold that solidarity is not something newly grafted onto Christian faith by Marxian philosophy. In fact, solidarity may be understood as essential to the Christian notion of redemption, applied to social situations of suffering and injustice. As Soelle has argued, Christian faith in a God of love must be enacted as world-transforming praxis in order to be internally consistent. Without such practical translation, faith in a loving God becomes a lie and a sham.[14] Specifically, faith in God must be translated into solidarity that seeks the liberation of creation from violence and exploitation.

There is a circular relationship between living in solidarity and developing a critical consciousness of suffering. Solidarity involves commitment that increases awareness and identification with the oppressed and motivates political action. In the praxis of solidarity, critical reflection and participation in collective struggles are integrated. For liberation theologians, theology itself is understood as praxis, namely, the correlation of reflection on Christian doctrines and faith practices including solidarity in struggles against suffering.[15] Solidarity is a critical posture that enables recognition of the exclusion of particular groups of people by the church and other social institutions.

While for Bloch, and to a lesser extent Metz, solidarity tends to be associated rather abstractly with the bourgeois awareness of the plight of the proletariat, contextual thinkers pay more nuanced attention to social location. In fact, many liberation and feminist theologians write theology from the perspective of marginal or oppressed social groups. Liberation thinkers caution political theologians, such as Metz, about their propensity to idealize the poor and speak for them. To take a leading example, Catholic theologian Gustavo Gutiérrez explores solidarity as directed toward the poor of Latin America: the exploited, the malnourished, the penniless, all of those whom the prevailing social order systematically treats as nonpersons. Reflecting on struggles against poverty in Peru, Gutiérrez articulates an emerging spirituality of suffering and liberation representing the viewpoint of the poor.[16] He seeks to be accurate in presenting their situation, but, at the same time, he is admittedly selective in choosing responses to suffering that seem both truly liberating and consistent with the Catholic tradition. He recognizes critically that liberation theology is not a matter of simply quoting the perspective of the poor, as if there were only one perspective, but interpreting their situation from a position of close involvement and solidarity.

In the work of Gutiérrez, Latin American poverty provides a standpoint from which to criticize the pious affirmation of poverty in traditional Christian thought. Using biblical exegesis, Gutiérrez clarifies the commonly misunderstood statement of Jesus that the poor are "blessed" (Matt. 5:1; Lk. 6:20). He argues that what precisely is blessed is "spiritual poverty," which is an attitude of openness to God, not "material poverty," which is a social evil. The poor should not piously accept poverty as a blessing, nor should church leaders encourage political passivity. Gutiérrez challenges bourgeois middle-class comfort by insisting that Christian solidarity requires relinquishing social-class privilege and embracing poverty voluntarily. Poverty is not to be sought for its own sake, but it may be accepted in solidarity as an authentic imitation of Christ.[17] Gutiérrez does not employ a theodicy justification of poverty, as if the suffering of the poor is intended by God for the sake of moral development or soul-making. That would be morally scandalous. But suffering potentially does have meaning, he admits, when it is accepted in solidarity with others. Both persons who live in poverty involuntarily and those who live with the poor voluntarily can confer meaning on suffering when struggle against it is dedicated to the redemption of creation.

Using traditional theological terms, solidarity can be identified with the love of one's neighbor, as Hispanic feminist theologian Ada María Isasi-Díaz explores. In her mujerista theology, she notes that solidarity must go beyond the Marxist idea of critical consciousness of oppression in society. Solidarity involves more than identifying with an oppressed group and proposing strategies to remedy social ills. This political viewpoint is too thin a description of solidarity because it leaves out the importance of love and friendship within communities. Her interviews with Hispanic women from different backgrounds show that interpersonal dialogue is a key component of solidarity.[18] I-Thou relation functions within the practice of solidarity in three different ways. First, I-Thou relation with victims motivates solidarity. Direct contact with persons who suffer creates bonds of fidelity and empathy, bonds that commit me to helping others, perhaps by joining a political struggle, seeking aid, or providing support. Second, I-Thou relation among persons working together for the cause of resistance is necessary. Friendships among members of a protesting group can foster loyalty to the individuals involved and hence stronger commitment to the cause of resistance when things are difficult. Resistance efforts require unity among comrades that is fostered by I-Thou relation. Third, I-Thou dialogue advances understanding and cooperation among persons struggling against suffering that helps them formulate shared priorities and goals. Within a solidarity group, plans and strategies must be worked out through effective communication, especially the capacity for empathetic listening.

In recent feminist theology, solidarity between different groups is promoted using novels that portray narratives of suffering and faith responses. African-American women's literature has been a point of focus for both womanist theologians and white feminists. For womanist thinkers, this literature opens numerous avenues for understanding faith responses to suffering. Narratives personalize the immense social sufferings caused by slavery, racism, and sexism; articulate various forms of women's agency; and show how resistance occurs in complex subtle and overt forms.[19] For white feminist theologians, black women's literature is important because it gives access to a new range of social experience and moral resistance. Sharon Welch draws on such literature to develop a "feminist ethic of risk" as a middle-class Christian response to suffering in solidarity with African Americans. Welch remarks that becoming discouraged and giving up on resistance when confronted with social problems is the privilege of the white middle class to which she belongs; whereas, for many black women and others, resistance is not optional, but absolutely necessary for survival.[20] African-American literature exposes social evils and racism perpetrated by white privilege, as well as the difficulties in achieving "liberation" under changing forms of racial prejudice.

From my social position, I identify with Welch and admire her commitment to learning from other standpoints. Yet the theological employment of African-American women's literature and the literature of other "marginal" groups requires caution. One problem in such use of narrative is the danger of appropriating the voices of others. Many post-Holocaust thinkers have drawn attention to the imperialism of Christian theology. Dominant Christian discourses have promoted negative views about Jews and Judaism since the birth of Christianity. The Holocaust has forced reexamination of traditional claims for the supersession of Christianity over Judaism. Post-Holocaust Christian theologians are sensitive to the need to understand Judaism in its own terms, rather than only through a Christian lens. They strive to allow Jewish victims and survivors to determine the meaning of Holocaust suffering and not hastily impose a Christian redemptive framework.[21] Such openness to others' perspectives and recognition of marginalized voices has been a major challenge in Christian theology, as post-Holocaust and other liberation theologians have recognized. The dominance of white Christian voices over Jewish voices, among others, creates an imbalance that can be addressed through academic, congregational, and personal dialogues that build solidarity.

From an African-American Christian perspective, it is the dominance of white theology that is overbearing. As black theologian James Cone has argued, there should be less emphasis on the Western theological tradition, although that is what is taught in most seminaries, in order for theologians to appreciate the significance of black history and culture for Christian thought. Cone puts the point quite bluntly when he writes that "the people responsible for or indifferent to the oppression of blacks are not likely to provide the theological resources for our liberation. If oppressed peoples are to be liberated, they must themselves create the means for it to happen."[22] White theologians may want to learn from oppressed groups, but they must be sensitive to how such narratives are employed. Clearly, African-American literature has widened the scope of white feminist Christian thought. As theologian Kathleen Sands describes it, "a world of color" is made available that can effectively illuminate moral consciousness and the aesthetic and mystical dimensions of the struggle with suffering.[23] But it must be recognized that both black and white theologians are selective in identifying helpful narratives that pair solidarity with faith, for these two elements are not always found together in narratives of suffering. Solidarity and resistance are not necessarily based on faith in God. They may be motivated by humanistic convictions about the value of every person and demands for justice and equality.[24]

Solidarity functions as a universal goal and ideal in Marxian and political thought, but contextual thinkers make an important corrective to this abstract universality. They stress the partiality and incompleteness of all solidarity and recognize social differences that create barriers to solidarity. This point is emphasized in Hispanic feminist theology by Isasi-Díaz, whose ethnographic interview method reveals striking differences among Latinas based on factors such as age, race, immigration status, and country of origin, such as Mexico, Cuba, or Puerto Rico. Seeking to build solidarity among Hispanic women, Isasi-Díaz interviews subjects to explore moral agency and consciousness that undergird liberation hopes and activities.[25] However, her fieldwork exposes that the divisions within a given group are profound and perhaps as challenging as differences between separate ethnic or social groups. Solidarity is not only difficult and partial, but, given diversity within an oppressed group and conditions of suffering, it may be nearly impossible.

Reflection on Holocaust memoirs and oral testimonies reveals that in concentration camp situations, solidarity among inmates was mainly

small-scale and local, centering on family ties or friendship with a few comrades. Severe suffering drives persons toward individualism because under
threat of death, self-protection and self-preservation become the primary necessities.[26] To practice solidarity requires that victims identify with one another and act together as agents of change, but such identification may be
blocked by the crushing physical and psychological effects of suffering,
where morals values are compromised for the sake of survival. Moreover,
solidarity is challenging because shared memories or circumstances of suffering might not effectively overcome differences of class or family background. The difficulty of solidarity often increases in proportion to the
severity of suffering, as Holocaust narratives illustrate.

Just as memory does not provide a universal purview, solidarity is universal only as a hope or ideal. In practice, solidarity is always limited. As efforts for liberation are strategic and partial, so is the ability to join together in
solidarity with others. Consciousness of solidarity exposes the subject's multiple identities and participation in multiple forms of social control. It also dis-
closes that there are communities and individuals affected by my social group
and myself, both for good and for ill.[27] I-It analysis of systemic injustice is a
precondition for awareness of the need to build bridges between different
groups, while I-Thou relation can help overcome barriers. Mutual listening
must exist for differences to be articulated and understanding to occur between economic classes or marginal groups. Solidarity requires openness to
dialogue in order to formulate shared strategies of resistance and survival.

Hope

The political model of hope promoted by German theologians Moltmann
and Metz has been influential for contextual liberation theologians such as
James Cone, whose black theology emerged alongside political theology in
the late 1960s. Like political thinkers, Cone is insistent that faith in God
should entail hope for social and political liberation, and he rejects all seemingly apolitical versions of Christianity. Cone cites Moltmann, and implicitly
Marx, in criticizing individual and escapist "otherworldly" interpretations of
eschatological hope that act as opiates for the oppressed.[28] As an example
of quiescent faith, he quotes lyrics from the spirituals sung by African-
American slaves. He finds that the lyrics do not call for protest and liberation, but instead emphasize the otherworldly hope to "go home to heaven"
and escape this world of suffering. More recently, historians of slave religion
and womanist theologians have contested this negative view, arguing that
the spirituals contain coded language that unmasks oppression and empowers resistance to suffering.[29]

Cone challenges political Marxian-influenced thought by questioning the identification of religious hope with absolute liberation. He finds this model of hope too closely bound to the Marxian preoccupation with revolution and the establishment of a perfect socioeconomic system, communism. Cone poses the rhetorical question: Is hope for the transformation of society, the removal of all structures of oppression, and liberation a white man's hope? Yes, in large part. Behind this utopian hope for liberation lies the assumption, according to Cone, that I see myself as part of a group with the political power to change history, and I see repeated patterns of oppression as eradicable. Cone remarks that the white attitude toward history assumes with hubris that history can be engineered and mastered by human planning, an attitude of "having" to use Marcel's vocabulary. This colonizing attitude toward history is not religious hope that views the future as open, as promoted by Marcel and Bloch, but confidence like that of Hegelian and orthodox Marxist determinists who view human beings as cogs in the mechanism of history. Whether this attitude of mastery is based on confidence in dialectical historical progress or human planning, it is an attitude that dehumanizes the victims of history and effaces their historical agency.[30]

Bloch and Metz are middle-class white males and members of the German intellectual elite. They do not display the arrogant confidence in transforming history that Cone seems to expect, for they make clear that hope is not equivalent to certainty. Nevertheless, Bloch in particular emphasizes that radical change is a real possibility. Cone's point is that within the African-American community even a modest hope in the possibility of institutional change may not exist, given the community's history of oppression. He differs from European political thinkers in recognizing the magnitude of hopelessness among oppressed persons. Cone observes that despair and cynicism prevail among some African Americans living in poverty-stricken neighborhoods. He does not condone such hopelessness as positive. But recognition of the severity of black oppression leads Cone to formulate his goals of liberation as centering around more local political objectives, rather than utopian schemes.

Cone, like Metz, recognizes that religious narratives of freedom, such as the Exodus from Egypt or the biography of Martin Luther King Jr., promote hope that liberation is possible for God's people. Such narratives also affirm the identity of the subject as an agent in history and the value of all persons as subjects before God. Cone endorses King's famous dream of peace and tolerance as a religious hope that has motivating power. For Cone, resistance is worthwhile in order to bring changes to American society, and he condones some measure of violence, at least in principle, as a response to the racist violence perpetrated against African Americans.[31] In contrast, Martin Luther King Jr. recommends a nonviolent strategy, recognizing that such resistance is valuable politically as a way to fight racism, but it is also a testimony to hope and the ideas of universal love and peace. Such hope has value even if it does not succeed as the means to abolish oppression. Resistance is important as a witness to the truth, exposing socially caused suffering. It proclaims the dignity of persons, created in God's image, who have the courage to protest in solidarity. The special moral significance of nonviolent protest is that it shows an alternative mode of social relations, where persons refuse to be the cause of suffering for others.[32]

Despite their differences, Cone and King both represent a Christian "liberation" perspective, which aims to radically transform society and ultimately end racism. However, objections to liberation hope are raised from the perspective of African-American women by Delores Williams. Williams argues that hope for liberation is appropriate under some circumstances, but under other conditions subdued hope for survival is more appropriate, particularly under extreme circumstances of oppression. The posture of survival hope lies between two extremes: revolutionary liberatory activity and political apathy or resignation. The biblical narratives of Moses and Hagar are used to illustrate the contrast between "liberation" and "survival" types of hope. Moses fights unjust social and economic structures and succeeds in liberating the descendants of Abraham from captivity in Egypt. He is a freedom fighter and a hero. Hagar is a slave belonging to Abraham, the first patriarch of the people of Israel, who makes a covenant with God and journeys to the Promised Land. As the concubine of Abraham, Hagar bears a son Ishmael. But she and her son are perceived as a threat to the privileges of Abraham's legitimate son, Isaac, and at the request of his wife Sarah, Abraham sends Hagar into exile with her baby. Wandering in the desert, Hagar's hope is for the necessities of survival: food and water, protection from robbery or rape, and the strength to care for her son without a husband, a home, or wealth.

Williams considers the story of Hagar's hope as a model for African-American women who seek to find a way out of no way, and for others in extreme need.[33] In a desperate situation, the posture of hope in God does not necessarily entail participation in revolutionary resistance, although the story of Moses, which is thematic in the writings of political and liberation thinkers, implies the contrary. Pragmatically, survival hope sanctions the acceptance of certain conditions of suffering to strategically combat others. It does endorse resistance to suffering, but resistance is not necessarily collective or political in scope.

The framework of I-Thou relation is not employed by Williams, but it is a helpful tool to describe the kind of interpersonal relations that she calls for among members of an oppressed group. Williams's model of survival hope focuses on the maintenance of personal family and community bonds. She identifies a network of supportive relations as necessary for survival under conditions of economic oppression and social prejudice. In some cases, building a close family unit or getting a good education for one's children might seem like ambitious hopes. Survival under circumstances of oppression is aided by I-Thou relations that create trust and sharing. Dialogue with God can also strengthen hope because prayer can give experiential certainty of God's presence in the face of suffering. As in the case of Job, encounter with God can confirm faith.

Existentialist thinkers Marcel and Buber would agree with Williams's refusal to equate religious hope with political hope for liberation in history. Drawing on stories of contemporary black women's experience, Williams validates religious hope that does not entail engagement in liberation activities designed to overthrow the causes of suffering, as if it were even possible to achieve total liberation. Williams's critique of the political model of hope is convincing. Her insights are applicable to a broad range of situations, including the Holocaust, where social suffering is chronic and persons are harmed to the extent that they have neither the material or personal resources to attempt to overthrow suffering's causes.

The testimony of Jewish Holocaust survivor and psychiatrist Viktor Frankl confirms Williams's observations about more modest types of hope as appropriate in situations of severe suffering. Frankl notes that, under the extreme suffering and oppression experienced by concentration camp inmates in Auschwitz, Jewish hope was predominantly survival hope.[34] The central hopes expressed by camp inmates were to stay together with family members in the camp and be reunited with family and loved ones after the war. These are existentialist types of hope for the endurance of I-Thou relations geared toward survival. Many camp inmates hoped for liberation, but they expected it to come as rescue from outside the camp by Allied soldiers. Frankl reports that many prisoners could not even muster hope for external rescue from Nazi brutality because they were physically and psychologically traumatized. It is interesting that Frankl does not report the case of even one prisoner who had hope that liberation could be achieved by concentration camp inmates heroically mounting resistance against their Nazi oppressors. The difficulty of survival hope is especially relevant as applied to settings where systemic oppression seems too entrenched and brutal to be overcome from within by rebellion.

To complicate the issue, it must be noted that Holocaust history contains examples of solidarity and resistance even in dire situations where hope for success or survival seemed impossible. There were persons under surveillance in Jewish ghettoes and concentration camp inmates who managed to find the hope, courage, and resources to organize and enact collective strategies of resistance. For instance, in 1941 a group of over thirty Jews in the heavily guarded Krakow ghetto—under what might seem like hopeless conditions—organized themselves as an armed resistance movement. The group was discovered and extinguished in 1943, but only after engineering numerous resistance operations outside the Krakow ghetto, including a café bomb that killed eleven Germans.[35] Another remarkable example of hope is the uprising that occurred in the Auschwitz-Birkenau death camp on October 7, 1944. This act of resistance was sparked by the selection of 300 *Sonderkommando* workers for death, mostly Hungarian and Greek Jews. Approximately 650 prisoners participated in violent protest and revolt. Handbuilt explosives were used to burn crematorium number four, and several SS guards were killed or wounded. Those rebels who planned the operation were either killed in the fighting or by Nazi guards afterwards, and hundreds of other prisoners died as punishment for the rebellion. Altogether, approximately 450 camp inmates lost their lives as a result of this resistance effort and no one successfully escaped to freedom.[36]

These varied examples from the European Holocaust and African-American history show how difficult it is to determine whether "survival" or "liberation" hope is appropriate in a given situation. The question also arises whether resistance is always linked with hope for real political change, as Marxian religious thinkers assume. Perhaps, persons might choose to resist, either violently or nonviolently, without hope for successfully overcoming suffering. They might consider their deaths as martyrdom or symbolic opposition to injustice. Resistance, even leading to death, might be a way of asserting one's individual dignity and courage in defiance of those in power, thus making suffering and death meaningful. It might also serve the political aims of drawing attention to the plight of one's fellow victims, shaming those who perpetrate injustice, and testifying to the world that oppression is wrong. Radical acts of resistance such as the Warsaw ghetto uprising presuppose the hope that one's own death can impact the future as a witness to injustice.[37] Willingness to die can be an act of hope when a person undergoes danger in solidarity with those who suffer. Resistance can be meaningful apart from successfully removing conditions of suffering.

Hope and resistance are conjoined, even in situations when persons involved in resistance do not seem to hope for heroic achievements or dramatic results. Both liberation and survival types of hope are central to faith, although political thinkers do not recognize survival as a form of resistance because of its personal scope. Even seemingly mundane matters of survival, such as rejecting negative self-representations or speaking publicly about past trauma, are acts of resistance in response to the damaging effects of suffering.

Hagar's exile in the desert with her child is an act of survival that displays resistance to the norms of slavery that denied her worth as a human being. The embrace of hope by Frankl affirms that suffering can be made meaningful by individuals who approach it as a trial, to use Marcel's term, that calls on their moral and spiritual resources.[38] These examples are acts of resistance by individuals under drastic conditions. Apart from whether hope lies in survival or liberation, acts of resistance show commitment to life in relation to other persons and future generations. Remembering hope-filled narratives of resistance, whether centering on survival or liberation, can encourage protest and commitment among future agents of resistance.

Political thinkers like Bloch and Metz insist that religious hope affirms the real possibility of historical change. But in response to the Holocaust and other situations of extreme suffering, a person might simply hope for the chance to perform, prior to death or while dying, some symbolic act affirming personal dignity. It is legitimate for hope to take more modest, less politically ambitious forms depending on the situation. Such contextual decisions cannot be made abstractly, but must be discerned specifically by suffering persons themselves. Just as there are different types of hope in God, there are various modes of resistance along the spectrum between basic survival and full liberation. In comparison with the Marxian emphasis on collectively organized action to liberate economic and political structures, survival hope relies on interpersonal strategies to cope with suffering, strategies that function as a significant means of resistance.

Mystical Faith

The practical approaches studied expose a "mystical" dimension to faith that involves the discovery of divine transcendence in all things, even in suffering. According to my definition, mystical faith deeply and vividly perceives divine reality pervading everyday reality. Moreover, it accepts that God is ultimately beyond understanding. To maintain faith despite lack of explanation or justification for evil displays mystical appreciation for the value and beauty of life, and mystical assurance that transcends oppressive conditions. Contrary to stereotypes of mysticism as elitist and esoteric, I hold that the mystical dimension of faith is broadly accessible. Also contrary to stereotypes, mystical faith is not essentially apolitical or isolated. Rather, mystical faith discovers God in human and natural reality and recognizes connections and interdependence among living beings, which entails solidarity, social involvement, and resistance to suffering and exploitation.[39]

Metz recognizes this socially activist element in his portrait of mystical-political faith, which has a prophetic character. Such faith is portrayed in narratives about Jesus, whose messianic praxis involves the memory of suffering, solidarity, and hope. Each of these practical postures of faith provides political models of transcendence. Memory transcends the naiveté and solipsism of the unreflective self by encompassing oppressed groups in the past and present while remembering narratives of suffering and resistance that spark critique of oppression. Solidarity transcends the limits of social location by continually expanding outward toward all-inclusive universality, even though it always remains partial. In hope, temporal limits are transcended because the aims of hope extend toward God's Kingdom and the promise of redemption. Even suffering itself is potentially an occasion for transcendence when it is dedicated to the process of redemption, defined negatively as the absence of suffering, violence, and injustice, and positively in analogy with earthly reconciliation and wholeness.

Despite appearances to the contrary, Metz's political response to suffering does not focus on collective aspects of suffering to the exclusion of personal or mystical aspects. His political approach targets resistance to suffering among oppressed groups of people, but Metz would not deny that love for other persons is expressed in I-Thou relation with individuals. His emphasis on solidarity is strategically designed to compensate for bourgeois overemphasis on faith as personal. In fact, there are striking parallels between the "prophetic" models of prayer portrayed by Metz and Buber. Both authors focus on Job and the Hebrew prophets, as well as other narratives specific to their respective traditions, to show how faith endures suffering. Prayer is important as dialogue that expresses lament and protest against suffering as well as trust in God. Buber and Metz agree that speech addressed to God, not about God, can articulate theodicy questions and provide a powerful source of divine reassurance. God addresses individuals through biblical texts and narratives, as well as in person. In prayer, where God is sought, divine transcendence intersects with human history. The mystical assurance founded on recognition of divine immanence in relation is communicated through narratives of Jewish and Christian faith responses to suffering.

The complementary mystical and political elements of faith are identified and developed independently of Metz in the work of Soelle. Like Metz, Soelle prioritizes narrative as a central resource for a Christian response to Auschwitz. In her theology, the memory of Jesus Christ centers on his resistance to social injustice and his attention to poor and marginal persons, not on the cross as emphasized by Metz or Moltmann. Using biblical texts situated alongside other narratives exhibiting faith responses to suffering, Soelle explores varieties of mystical faith that discover God in the world and find hope in situations of survival and resistance. Soelle directly incorporates aspects of Buber's thought into her theology, such as the priority of language addressed to God and the lived meaning that arises from faith, independent of understanding God's reasons for permitting suffering.[40] She considers I-Thou relation to be a mystical attitude, although Buber denies this conclusion based on his narrow conception of mysticism as a primordial and otherworldly experience of ecstasy.[41] According to Soelle, I-Thou relation is mystical because the "I" transcends its self-orientation and becomes radically open to creation viewed as infused with the divine. Buber's admiration for Hasidism, which is commonly considered a mystical branch of Judaism, directly supports this conclusion.[42] In my view, I-Thou relation indeed exhibits mystical openness and trust in God. Mutual interdependence between God and human beings becomes a conversation in which persons call to God and are called by God to seek reconciliation.

Building a mystical and political portrait of faith, Soelle places Buber's I-Thou philosophy alongside medieval, Quaker, Hasidic, and liberation writers (among others) to explore the mystical dimension implicit in resistance to suffering. She cites Bloch's *Principle of Hope* to illustrate the mystical impulse that projects inner visions and dreams of redemption onto history, drawing on the imagination and what is "not yet" real to transcend present oppression and motivate the alleviation of suffering and injustice.[43] Mystical faith strengthens hope and resistance. It is not cowed by fears of failure, nor does it depend on achieving politically successful results for its sustenance. Such faith does not expect the intervention of God, but recognizes human subjects as divine agents. Prayer is not used as a means to obtain favors from God, but it is an end in itself. From a mystical perspective, prayer is a direct response to divine-worldly reality. There is certainty of God in mystical faith that sustains survival and liberation hope and evokes deep love and joy.[44]

In Holocaust-era diaries from 1941 to 1943, Jewish writer Etty Hillesum articulates a mystical response to suffering that bears striking parallels to Soelle's viewpoint. Living in the Netherlands under Nazi occupation as the persecution of Dutch Jews steadily increased, Hillesum's journal entries articulate the development of faith and nearness to God, rather than protest in the face of suffering. Although she could have tried to avoid deportation, she is willing to share the fate of the majority of Jews because of solidarity with those lacking the money or connections to flee or gain privileged treatment. Interned in Westerbork transit camp, Hillesum reflects on her inner spiritual condition and her opportunities to help and encourage others. In the camp, she finds God present within herself, other persons, and nature. Her mystical response to Nazi-propagated violence and inhumanity affirms the sanctification of daily life.[45] Reflecting on camp conditions in Westerbork, she writes: "I am not afraid to look suffering straight in the eyes. And at the end of each day, there [is] always the feeling: I love people so much."[46] Up until the end, she continues to find meaning in assisting fellow camp prisoners and in appreciating beauty in existence, past and present. In September 1943, Hillesum was deported to Auschwitz where she died two months later.

Mystical faith can transform personal suffering into something meaningful, although not all suffering is thereby made meaningful. God can be found in one's own pain only by choosing to exercise agency, when suffering is embraced with hope and solidarity. In response to the Holocaust, Hillesum and Soelle propose mystical responses that view God not as distant or in eclipse, but as accompanying human beings in their suffering. Rejecting theodicy justification, which exonerates God for permitting suffering for good purposes, they blame human evils for causing the Holocaust. Rather than understanding God as controlling, Hillesum sees God as immanent, sharing her suffering and dependent on persons. Suffering has mystical meaning for the person of faith who perceives connectedness with the web of life, where love of reality and love of God are coextensive. Soelle affirms that God suffers along with human beings who refer their suffering to God, although suffering is not posited ontologically in God's being but taken up in the relations between God and the world.[47] Soelle does not privilege suffering or the cross as the deepest point of mystical contact with God, unlike Christian theologians such as Metz and Moltmann, because that elevates suffering wrongly as the chief indication of divine involvement in history. Rather, suffering is one potential locus of mystical faith alongside others, such as nature, love, or communal solidarity.[48]

Hillesum and Soelle both exhibit mystical faith in God that activates individual suffering as a means of sharing in divine love. The religious meaning of suffering can be parsed in different ways. For some mystics, suffering has a prophetic role, while for others suffering is considered direct participation in divine suffering, completing the process of redemption.[49] Suffering acquires meaning when the subject's suffering is understood as suffering unto God, or what Metz calls "*Leiden an Gott.*" Moreover, when individual suffering is viewed as part of a wider context, such as the suffering of a religious community or an oppressed group, it can be given meaning as an act of solidarity. Suffering can be intentionally directed, individually or collectively, for the sake of serving God.

In exploring how human suffering takes on divine meaning, the image of God's "suffering servant" in the Hebrew Bible is central. In Buber's interpretation of the famous "suffering servant" passage from the book of Isaiah (Is. 52:13–53:12), he explains that suffering, both voluntary and involuntary, can be dedicated to realizing God's redemptive promises of justice and peace. In the context of the Hebrew Bible, the servant figure represents the people of Israel who play a special role in history. Jewish interpreters of the text commonly focus on communal Jewish suffering in history, where the servant represents the people of Israel, while Christian theologians read the same passage as a prophecy about Jesus, the messiah who suffers for the sake of redemption. In either case, suffering is understood as having transcendent meaning when it is intentionally directed toward God. Although much suffering in the world is without meaning, human agency can give particular instances of suffering a mystical significance that transforms it into something productive.

Although I do not at all want to minimize the inter- and intrareligious differences in interpreting this crucial and contested passage from Isaiah, I am intrigued by the potential convergence between Jewish and Christian understandings of the idea of meaningful suffering connected with the suffering servant image. In his essay on Jewish and Christian responses to suffering, Jewish thinker Robert Gibbs asserts that this passage indicates a type of representative suffering that possibly can be affirmed by both traditions. According to Gibbs's definition, "representative" suffering is suffering taken on voluntarily for the sake of others. In viewing suffering as representative, the particularity of suffering is not lost in a universal historical scheme, nor is suffering justified as part of the machinery of history, as theodicy would have it. Nevertheless, suffering gains meaning when a "servant" of God accepts suffering. The intentional designation of suffering as representative has moral implications because it connects the suffering self with others for whose sake it is endured. Gibbs emphasizes the moral meaning of representative suffering, stating that "as representatives, we are called to fight against other's suffering, as well as against our own. We are called to treat the stranger fairly, even to prevent genocide against other peoples."[50] For suffering to be representative, it must be deliberately dedicated to serving others, and thus to God. I agree that this faith posture can potentially be affirmed by both Christians and Jews, as the preceding chapters confirm. Representative suffering is mystical because it identifies the subject in relation to God, displays solidarity with others who suffer, and evidences hope for resisting suffering.

The book of Job illustrates mystical faith in which existential and political aspects of faith are reciprocal. As Gutiérrez points out, Job recognizes his condition as unjust suffering broadly shared among humanity. Commonly, attention focuses on the existential side of Job's struggle: his doubts, the accusations by his friends, and God's absence. But, from a political perspective, the book of Job is a narrative showing exemplary commitment to the suffering of others. Gutiérrez observes that, through his suffering, Job becomes keenly aware of the suffering of the poor and the hardships of peasants, widows, and orphans. Job also protests such suffering, yet he trusts that God loves both himself and the poor, although they do not appear blessed. The book of Job shows the necessity of two complementary types of response to suffering: prophetic language and mystical expression. Prophetic language articulates the moral scandal of suffering, while mystical speech praises the grace of God that sustains life and promises human fulfillment.[51] Even after God speaks from the whirlwind, God's mystery still transcends human understanding. In the end, Job displays a mystical faith that places no conditions on commitment to God and demands no recompense for suffering.

Divine transcendence is crucial to mystical faith, yet overemphasis on transcendence is problematic if it appears to distance God from historical struggle. For Job, God is paradoxically far and near. Job hears God speak, yet theodicy answers remain beyond human scope. The major figures studied in the previous chapters affirm God's transcendence, which functions as a symbol and anchor for hope. Their reluctance to reflect on God abstractly, apart from faith practice, implies that God transcends theoretical knowledge. But the discovery of God in religious postures and practices suggests that God is near to persons. Indeed, God may be discovered as immanent in human resistance to suffering and liberation struggles. Reflection on divine transcendence in immanence, as pursued by feminist theologians and others, integrates political and mystical aspects of faith in God. Patriarchal concepts of God as an omnipotent ruler are rejected in favor of nonhierarchical human and natural images, such as companion or breath of life.[52] The divine is embodied in reality whenever a person acts as a co-creator with God promoting solidarity and care for creatures. Practically, God's transcendence and immanence are interlaced in work for justice, love, creativity, and joy. Alongside divine immanence, liberation hope appeals to the divine source of life as deeper and broader than human reality. Faith in a God who transcends the world is crucial for mystical faith because the ideals of faith themselves exceed the limits of human efforts.

Divine transcendence motivates resistance and assurance even in the face of failure, when social activism seems more like a symbolic token than a viable means of change, and it sustains solidarity because it affirms connections among all creatures as part of God's world. While divine transcendence anchors hope for overcoming suffering and injustice, divine immanence gives struggles with suffering intimate meaning. Mystical faith can enable persons to accept representative suffering for the sake of others, alongside protest and resistance. Recognition of the magnitude of suffering in the Holocaust and other historical horrors challenges faith, as theodicy has always recognized, because in many cases of suffering the victims do not find meaning. Given the desperate circumstances of world history—where exploitation, pollution, genocide, abuse, apathy, prejudice, and injustice are interminably destructive—memory, solidarity, hope, and mystical faith embody compelling, contextual faith modes of survival and resistance.

8 Beyond Theodicy
Evaluating Theodicy from a Practical Perspective

THE CONTEXTUAL APPROACHES to suffering examined in the previous chapter are extensions of the political approach in their attention to social position. But they do not repeat the Marxian fixation on revolutionary resistance found in the work of Bloch and Metz. Instead, a dynamic balance between faith postures of acceptance and resistance emerges. Cumulatively, contemporary post-Holocaust, feminist, and liberation thinkers give subtle accounts of how the practices of memory, solidarity, hope, and mystical faith vary according to circumstances of suffering. Each one of these faith practices enables sufferers to find the resources to survive under difficult circumstances. In cases of voluntary suffering resulting from resistance, there is meaning found in the intentional effort to help one's self and others. Involuntary suffering may be accepted as meaningful or not, depending on the situation. Horrific suffering symbolized by the Holocaust, slavery, or Latin American poverty is not viewed retroactively as positive or justified, and global theodicy meanings are not projected onto suffering.

Granted that the insights of existentialist and political approaches are not mutually exclusive, this final chapter returns to the philosophical issues raised in chapter One. It reflects on the common intellectual commitments that motivate the rejection of theodicy, in the wake of the precedent set by Enlightenment philosopher Immanuel Kant. Despite their differences, it is striking that neither existentialist nor political thinkers address the logical problems that suffering raises for the rational plausibility of theism, nor do they engage in systematic reflection on God's nature. This chapter probes the main reasons for these omissions and the variety of objections to theodicy that have been raised. A key question at stake is whether practical approaches tolerate theodicy as an alternative approach or dismiss it entirely.

To conclude this comparative project, I will evaluate the overall possibility and appropriateness of theodicy from a practical perspective. The first part addresses a complex set of issues: (1) practical faith in God, (2) the epistemic impossibility of theodicy, and (3) the moral scandal of theodicy. The second part proposes four guidelines for religious approaches to evil and suffering that encourage philosophical and theological discussion of these themes to move beyond the shortcomings of theodicy.

THE POSSIBILITY AND APPROPRIATENESS OF THEODICY

Practical Faith in God

The epistemic possibility of theodicy is called into question by the Kantian distinction between *phenomena* and *noumena* and the division between scientific knowledge and moral faith. We have seen that Marcel and Buber endorse a Kantian-style epistemological dualism between the I-It realm of problem solving and the realm of I-Thou relation where God is encountered. Moreover, the Marxian thinkers studied posit a twofold distinction between the social sciences that analyze the facts of history and plan political strategies, and the practical postures of hope and faith that motivate resistance. Although these thinkers are by no means disciples of Kant, they operate with epistemic dualisms that echo the distinction between *phenomena* and *noumena* without using this terminology. In addition, existentialist and Marxian thinkers appear to share certain Kantian perspectives concerning God. They agree that God functions as a practical postulate necessary for faith and hope in the face of evil and suffering. Rejection of scientific knowledge of God is motivated by moral considerations—namely, that knowledge of history (such as Hegel advances) is counter to moral hope that goodness will be rewarded and perpetration of suffering punished. Theodicy is judged to be wrongheaded because it applies a theoretical approach to practical faith.

Kant rejects theodicy because it claims theistic knowledge that is impossible within the finitude of theoretical or speculative human reason. Similarly, a point of convergence among existentialist and political thinkers in their rejection of theodicy is the theistic conviction that God is a mystery remote to theoretical knowledge. They seem to agree that God is not a *phenomenon* in the spatiotemporal realm. Indeed, Hebrew scriptures support the view that there is a sizable ontological and epistemic gap between God and creatures. The commandment prohibiting images or idols representing God is commonly understood by Jewish and Christian thinkers to signify that

God's being transcends what is physical or material (Ex. 20:4). Corresponding to God's transcendence is God's mysteriousness and partial hiddenness.[1] The theme of divine hiddenness is thematic in the writings of the Psalms, the prophets, and the book of Job. In the Jewish tradition, this theme is also prevalent in rabbinic writings, the negative theology of Maimonides, and the mysticism of the Kabbalah. In the New Testament, narratives of the crucifixion suggest that Jesus becomes estranged from God the Father who seems absent, while the apostle Paul is famous for his dictum that, in this life, our knowledge of God is a dim and dark reflection of divine reality (I Cor. 13:12). Many Jewish and Christian thinkers, and not only those categorized as mystics, hold that God is so great as to exceed conceptualization.[2] The transcendence of God's being makes it inevitable that there is a wide epistemic gap between human subjects and God's mystery. It is not necessary to categorize God as noumenal to maintain this position. In contrast to Kant's approach, existentialist and political thinkers bracket speculation about God's nature and do not exploit the claim that God's hiddenness is beneficial for morality.

The acknowledgment of divine hiddenness or mystery denies success to theodicy because God cannot be understood, and motivates a practical approach that focuses on faith postures and on how faith fulfills practical and moral needs. In response to evil, faith in God is necessary for hope in certain highest goods, such as the alleviation of suffering, the achievement of moral goodness, or the establishment of a just society. When one reflects on what kind of God would meet these needs and hopes, practical postulates about God arise. The Jewish and Christian types of hope, explored in previous chapters, implicitly assume certain features of God. The authors studied affirm that God cares about creatures, God values moral goodness, and God promises redemption. They presume that God is accessible to persons in prayer or I-Thou relation; thus, faith has a mystical dimension of contact with the divine. The view that God is beyond epistemic reach is recurrent in the Jewish and Christian traditions, but it does not imply that God is beyond direct personal contact.

In contrast, Kant's practical faith does not make room for encounter with God and it is dismissive of mystical experience. This prejudice reflects disapproval of what Kant perceives as the emotional excesses of eighteenth-century German Pietism.[3] One reason for his objections to mysticism is the fact that, for Kant, "experience" in space and time occurs only within the phenomenal realm. As noumenal, God cannot be an object of possible experience but only a subject of practical moral reflection. Kant also discounts the possibility of religious encounter because it seems to compromise moral autonomy. Just as knowledge of God would emphasize a morality based on desire for reward or fear of punishment, direct encounter with God might give experiential proof of God's existence with the same deleterious effects. However, these objections do not hold if divine-human encounters are noumenal and not determined by natural causality. The mere possibility of I-Thou encounter with God requires the exercise of freedom because the individual must choose to be open and receptive to God, and the initiative of divine freedom and grace is required to make opportunities for persons to encounter God. The "I" encounters God as a free, moral, and noumenal self. Such encounter with God does not produce scientific knowledge and is compatible with divine hiddenness affirmed by mystical faith.

In interpreting the book of Job, Kant refuses to credit religious experience. In his essay on the failure of theodicy, he admits the importance of Job's encounter with God, which trumps Job's many questions about God's reasons for allowing suffering. But Kant evades the significance and reality of the divine voice from the whirlwind. Instead, he moralistically concludes that what Job learns is simply the limitations of human understanding of God. Kant holds up Job as an example of practical faith, uncompromising in demands for justice and unflinchingly honest about epistemic limits. Job is a model of sincerity, humility, and moral conscience.[4]

Reading Job, existentialist and political thinkers reject the theodicy of Job's friends and admire his moral protest, but they do not deny the possibility or reality of encounter with God. Although divine encounter seems to indicate a noumenal dimension beyond the physical world, practical thinkers rely on narrative language to speak of God and do not use the framework of metaphysical categories. Narratives situate faith in a historical context. Scriptural and traditional narratives are the sources of concepts, metaphors, and doctrines. As such, they are not dispensable portrayals of faith but primary sources for theological discourse.[5] Alongside hope-filled narratives, firsthand encounters with God are a possibility for individuals, vital for sustaining moral, mystical, and liberatory faith in the face of suffering.

The Epistemic Impossibility of Theodicy

The practical authors studied tend to be conceptually reticent, even agnostic, about God's nature and attributes. Their work emphasizes the importance of religious postures directed toward God and language addressed to God in prayer or protest. They do not debate whether encounter with God is noumenal or whether God is real as independent and transcendent over history.[6] However, it is important to distinguish between levels of theological reticence. The thinkers studied do not entirely lack concepts of God. They clearly assume God's attributes of love and moral justice. But, interestingly, they do not exploit the attribute of divine suffering to make evil comprehensible or bearable. Marcel, Buber, Bloch, and Metz all refuse to justify God conceptually. We have seen that Metz sharply criticizes Moltmann for eternalizing and mythologizing suffering in God, a Trinitarian understanding of divine suffering intended to rebut accusations of divine cruelty magnified by Auschwitz. Moltmann's approach is primarily that of systematic theology, although he articulates political concerns. Conceptual explication of theism is Moltmann's key response to theodicy questions that challenge God's goodness and power, whereas practical approaches scrutinize faith practice without developing the attributes of God.

The work of German liberation theologian Dorothee Soelle is instructive in overcoming this impasse. Like Moltmann, she affirms divine suffering because for God to be an omnipotent spectator is a moral scandal from the perspective of Auschwitz. Yet like political thinkers, she takes a praxis-centered approach. In her theology, conceptual discussion of God is not developed apart from articulation of human relation to God. She situates divine suffering as immanent within human history, shared by persons who resist suffering and injustice. Citing Buber, she insists that theology is wrong to theorize about God abstractly, apart from the world. Reflection on doctrine tends to reify and reduce God to an object, in contrast to more adequate forms of discourse—narrative and prayer—where God acts and is addressed. Her narrative approach is nonsystematic, theologically speaking, but centers on analyzing religious life and how persons of faith seek God. Soelle does not posit suffering in God's being, as Moltmann does, but she uses the image of divine suffering to indicate the discovery of representative meaning in suffering. Her theology does not hinge on divine suffering but divine relationality: the sharing of divine power with humanity in mutual interdependence. God is found in human suffering, but God also transcends it as enduring love.[7]

In surveying post-Holocaust and liberation responses to suffering, there is no consensus among Jews or Christians as to whether divine suffering substantially helps persons of faith cope with massive evils. Judged by practical criteria, the idea of a suffering God does not necessarily make human suffering meaningful, nor does it motivate stronger hope or protest.[8] After all, a God who is not enmeshed in suffering can help persons rise above its damaging effects and see themselves as God's partners in alleviating suffering. In contrast, emphasis on divine suffering can glorify suffering as exemplary for persons of faith, whereas most human suffering is involuntary and damaging. In my view, suffering can be given representative meaning when dedicated to God, but only by the agency of the person who suffers. There is no necessity to posit divine suffering to give human suffering meaning. What is necessary is that human suffering is related to God.

Although Marcel, Buber, Bloch, and Metz refuse systematic development of God's attributes, their practical approaches involve certain posits about God. Questions about God's goodness and justice can begin at a practical level even though it is the case, as Kant recognized, that God's reasons for evil cannot be made intelligible and theodicy fails.[9] It is striking that many philosophers working on theodicy would in fact concede that theodicy is not sufficient for a religious response to suffering. They would admit that evil and suffering raise existential and moral challenges that theodicy does not address, but which deserve to be addressed by other kinds of responses. However, they disagree about whether responses to these practical challenges fall within the discipline of philosophy, rather than psychology or pastoral care. Among many analytic philosophers of religion, moral or practical faith issues are divorced from logical argumentation about God and evil.[10] The preceding chapters show that continental thinkers, who address practical faith through philosophical lenses, have much to contribute to reflection on coping with suffering. I do not condone the division between theodicy and practical issues, where the former lies in the domain of philosophy and the latter is relegated to the pastoral domain. Unlike most analytic philosophers of religion, I hold that theodicy is neither central nor sufficient for upholding faith intellectually because it cannot achieve what it sets out to do: to find actual or possible divine reasons for evil. In my view, practical coping postures such as hope and solidarity, not theodicy reasons, sustain faith in response to evil and suffering.

The question remains, Is theodicy discourse that attempts to understand God's nature and plans for history ruled out by a practical approach? Most basically yes, in the case of theoretical theodicy that uses theories about divine agency, impassibility, sin, salvation, or postmortem existence to explain or justify evil and suffering. Universalizing religious discourses efface the ruptures of suffering in history. Moreover, faith does not warrant the knowledge base that is needed for theodicy.[11]

However, the rejection of theodicy does not entirely dismiss religious reflection about evil and suffering or the issues that theodicy raises. As philosopher Paul Ricoeur has observed, evil creates an intellectual *aporia* that a practical response can make productive. While he rejects theodicy as a vestige of modern Enlightenment philosophy, he affirms that the myths and symbols of evil give rise to thought.[12] In Ricoeur's practical response to evil, reflection on evil and suffering centers on the interpretation of scripture and myths through which persons create a narrative religious self-understanding. He distinguishes between a religious "response" and a theodicy "solution" to evil. A response involves the individual taking action to resist evil and its causes, and discovering the spiritual wisdom to love God without seeking protection or reward.

I hold that the discussion of theodicy issues—as opposed to "theodicy" as represented by Leibniz, Hegel, and analytic philosophers—can and does occur in a practical context where the faith subject struggles with God, evil, and suffering. We have seen that one of the major questions raised in practical reflection is: How can my suffering serve God? Such a question may lead to conversations about God's involvement in my suffering and the theological issue of whether God suffers. The focus of such reflection is primarily on coping with personal suffering, surviving, and practicing resistance. As God's companionship is sought, understandings of God and creation can emerge, drawn from Scripture and tradition. Suffering can be dedicated to serving God and designated as representative for the sake of others.

Academic discussion of theodicy issues reflects, explicitly and implicitly, the political interests and cultural assumptions of particular communities at particular times. This historicist insight is a Marxian one, but it is also found among the contextual theological approaches examined in the previous chapter. Although Marx's opium metaphor is discredited as a stereotype of religion, his conviction that religion arises within social and economic conditions and reflects class interests is widely accepted by social scientists and scholars of religion, although less widely by analytic philosophers of religion. As cultural anthropologist Clifford Geertz defines it, "religion" is a cultural-linguistic system that interprets reality and creates "long lasting moods and motivations" within a given community. From this perspective, responses to evil and suffering appear as culture-bound discourses, or language-games, that continuously shift between cultures and evolve as religious traditions engage present conditions.[13] Viewed in relation to Marxian thought and cultural anthropology, my investigation of practical thinkers studies how discourses about suffering and the Holocaust reflect cultural and intellectual assumptions. My approach centers on faith postures, such as solidarity or hope, as these postures are articulated in written texts or narratives interpreted in response to the Holocaust. Practical faith responses are plural and intratextual, revealing conflicting philosophical, and traditional religious presuppositions.

The Moral Scandal of Theodicy

Moral objections are directed at the global, justifying reasons proposed by theodicy.[14] Theodicies persist in giving all-encompassing explanations on a theoretical level that do not engage the actual process of finding meaning for individuals. Some philosophers try to give theodicy a practical slant, but the problems of universal justification remain. In the theodicy of John Hick, for example, the moral and spiritual development of individuals justifies God's permission of evil and suffering. However, his theodicy glosses over worst-case scenarios where suffering warps and destroys persons rather than fosters soul-making. He does not deal with how theodicy discourse functions morally in situations of suffering, nor does Hick give attention to the uneven distribution of suffering among groups, such as Jews or African Americans. Especially for such groups, to say that suffering is for the sake of moral training and faith building ignores the institutionalization of prejudice and violence against them and its lethal effects.

The unsatisfactory treatment of horrendous evils in Hick's theodicy is criticized by Marilyn McCord Adams, who seeks to combine theoretical and practical considerations in responding to evil. She criticizes impersonal global justifications of evil, which ignore the plight of individuals whose lives are ruined by horrendous suffering. Her theodicy argues that God's overwhelming goodness toward persons who suffer provides a source of positive meaning that engulfs the suffering of each individual in the context of one's life as a whole. Adams justifies horrendous suffering on a personal level, on the basis of God's goodness to each person during or after the occurrence of suffering. In defending her position against potential criticism by post-Holocaust and liberation theologians, she insists that her theodicy is not insensitive to moral responses but is "complementary" to practical resistance to suffering and oppression.[15] However, this disclaimer is defensive and unconvincing because moral opposition to suffering is not integrated with the redemptive meaning found in suffering. Human agency is portrayed as diminutive and weak, since the overcoming of suffering is primarily accomplished by God. Adams's theodicy promotes acceptance of suffering and reliance on God for persons of faith, without the counterweight of individual or collective resistance to social suffering that makes protest imperative.

In post-Holocaust thought, global theodicy answers are put to the test as applied to Nazi concentration camps. Jewish thinker Irving Greenberg makes the dramatic statement that no theological reasons for suffering should be made that are not "credible in the presence of the burning children" in Auschwitz.[16] His litmus test for theodicy is that if its reasons cannot be asserted in the face of such suffering, it is a scandal to apply such justifying rationale. I understand Greenberg's statement as having two distinct implications: (1) theodicy is inappropriate in the actual presence of such suffering (at the time it occurs), and (2) it is inappropriate to project theodicy onto such a situation after the fact.

It is not difficult to accept his first point, that theodicy would be inappropriate in an actual concentration camp setting. It is insensitive to bring up theodicy reasons when persons are in the throes of pain or barely surviving desperate circumstances. Instead of providing comfort, theodicy reasons would be more likely to provoke anger, tears, or accusations directed at God. The theodicy claim that God intends suffering for some greater good would make the sufferer feel abandoned and abused by God.[17] It might not even be possible for victims to sustain faith under such grave circumstances. A survey of the writings of Holocaust survivors and post-Holocaust thinkers show that camp victims were not inclined to accept that justifying reasons, advanced by theodicy, could logically reconcile God's goodness with the evil experienced in the camps.[18] Yet many persons continued to pray to God and hope that God would end their suffering and heal its scars. Faith and hope were (and are) practical postures necessary for coping with suffering.

But why not discuss theodicy reasons after suffering has ended? After all, persons generally need to make some sense of what happens. Looking back on the Holocaust in a reflective moment, a person may well be interested in God's reasons for permitting evil. Surely concentration camp survivors might, some time after the fact, reflect on why God allowed their suffering and the suffering of millions, including burning babies. In conversation or I-Thou dialogue with a person who has suffered, it may indeed be appropriate for me to discuss possible divine reasons or religious meanings for suffering, if asked to do so. For example, psychiatrist Viktor Frankl took it on himself to encourage fellow inmates at Auschwitz to find hope and meaning in suffering when he was asked for advice.[19] But like the existentialist writers studied, Frankl emphasizes that only the individual can apply reasons or meaning to personal suffering. He would agree with Emmanuel Levinas that the suffering of the other is "useless" and unjustified suffering that should be resisted and not condoned by bystanders.[20] For individual agents, personal suffering may be voluntarily given religious meaning, as it happens or in retrospect, but it is a moral scandal to impose meaning (including theodicy reasons) on the suffering of others. To do so is illicitly to exercise the privilege and responsibility of the actual victims. Hence, as Greenberg would agree, the suffering of the children who died in the flames at Auschwitz should remain unjustified. There is no intrinsic value to suffering because ethical or theological value is conferred only by the assent of the sufferer. Most post-Holocaust Jewish and Christian thinkers reject assigning any intrinsic value to suffering, although many orthodox Jewish and conservative Christian thinkers still maintain that all suffering is redemptive.[21]

Holocaust suffering and other suffering in the past need not be remote for nonvictims here and now. It can be made present by means of memory. Sensitivity to the past requires a moral consciousness of history, which ensures that we never become dispassionate or distant regarding the suffering of others who are removed from us by time or geographical distance. The person who reflects on suffering with moral sensitivity is *always* in the presence of burning babies.

Memory of the Holocaust is not simple repetition of the past, but rather is constituted by cultural assumptions and media images. For North Americans and Europeans, remembrance of the Holocaust is mediated through countless novels, films, plays, photographs, histories, newspaper articles, lectures, and so on.[22] Now more than fifty years after the event, the witness of Holocaust survivors is rarely available through personal I-Thou conversation. Remembering entails vicarious listening involving multiple layers of memory removed from the event of the Holocaust. Yet memories are not doomed by the passage of time to be remote and dispassionate. Memory can raise moral consciousness of the violence of the past and connect me in solidarity with others. Without endorsing redemptory closure or justification, memory exposes the ambiguities of history and implications for how history is memorialized in the present.

In contrast, theodicy effaces the testimonies of victims of the Holocaust and other historical catastrophes. It also sanctions the suffering of others, adopting the perspective of a dispassionate bystander. As a corrective, narratives of suffering deserve primary attention and should serve as a critique for meta-level philosophical or theological discourse.[23] Post-Holocaust and Marxian thinkers converge on the insight that morally acute, historical memory motivates the moral faith postures of solidarity, protest, hope, and resistance. Theodicy is harmful because it condones evils by ignoring their social dimensions. This moral criticism is not directed toward the authors of theodicy, but toward theodicy as an intellectual product. The academic discourse of theodicy itself has moral force. Theodicy names what is evil in a manner that prioritizes certain areas of reflection, such as God's nature or human freedom, and neglects others, such as the material analysis of social evils. It must be recognized that academic discussions of God and evil have declarative power that usually goes unrecognized by those who propose theodicies: the power to name and focus on certain types of evil and to silence other memories of suffering.[24] Narratives of suffering from the margins are needed to disrupt the false totality of the discourse of theodicy and to counteract its moral evasions.

GUIDELINES FOR FAITH RESPONSES TO EVIL AND SUFFERING AFTER AUSCHWITZ

Based on the analysis of post-Holocaust continental thinkers, I argue that philosophical religious approaches to evil and suffering need to move beyond the theoretical theodicy approach in order to situate discourse about evil socially and to respond morally to the suffering of individuals and groups. As a philosopher of religion, I choose to devote my attention to developing practical approaches. It is my recommendation that this area of reflection deserves attention by all religious thinkers who address the themes of evil and suffering.

In conclusion, I propose four desiderata that are intended as guidelines for philosophical and theological approaches to evil and suffering. They deal with the following themes: (1) epistemic humility, (2) moral sensitivity, (3) religious practice, and (4) narrative memory. The first two points are essentially prohibitions against intellectual immodesty and immorality, while the second two indicate constructive moves toward a situated religious discourse in response to theodicy issues.

Epistemic Humility

I join existentialist and political approaches in affirming the appropriateness of epistemic humility regarding theories about God's nature, acts, and purposes. It should be noted that epistemic modesty comes in various degrees and does not require Kantian convictions. For Kant, ideas of God can be posited according to the needs of morality, but knowledge of God is impossible since God is noumenal. Philosophers who are "realists" take the commonsense view that persons can have knowledge of what is the real fact of the matter concerning the world and God. Analytic philosophers who are epistemic realists, such as Alvin Plantinga and John Hick, do not necessarily think that it is possible to know the actual or complete reasons God has for creating a world containing evil, but only possible or plausible reasons. Pursuing theodicy justifications, analytic philosophers who are "skeptical realists," such as Marilyn McCord Adams, hold that one can develop theoretical frameworks aiming for maximum consistency, coherence, and explanatory power without presuming that one can know reality with certainty and without assuming that the truth about reality can be demonstrated to convince every reasonable person. In contrast, the cultural-linguistic or narrative approach examines intratextual meanings of God-language and the function of religious discourses in faith communities. Theodicy questions are raised centering on what Ricouer calls a faith response to suffering and evil, as opposed to a solution. Then there are nonrealist philosophers of religion such as D.Z. Phillips who view "God" as a word that refers to human spiritual dispositions, thus ruling out the possibility of theodicy altogether.

Along the spectrum of theistic realism and nonrealism, I counsel that in the interests of epistemic modesty philosophers and theologians should recognize that theodicy, which explains or justifies God's permission of evil and suffering, aims at an unreachable goal.

Moral Sensitivity

Theodicy discussion is charged with moral failure for not recognizing suffering that specifically afflicts oppressed groups. From Augustine onward, evil in the world has been categorized as either "natural" or "moral." The flaw in this typology is that systemic or institutional suffering has been masked under the category of moral evil. Only in the twentieth century have religious thinkers proposed that evil caused by social, economic, and political systems should be differentiated from evil attributed to the sins of individuals. Individual repentance is not the whole answer to problems such as racism, sexism, and poverty because they are structurally imbedded in political and economic systems. As an antidote, religious thinkers should attend to memories of evil and suffering that provide critiques of social and political systems. Narratives can expose the subjugated memories of those who suffer and teach faith communities about the realities of prejudice and violence.

Especially after Auschwitz, philosophers should take care to reflect on the application of theodicy reasons to mass suffering. It is morally objectionable to apply theodicy reasons to the suffering of others, unless requested to explore such reasoning in conversation with a person who suffers. When philosophical discourse on evil is situated in the interpersonal dimension, it becomes apparent that theodicy is an inappropriate response to the appeal of the Thou who suffers, which is an urgent appeal demanding a practical moral response. Although philosophers who advocate theodicy doubtless do not intend immorally to condone others' suffering, by giving reasons they presume that others' suffering is ultimately positive or useful. The justification of suffering serves to corroborate bourgeois apathy toward the need to make large-scale changes in institutions.

On the other hand, it is not morally insensitive for victims to respond to suffering by reflecting on its religious meaning, which raises theodicy issues. A person can designate suffering as prophetic or representative, endured for the sake of others. Suffering can be framed as a trial or challenge for God's sake, both when suffering is voluntary, due to acts of chosen resistance, and also when it is involuntary, due to social oppression or natural causes. The search for meaning takes place in the context of individual and communal religious practices, such as prayer, I-Thou relation, hope, and solidarity. Moral sensitivity is empty without action against the causes of suffering. Every response to suffering is context-dependent and should be attentive to the possibility of faith resistance to suffering on political and personal levels.

Religious Practice

For religious thought to move beyond theodicy means that philosophical effort should shift from global, conceptual theodicy treatments of God and evil to concentrate on situated practices of faith response to suffering. Practice does not exclude theory, for a practical approach requires a methodology to study faith practices. This paradigm shift signals the recognition that it is artificial to separate theoretical discussions of God and evil from discussion of personal context and moral issues, as if conceptual concerns can be treated independently from ethical ones. As shown previously, even abstract global theodicy has unrecognized practical implications for condoning the acceptance of suffering.

Inspired by existentialist and political thinkers, I urge that reflection on practice should guide the formulation of religious meanings in response to suffering. For instance, both Buber and Metz, despite their different philosophical motivations, approach discussion of God's promised redemption through examining the religious postures of hope and solidarity or I-Thou relation. They do not treat the idea of redemption theoretically as a set of propositions giving knowledge of the end of history, but as embodied in narratives that extrapolate a hopeful future. Focus on faith practice is also found in recent writings on spirituality and mysticism, where liberation and feminist theologians seek meaning in suffering without theistic justification.[25] Given attention to practice, faith is understood as centrally involving prophetic and moral postures and not propositional assent or belief. In contemporary Jewish thought, there has not been a dramatic turn toward "practice" parallel to the political and liberation movements in Christian thought, although there are currents of Jewish liberation theology in dialogue with Christian thinkers.[26] In Jewish thought from biblical and rabbinic times to the present, practice has been an integral component of reflection on community and commandments. Post-Holocaust Jewish thinkers regularly discuss practice when they reflect on such central issues as covenant identity, God's involvement in history, and religious observance.[27] In recent Jewish and Christian thought, the call for attention to practice follows on the heels of developments in philosophy and theology that emphasize the cultural and textual imbeddedness of religious discourses. In a practical context, theodicy issues can be raised in dialogue without abstracting and systematizing religious ideas to legitimize evil and suffering.

Narrative Memory

A corollary of attention to religious practice is attention to "narrative" that broadly includes written or oral memories, histories, Scripture, poems, dramas, liturgies, biographies, and reports of prayer and dialogue. Reflection on the stories of persons who face severe suffering shows that theodicy reasons fail to satisfy and are scandalous when applied to cases of extreme suffering such as the Holocaust. The narrative of Job confirms that perplexity concerning God's goodness and justice is valid, even for persons with exemplary faith in God, and that attempts at cognitive comfort are unconvincing. The writings of Holocaust survivors and post-Holocaust thinkers suggest that the most probing, honest faith responses to suffering include substantial protest and questioning of God. Responses to the Holocaust involve wrestling with traditional religious texts that affirm God's goodness.[28] The accounts of persons who face systematic oppression based on class, gender, or race, such as African-American writers or "Third World" theologians, display that the coexistence of faith and suffering does not hinge on finding plausible accounts of how God's goodness is logically compatible with evil. Such voices are dangerous memories that disillusion philosophical ambitions for discovering final answers.

Practically speaking, religious responses to evil and suffering are situated discourses that should center on narratives. Responses to suffering are commonly recorded and written as third-person narrative reports, but they also take the form of first-person discourse in which I express my own suffering and faith. Moreover, responses may occur within I-Thou dialogue that consists in second-person address and response, recorded as a conversation or drama. Since my own experience and that of my personal contacts may be limited to a middle-class environment, memory of suffering is critically important. Attention to narrative offers a wide spectrum of viewpoints about how suffering occurs and how faith responds, although memory can never give complete or universal awareness. Existentialists use narrative reports of I-Thou dialogue to examine how meaning-making can take place in interpersonal contexts, while Marxian-influenced thinkers employ methods of the social sciences to analyze the causes of collective suffering using the narrative histories of oppressed groups. In my view, narrative should be a primary source for reflection on faith responses to suffering because it can encompass both personal and political components of faith postures. It allows for distinctions between liberation and survival hope, as well as contextual reflection on how faith in God and hope are intertwined in various concrete situations. Narrative is a mode of remembrance that brings the truth of the past into present consciousness. Overall, it is in reference to narratives, whether they are articulated in first-, second-, or third-person language, that the context-dependent variables of religious acceptance and resistance to suffering are exposed.

In addition to serving as a resource for awareness and reflection, narrative also functions to inspire faith and hope. Stories showing persons responding to suffering with active hope, love, and justice, such as biblical narratives, can motivate political protest through their examples. For instance, the "slave narratives" of African-American spirituals are song lyrics with multiple coded meanings that speak of coping with oppression, hoping for justice, and trusting in God. When persons sing the spirituals, they can tell these stories of struggle as their own story, projecting themselves into the situation of slaves singing songs of freedom.[29] The memory of faith withstanding the oppression of slavery is dangerous and sustaining. Because narratives can display the meanings of hope, solidarity, and love, they are primary sources for examining religious practices for surviving suffering.

An example of biblical narrative that offers assistance in coping with suffering is the book of Job. The story of Job can provide a person who suffers with words of lament and complaint to God. If I read the text as a Thou and project myself into Job's drama, I can hear God's voice from the whirlwind as addressed to myself. As I imaginatively enter the story, I face my own suffering with protest to God, as Job did, I become aware of others' suffering, and I am encouraged to hope. The biblical text mediates dialogue with God. Contemporary narratives of religious persons coping with suffering also express protest alongside God's sustenance. In reading the first-person reflections of a Christian father who lost his twenty-five-year-old son in a mountain-climbing accident, I may find encouragement to dialogue with God even when coping with wrenching grief. The father's struggles with the insufficiency of theodicy explanations may assist me to voice my own lament and find the presence of God in love, even bereaved love.[30]

Although in most post-Holocaust theology the narratives of victims and survivors are central, I have found that narratives of German women who lived under Nazi rule also provoke challenging reflection on suffering.[31] These women, protected from anti-Jewish prejudice as Aryans, speak of bombing raids, hunger, bereavement, and the threat of punishment for breaking Nazi laws. They are not Holocaust victims subject to genocidal governmental policies, yet they experience and witness suffering. Some of their narratives speak sympathetically about Jews, while other women are evasive in sharing memories of their Jewish neighbors or their knowledge of the concentration camps. As a gentile, I read these women's stories with questions about the ease of moral complicity in prejudice and social persecution. Although faith is not frequently mentioned, I remember these narratives in order to examine the reactions of Holocaust "bystanders" and the Christian cultural heritage that shapes my perspective on the Holocaust and its victims. Not only am I a bystander to Holocaust history, but in the present I am a bystander to local, national, and global suffering and oppression that I remember, but am not directly involved in. While the testimonies of victims recall how brutal and useless much suffering is, by remembering the stories of German women, I reflect on how bystanders to suffering can also be victims of suffering and how religious affiliation may fail to spur resistance to the suffering of others. The exploration of practical faith responses undertaken in this project can be expanded to include consideration of non-exemplary faith responses to suffering, by perpetrators and bystanders, where others' suffering is not resisted. Reflection on narratives from multiple sources not only potentially deepens but also broadens academic approaches to the study of evil and suffering.

To conclude the book, I propose these four guidelines as correctives that challenge theodicy and open up alternate philosophical and theological avenues. In moving beyond logical and metaphysical approaches typical of modern and analytic philosophy, existentialist and political responses provide an opportunity to explore objections to theodicy. However, they do not provide adequate practical alternatives. Fortunately, such alternatives are developing, and have been developed, in response to the Holocaust and the challenge of massive social suffering, where contemporary Jewish and Christian theologians recognize the centrality of practice and narrative for religious reflection. There is no single uniform appropriate faith response to suffering and evil, nor should there be. Responses to evil and suffering take on different configurations appropriate to different religious communities, given the complex dynamics of coping with evil.

This project has mapped an intellectual history of selected continental figures, who respond to the Holocaust without theodicy comfort. In so doing, it has identified common convictions and directions among a wide range of scholars. Given this critical and comparative orientation, it is fitting to close with methodological desiderata warning against epistemic immodesty and moral insensitivity and encouraging attention to faith practice and narrative, rather than with a normative synthesis of practical responses. To take these four guidelines seriously is to affirm that the plausibility of faith in God must not be defended at the price of concealing the unresolved practical and conceptual tensions between faith and suffering.

Notes

CHAPTER ONE

1. I have chosen to use the term "Holocaust" throughout the book, rather than "Shoah," because it has become standard in scholarly and popular English usage.

2. A similar fourfold typology of responses to evil is proposed by liberation theologian Jon Sobrino in *The Principle of Mercy: Taking the Crucified People from the Cross* (Maryknoll, NY: Orbis Press, 1994), 29. Issues three and four can be viewed as roughly corresponding to the emphasis of "existentialist" and "political" approaches, respectively, although this dichotomy oversimplifies the resources of each in responding to suffering.

3. A definitive statement of the terms of the theodicy debate is made by J. L. Mackie, an atheist philosopher who throws down the gauntlet to theists by arguing for the logical inconsistency of the aforementioned triad of propositions. J. L. Mackie, "Evil and Omnipotence," [1955] in *The Problem of Evil*, ed. Marilyn McCord Adams and Robert Merrihew Adams (Oxford: Oxford University Press, 1990), 25–37.

4. The distinction between a free will "defense" and "theodicy" is proposed by Alvin Plantinga in *God, Freedom and Evil* (Grand Rapids: Eerdmans, 1974), 28. The contrast between "defensive" and "explanatory" approaches is delineated in the Introduction to *The Problem of Evil*, 3.

5. Gottfried Wilhelm Leibniz, *Essais de Theodicée sur la bonté de Dieu, la liberté de l'homme et l'origine du mal* [1710] (Paris: Erdmann, 1946).

6. Eighteenth-century skeptic David Hume raises the existence of evil numerous times as counterevidence to belief in the existence of a good, omnipotent creator. David Hume, *Dialogues Concerning Natural Religion* [1779] (New York: Harper, 1948).

7. Chisolm focuses on analyzing the notions of "balancing off" and "defeat" as applied to global judgments about whether the world is good or evil. Chisolm considers "defeat" as superior, for theodicy purposes, to "balancing off" because if evil elements are "balanced off" by good elements, the evil parts are not inherently necessary for what is good. Roderick Chisolm, "The Defeat of Good and Evil," in *The Problem of Evil*, 53–68.

8. Marilyn McCord Adams, *Horrendous Evils and the Goodness of God* (Cornell: Cornell University Press, 1999), 26–31.

9. To assert that the existence of God and evil are "compossible" means that these assertions together are logically possible and consistent with each other. Alvin Plantinga, "God, Evil and the Metaphysics of Freedom," in *The Problem of Evil*, 83–109.

10. Plantinga takes an "incompatiblist" view of freedom: by definition, it is a logical impossibility for a free act to be caused. God's omnipotence does not give God the power to cause a person to do good freely because God cannot do what is logically contradictory. For an overview of Plantinga's argument, see Kelly James Clark, *Return to Reason* (Grand Rapids: Eerdmans, 1990), 68–91.

11. Not only can God not control free beings by causally determining free choices, but divine omniscience does not enable God to know the truth of the outcomes of free choices. Therefore, omniscience does not enable God to secure the actuality of (i.e., "weakly actualize") a morally perfect world where certain possible free creatures always do moral good and never evil. Mackie's atheistic objection that an omnipotent, omniscient, perfectly good God could know the outcome of free acts and prevent evil is refuted. Plantinga, "God, Evil and the Metaphysics of Freedom," in *The Problem of Evil*, 90–91.

12. John Hick, *Evil and the God of Love* (New York: Harper and Row, 1966). Comparable in importance to Hick's proposal is the theodicy of fellow Englishman Richard Swinburne. Both philosophers place a high value on freedom and both employ instrumental explanations for evil, viewing evil as a means to a good end. Richard Swinburne, *The Existence of God* (Oxford: Oxford University Press, 1979).

13. Hick claims that hard-won moral and spiritual development has greater value than ready-made perfection. He also affirms the metaphysical presupposition that God could not make persons who, from the beginning, were spiritually mature. Soul-making maturity requires willingness and uncompelled responses on the part of persons. For a concise analysis of Hick's position, see the Introduction to *The Problem of Evil*, 18–20.

14. Hick, *Evil and the God of Love*, 363–372.

15. In contrast, contemporary Thomist philosophers propose an understanding of divine omnipotence as God's power to act intimately in all things. They claim that human free actions are co-caused by God, proposing a "compatiblist" notion of freedom and omnipotence. All medieval philosophers thought that God concurred with created causes, but not all of them thought that divine co-causation is deterministic, and it is not clear from the writings of Thomas Aquinas whether he embraced determinism. Brian Davies, ed., *Philosophy of Religion* (Washington, DC: Georgetown University Press, 1998), 163–201.

16. Hartshorne's metaphysics, based on Whitehead's philosophy, involves a complex concept of God as the "being" who is the sum of all events or occasions, past and present. God influences the world by presenting "initial aims" to creatures who may choose to actualize those aims. God's plan is to lure self-determining creatures to seek integration into the universe and to thus maximize its beauty and variety. Process thinkers are adamant that God is not responsible for evil, nor is it possible for God to prevent it. Charles Hartshorne, *Omnipotence and Other Theological Mistakes* (Albany: SUNY Press, 1984), 31–38; and David Griffin, *God, Power and Evil: A Process Theodicy* (Philadelphia: Westminster, 1976).

17. For an overview of Christian authors who reject divine omnipotence and impassibility, such as feminist, process, and post-Holocaust thinkers, see Günther Schiwy, *Abschied vom allmächtigen Gott* (Munich: Kösel Verlag, 1995); and Thomas G. Weinandy, *Does God Suffer?* (Notre Dame: University of Notre Dame Press, 2000), 1–26.

18. Developing the New Testament idea of "principalities and powers," Wink defines evil as a system of violence and domination that operates among individuals, groups, and nations. Walter Wink, *Engaging the Powers: Discernment and Resistance in a World of Domination* (Minneapolis: Fortress Press, 1992), ch. 1.

19. Global analytic approaches are criticized by Marilyn McCord Adams in "Problems of Evil: More Advice to Christian Philosophers," *Faith and Philosophy* 5 (April 1988): 121–143. From a nonrealist position indebted to the philosophy of Wittgenstein, epistemic and moral objections to analytic theodicy are argued in D. Z. Phillips, "The Problem of Evil," in *Reason and Religion*, ed. Stuart C. Brown (Ithaca: Cornell University Press, 1977), 103–121.

20. For an overview of Christian and Jewish anti-theodicy positions, respectively, see Kenneth Surin, *Theology and the Problem of Evil* (Oxford: Blackwell, 1986); and Zachary Braiterman, *(God) After Auschwitz: Tradition and Change in Post-Holocaust Jewish Thought* (Princeton: Princeton University Press, 1998). Other authors who raise decisive methodological objections to theology are Paul Ricoeur, "Evil, a Challenge to Philosophy and Theology" [1985], in *Figuring the Sacred* (Minneapolis: Fortress Press, 1995), 249–261; D. Z. Phillips, "The Problem of Evil"; Terrence W. Tilley, *The Evils of Theodicy* (Washington DC: Georgetown University Press, 1991); and Kathleen M. Sands, *Escape from Paradise: Evil and Tragedy in Feminist Theology* (Minneapolis: Fortress Press, 1994).

21. Among early and mid-twentieth-century continental Jewish and Christian thinkers, the trend toward rejecting theodicy is represented by thinkers such as Herman Cohen, Franz Rosenzweig, Martin Buber, Gabriel Marcel, Ernst Bloch, Walter Benjamin, Theodor Adorno, Emmanuel Levinas, Elie Wiesel, Paul Ricoeur, Johann Baptist Metz, Jürgen Moltmann, and Dorothee Soelle.

22. A recent comparative approach to Jewish and Christian theology that explores areas of commonality rather than difference on the topic of suffering is the essay by Leora Batnitzky, "On the Suffering of God's Chosen: Christian Views in Jewish Terms," in *Christianity in Jewish Terms*, ed. Tikva Frymer-Kensky et al. (Boulder: Westview Press, 2000), 203–237.

23. Marcel, Buber, and Bloch formulated their responses to the Holocaust before the 1970s, when Holocaust Studies developed as a major area of study, and Metz was part of the early vanguard of post-Holocaust theology in the late 1960s. For an overview of the development of post-Holocaust theology, see Braiterman, *(God) After Auschwitz*, 6–11.

24. Here is a sampling of post-Holocaust and liberation authors who criticize theodicy that have particularly influenced my thinking: Richard Rubenstein, *After Auschwitz: Radical Theology and Contemporary Judaism* (Indianapolis: Bobbs-Merrill, 1966); David R. Blumenthal, *Facing the Abusing God: A Theology of Protest* (Louisville, KY: Westminster/John Knox Press, 1993); Marc H. Ellis, *Ending Auschwitz: The Future of Jewish and Christian Life* (Louisville, KY: Westminster/John Knox Press, 1994; Dorothee Soelle, *Suffering* (Minneapolis: Fortress Press, 1975); Rebecca S. Chopp, *The Praxis of Suffering* (Maryknoll, NY: Orbis Books, 1992); Gustavo Gutiérrez, *On Job: God-Talk and the Suffering of the Innocent* (Maryknoll, NY: Orbis Books, 1995); and Cheryl A. Kirk-Duggan, *Exorcizing Evil: A Womanist Perspective on the Spirituals* (Maryknoll, NY: Orbis Books, 1997).

25. With reference to the social theories of Peter Berger and Jürgen Habermas, philosopher Regina Ammicht-Quinn argues that in twentieth-century society the need to justify faith by showing its pragmatic capacity to respond to suffering in solidarity-praxis, which gives existence meaning, is more relevant than the need to justify God speculatively, systematizing the conceptual contents of faith. Regina Ammicht-Quinn, *Von Lissabon bis Auschwitz: Zum Paradigmawechsel in der Theodizeefrage* (Freiburg: Herder Verlag, 1992), 253–264.

26. The role of this phrase in the attempt to throw off the legacy of Holocaust memory is explored in Michael Geyer, "The Politics of Contemporary Germany," in *Radical Evil*, ed. Joan Copjec (New York: Verso, 1996), 189–190.

27. Peter L. Berger, *The Sacred Canopy: Elements of a Sociological Theory of Religion* (Garden City, NY: Doubleday and Co., 1967), 3–6.

28. As anthropologist Clifford Geertz asserts in his well-known definition of religion, religion is not exclusively theoretical. It functions as a set of "powerful, pervasive and long-lasting moods and motivations" that shape self-identity and guide action. Clifford Geertz, "Religion as a Cultural System," in *Reader in Comparative Religion*, ed. William A. Lessa (New York: Harper and Row, 1965), 206.

29. The distinction between a "practical" response and a "theodicy" solution is formulated by Paul Ricoeur in "Evil, a Challenge to Philosophy and Theology" [1985], in *Figuring the Sacred*, ed. Mark I. Wallace (Minneapolis: Fortress Press, 1995), 258.

30. The distinctive feature of a practical approach to suffering is the study of "embodied behaviors and issues of value, meaning and practice" as pointed out by Peter Van Ness in "Philosophy and Suffering: A Contemporary Case for the Comparative Philosophy of Religion," *Union Seminary Quarterly Review* 50 (1996): 107–115.

31. Contextual theologies address the suffering of subjects who experience prejudice and who are socially marginal or oppressed: this group includes "Third World" liberation theology, Hispanic-American women's "mujerista" theology, black theology, African-American "womanist" theology, North American and European feminist thought, and post-Holocaust theology.

32. The liberation theologian who has been most strongly influenced by both of these intellectual currents, particularly by the writings of Martin Buber and Ernst Bloch, is German writer Dorothee Soelle. Dorothee Soelle, *Thinking about God* (Philadelphia: Trinity Press International, 1990), 127–131.

33. According to Hume's terminology, "ideas" are derived from "impressions," which are produced by the five senses and by reflection (i.e., feelings and sentiments). Ideas and impressions are the two branches of "perception." Hume defines "perception" broadly to embrace "everything that appears to the mind." David Hume, *A Treatise of Human Nature* [1739] (Oxford: Clarendon Press, 1946), Book 1, Part 1.

34. A useful discussion of the philosophical background of Kant's philosophy is found in Roger Scruton, *Kant* (Oxford: Oxford University Press, 1982), 11–21.

35. Immanuel Kant, *Critique of Pure Reason* [First edition 1781, Second edition 1787], trans. Norman Kemp Smith (New York: Macmillan, 1993), A442–496/ B470–524.

36. Kant proposes that "intellectual intuition" could, hypothetically, have a positive grasp of *noumena* without the use of mediating appearances or categories. However, only a higher intellect, such as that of God, could possess intellectual intuition (A250–255/B307–311).

37. Kant, *Critique of Pure Reason*, (A426–460/B454–488, A686/B714, A77–83/ B102–116).

38. Where Kant departs from traditional monotheism is in his conclusion that God cannot be experienced because God is not a *phenomenon* but a *noumenon* (A590–630/B618–658). James Collins, *The Emergence of Philosophy of Religion* (New Haven: Yale University Press, 1967), 89–128.

39. Kant, *Critique of Pure Reason*, B xxx.

40. Immanuel Kant, *Critique of Practical Reason* [1788], trans. Lewis White Beck (London: Macmillan, 1956), 150.

41. A helpful overview of how moral reason and faith hinge on Kant's distinction between *phenomena* and *noumena* is provided by Robert Merrihew Adams in the introduction to *Religion within the Boundaries of Mere Reason and Other Writings*, trans. and ed. Allen Wood and George DiGiovanni (London: Cambridge University Press, 1998), vii–xxxii.

42. Michael Despland, *Kant on History and Religion* (Montreal: McGill-Queens University Press, 1973), 269–282.

43. Kant considers the religion of the Bible as centering on morality. Immanuel Kant, *Religion within the Boundaries of Mere Reason* [1793], in *Religion within the Boundaries of Mere Reason and Other Writings*, 151–155.

44. Kant, *Critique of Practical Reason*, 120–126.

45. For a detailed explication of Kant's concept of God, see Allen W. Wood, *Kant's Rational Theology* (Ithaca: Cornell University Press, 1978), 16–23.

46. Kant, *Critique of Practical Reason*, 155.

47. Kant considers freedom of the will as a necessary condition for moral development. However, he does not endorse the theodicy explanation that evil and suffering happen for the sake of moral education. He remarks that such a response (similar to Hick's soul-making theodicy) "cuts the knot" rather than unties it rationally, as promised. Immanuel Kant, "On the Miscarriage of All Philosophical Trials in Theodicy" [1791], in *Religion within the Boundaries of Mere Reason and Other Writings*, 21.

48. His discussion of "radical evil" affirms a deep and pervasive propensity to evil in all persons, counter to moral reason. Kant, *Religion within the Boundaries of Mere Reason and Other Writings*, 45–73.

49. Kant, "On the Miscarriage of All Philosophical Trials in Theodicy," 26. For a comparative study of Kant's position on theodicy, see Christoph Schulte, "Judische Theodizee? Überlegungen zum Theodizee-Problem bei Immanuel Kant, Hermann Cohen und Max Weber," *Zeitschrift für Religions und Geistesgeschichte*, 49 (1997): 135–159.

50. A contemporary philosopher who appreciates the potential of Kant's alternative to theodicy is Paul Ricoeur. Invoking Kant's turn from knowledge to practice, Ricoeur articulates what he calls a "practical response to evil" that has three dimensions: action (solidarity, resistance), feeling (lament, protest), and reflection (wisdom, acceptance, gratitude). Faith has political, existential, and mystical aspects. Paul Ricoeur, "Evil, a Challenge to Philosophy and Theology," in *Figuring the Sacred*, ed. Mark I. Wallace (Minneapolis: Fortress Press, 1995), 258–261.

51. G. W. F. Hegel, *Reason in History* [1837], trans. Robert S. Hartman (New York: Macmillian, 1953), 68–87.

52. Hegel speaks of "subjective spirit," which is human thinking and will; "objective spirit," which includes customs, laws, and institutions; and "absolute spirit," which is the ultimate self-consciousness where the objective and subjective sides become perfectly harmonized. Spirit encompasses both the subjective and objective manifestations of reason. Michael Inwood, *A Hegel Dictionary* (Oxford: Basil Blackwell, 1992), 273–275.

53. Hegel departs from traditional Christian doctrine, however, in claiming that the narrative of salvation history exhausts the divine narrative. Hegel is radical, and heretical, in developing the idea of the "economic" Trinity manifest in creation and

history, while dismissing the idea of an "immanent" Trinity self-sufficient apart from creation. Cyril O'Regan, *The Heterodox Hegel* (Albany: SUNY Press, 1994), 63–80.

54. Hegel's Trinitarian scheme attributes pathos (suffering, negativity) as well as *kenosis* (emptying, incarnation) to God. O'Regan, *The Heterodox Hegel*, 205–207.

55. Hegel's theodicy involves detailed philosophical explication of theological terms, such as "Providence" and "God's Kingdom." For a comprehensive discussion of Hegel's theology, see O'Regan, *The Heterodox Hegel*, 318–326.

56. Marx accuses Hegel of promoting an "ideology" that serves the interests of the bourgeois, capitalist society of his own time. Sidney Hook, *From Hegel to Marx: Studies in the Intellectual Development of Karl Marx* (New York: Humanities Press, 1958), 22–28.

57. Many contemporary scholars of Hegel are embarrassed by these claims that they attribute to the "right-wing, religious, and conservative" side of Hegel's thought. Discarding this side of his work, they choose to read Hegel as a critical, secular historicist and a radical philosopher of change rather than a philosopher of the Absolute. For a profile of the split between the "two Hegels," see Robert C. Solomon, *In the Spirit of Hegel* (New York: Oxford University Press, 1983), 14–16.

58. Like Hegel, orthodox Marxists view suffering (within capitalism) as justified and necessary because it is a necessary step toward a better form of socioeconomic life. However, orthodox Marxists are atheists; hence, they do not employ a holistic justification of suffering as inherently good (see ch. 4).

59. A prominent post-Holocaust theological interpretation of suffering, which borrows from Hegel's Trinitarian philosophy of history, is the Protestant theology of Moltmann. Jürgen Moltmann, *The Crucified God*, trans. R. A. Wilson and John Bowden (New York: Harper and Row, 1974).

60. Hegel's dialectical holism bears passing resemblance to the rational optimism parodied in Voltaire's *Candide* because he denies that evil ruptures history or spoils its rational, teleological development. There is no irrationality or incomprehensibility of evil and no sense in which evil is radically opposed to good. William Desmond, "Evil and Dialectic," in *New Perspectives on Hegel's Philosophy of Religion*, ed. David Kolb (Albany: SUNY Press, 1992), 159–182.

CHAPTER TWO

1. Notable religious figures who have been termed "existentialists" are Jewish thinkers Martin Buber, Franz Rosenzweig, and Hermann Cohen, and Christian thinkers Soren Kierkegaard, Gabriel Marcel, Nicholas Berdyaev, Rudolf Bultmann, and Paul Tillich. James Collins, *The Existentialists* (Chicago: Henry Regnery Co., 1968).

2. Nathan A. Scott, Jr., *The Unquiet Vision: Mirrors of Man in Existentialism* (New York: World Publishing, 1969), 23–34.

3. Albert Camus, *The Myth of Sisyphus*, trans. Justin O'Brien (New York: Random House, 1955), 88–91.

4. Jean-Paul Sartre, *Being and Nothingness*, trans. Hazel Barnes (New York: Philosophical Library, 1956), 553. Sartre made an attempt to integrate existentialism and Marxism in his last major work, *Critique de la Raison Dialectique. I. Theorie des Ensembles Pratique* (Paris: Gallimard, 1960). He adopted the Marxist theory of the dialectic of history involving class struggle and revolution, while grafting on it the necessity of

the individual to realize freedom, affirmed in his earlier work. Willfrid Desan, *The Marxism of Jean Paul Sartre* (New York: Anchor Books, 1966), 235–241.

5. Buber is famous for coining the term "I-Thou" (*Ich-Du*) to designate authentic intersubjective relation. Marcel also uses the terms "I" and "thou" (*je* and *tu*) to describe authentic relation, although he does not employ these terms as consistently as Buber does. For both authors, authentic relation is defined as open, mutual, noninstrumental, and non-objectifying. Gabriel Marcel, "I and Thou," in *The Philosophy of Gabriel Marcel*, ed. Paul A. Schlipp and Lewis E. Hahn (La Salle, IL: Open Court, 1984), 41–48.

6. Marcel's conversion to Christianity in 1929, at age forty, was prompted by a letter from the prominent French Catholic writer Francois Mauriac. Marcel was baptized as a Roman Catholic, but he was always very ecumenical in outlook and strongly opposed to religious legalism and dogmatism. Gabriel Marcel, "An Autobiographical Essay," in *The Philosophy of Gabriel Marcel*, 28–31.

7. Albert Camus, *The Plague*, trans. Stuart Gilbert (New York: Modern Library, 1948).

8. Marcel's contrast between "having" and "being" distinguishes between an objective, instrumental perspective and an attitude of openness and appreciation of persons and objects. This division runs parallel to Buber's "I-It" and "I-Thou" attitudes (IT 53–57).

9. Kant's realm of *phenomena* is studied using speculative reason. *Phenomena* include nonliving and living things studied by the physical sciences and the human sciences such as empirical psychology and sociology. Like Kant, Marcel claims that philosophy can open up an alternate standpoint for understanding human existence, the standpoint of the free subject and moral faith. Immanuel Kant, *Critique of Pure Reason*, trans. Norman Kemp Smith (New York: St. Martin's Press, 1956), A 442/B 470.

10. Kenneth T. Gallagher, *The Philosophy of Gabriel Marcel* (New York: Fordham University Press, 1962), 30–49.

11. The moral significance of this distinction is promoted by Kant who formulates the categorical imperative of morality as the maxim that I should treat the other person as an end, not a means. Immanuel Kant, *Foundations of the Metaphysics of Morals*, trans. Lewis White Beck (Indianapolis: Bobbs-Merrill, 1973), 46–55.

12. Marcel does admit that evil poses a theoretical problem; however, he considers theodicy an inappropriate tactic of response. Marcel Nadeau, "Gabriel Marcel et la Signification du Mal," in *Gabriel Marcel: Colloque* (Paris: Bibliotheque Nationale, 1989), 185.

13. James Cone, founder of black theology, cites Marcel approvingly on this point. But Cone locates the experience of evil far more concretely than Marcel in "the struggle of an oppressed community for justice." James H. Cone, *God of the Oppressed* (San Francisco: Harper San Francisco, 1975), 180–184.

14. Psychologist Eric Fromm uses Marcel's distinction between "having" and "being" to profile two contrasting kinds of faith: faith that is essentially acceptance of a creed and faith that is not tied to fixed images but is open to God's mystery. In depicting the latter, Fromm draws on the writings of mystic Meister Eckhart. Eric Fromm, *To Have or to Be?* (New York: Bantam Books, 1981), ch. 1.

15. Marcel is imprecise on the issue of whether I-It language has any legitimate place in philosophy or theology. He appears to be a realist concerning God's existence, although the notion of real reference of divine names to God is problematic because it implies that God is an object rather than a subject encountered. Buber makes an

analogous point in *I and Thou* where he claims that concepts of God are reductive and inappropriate for describing God, who is "the Thou that by its nature cannot become It." (IT 75) Marcel does not develop I-It language about God, but he implies that theology based on revelation may do so. For further discussion, see C. Peter R. L. Slater, "The Question of Evil in Marcel, Some Philosophical Analysts and Saint Augustine" (Ph.D. diss., Harvard University, 1964), 28–38.

16. Gabriel Marcel, "An Autobiographical Essay" in *The Philosophy of Gabriel Marcel*, 20–21.

17. The significance of the "appeal" of the other, suggested by Marcel, is developed by Emmanuel Levinas who accentuates its ethical import. Levinas stresses the moral imperative of the appeal of the Thou by placing the Other at a commanding height and the self under the bondage of obligation. Levinas considers Marcel and Buber both mistaken in phenomenologically positing relational symmetry between I and Thou. Emmanuel Levinas, "Martin Buber and the Theory of Knowledge" in *The Philosophy of Martin Buber*, 133–150.

18. Marcel's play *La Signe de la Croix* (1948), a drama about Jewish families in occupied France during World War II, depicts a situation in which suffering is accepted as a "trial" as a result of understanding reached through I-Thou relation. The friendship between a Jewish man, Simon, and an elderly Jewish woman in exile, Lena, enables Simon to accept suffering voluntarily for the sake of others who suffer from Nazi persecution and to realize that such commitment is a form of religious faith. For commentary, see Katherine Rose Hanley, *Dramatic Approaches to Creative Fidelity* (New York: University Press of America, 1987), 134–151.

19. Marcel and Bloch both consider hope as central to faith. Bloch's treatment of hope is Marxian, while Marcel is politically more conservative, as evident in the published dialogue between Marcel and Bloch entitled "Gabriel Marcel et la Pensée Allemande," in *Présence de Gabriel Marcel* 1 (1979): 39–74.

20. For a comparison of Marcel's idea of hope with the Marxian position of Ernst Bloch, see Otto Friedrich Bollnow, "Marcel's Concept of Availability," in *The Philosophy of Gabriel Marcel*, 192–194.

21. Although there are degrees of hope in the future, according to individual disposition, Marcel argues that religious hope that considers interpersonal fidelity grounded in God's eternal mystery and love is by definition unconditional (HV 46).

22. Marcel's dismissal of protest in favor of acceptance is in stark contrast with the conclusions of Jewish and Christian Marxian and post-Holocaust thinkers. It is axiomatic in political and liberation theology that resistance to suffering on a collective social level is a religious responsibility, while in post-Holocaust theology the responses of protest and horror at the memory of suffering is unquestioned.

23. Gabriel Marcel, *Rome n'est plus dans Rome* (1951), quotation translated by Katherine Rose Hanley in *Dramatic Approaches to Creative Fidelity*, 152.

24. The endurance of Thou-relation beyond death accompanies religious hope in God and immortality (CF 167). Marcel emphasizes that his play *The Iconoclast* (1920) gives a concrete example of hope that displays how the presence of a deceased loved one remains real to the survivor and how the bond of fidelity lasts beyond death (CF 151–2; and EBHD 50–53).

25. Cone, *God of the Oppressed*, 181.

26. For instance, in recent feminist Christian theology, African-American women's literature has been used as a resource for the study of suffering, gender, and

faith by both black and white female authors. See Katie G. Cannon, *Black Womanist Ethics* (Atlanta: Scholars Press, 1988); Sharon D. Welch, *A Feminist Ethic of Risk* (Minneapolis: Fortress Press, 1990); and Kathleen M. Sands, *Escape from Paradise: Evil and Tragedy in Feminist Theology* (Minneapolis: Fortress Press, 1994).

27. The writings of concentration camp survivors describe many symptoms of dehumanization, including violent behavior and suicidal passivity. For example, see Primo Levi, *Survival in Auschwitz: The Nazi Assault on Humanity*, trans. Stuart Woolf (New York: Collier, 1993).

28. Viktor Frankl, *Man's Search For Meaning: An Introduction to Logotherapy*, 3d ed. trans. Ilse Lasch (New York: Simon and Schuster, 1984), 88–91. Marcel would likely concede that some persons are too broken to find meaning by an act of inner freedom, as Frankl points out, but his religious response to suffering clearly lacks reflection on situations in which the individual is unable to find hope or meaning in suffering.

CHAPTER THREE

1. Critics have questioned whether Buber's lack of attention to Jewish law and ritual and his apparently interreligious vision of faith indicate a lack of Jewishness in his work. His defenders point to his extensive studies of Hebrew scripture and Hasidism, and argue that in *I and Thou* Buber elaborates central historical strands of the Jewish tradition, such as dialogue with God and the hallowing of creation. Daniel Breslauer, *The Chrysalis of Religion: A Guide to the Jewishness of Buber's I and Thou* (Nashville: Abingdon, 1980), 1–16.

2. Buber's work exceeds the boundaries of "existentialist" philosophy dramatically. His impact on both Jewish and Christian thought has been deeper and more enduring than Marcel's. A former student of eminent Kantian Jewish philosopher Hermann Cohen, Buber is among the foremost Jewish thinkers of his generation. Buber and his collaborator Franz Rosenzweig (1886–1929) paved the way for the postmodern Jewish philosophy of Emmanuel Levinas and others. For comparative discussion of Jewish postmodern thinkers and their forebearers, such as Levinas, Rosenzweig, Marcel, Buber, and Cohen, see Robert Gibbs, *Correlations in Rosenzweig and Levinas* (Princeton: Princeton University Press, 1992).

3. Texts that are most central to Buber's coming to terms with the Holocaust and his response to suffering are the Hasidic novel *For the Sake of Heaven* [1945], *Prophetic Faith* [1949], the lecture entitled "The Dialogue between Earth and Heaven" [1951] (published in *On Judaism*), and *The Eclipse of God* [1952]. Buber's book *Good and Evil* [1953] deals less with faith responses to suffering than with existential interpretation of sin and myths of evil.

4. The Kantian dimensions of Buber's philosophy are affirmed and explored by Steven T. Katz in *Post Holocaust Dialogues* (New York: New York University Press, 1983), 19–21.

5. Parenthetical citations from *I and Thou* refer to the translation by Ronald Gregor Smith, which better captures the tone of Buber's lyrical German than the Walter Kaufmann translation. For a comparison of the two translations, see Maurice Friedman, *Martin Buber's Life and Work: The Early Years, 1878–1923* (New York: Dutton, 1983), 428–429.

6. Buber's critique of the damaging effects of the I-It attitude in society is echoed in the critique of technological attitudes by existentialist philosopher Martin

Heidegger. Martin Heidegger, "The Question Concerning Technology" [1955] in *The Question Concerning Technology and Other Essays*, trans. William Lovitt (New York: Harper and Row, 1977), 1–49.

7. Buber proposes the developmental thesis that in the earliest stages of human culture, the I-Thou attitude is primary, but it becomes overshadowed by I-It development (IT 26). His position on cultural development corresponds closely with Cassirer's theory that "mythical consciousness," which views reality as immediately present and dynamic, dominates primitive culture and is gradually superceded by objective consciousness. Ernst Cassirer, *The Philosophy of Symbolic Forms*, vol. II (New Haven: Yale University Press, 1955), 29–58.

8. Like Marcel, Buber rejects Sartre's depiction of freedom as a power of decision exerted by the isolated self, which competes with the freedom of the other. For Buber and Marcel, the "I" is defined as being-in-relation with others, and freedom involves the recognition of the participation of the self in relation. Sylvain Boni, *The Self and the Other in the Ontologies of Sartre and Buber* (Washington, DC: University Press of America, 1982), 72.

9. Emmanuel Levinas's depiction of relation to the Other, which is religious, moral, and aesthetic in character, bears some resemblance to Buber's philosophy of dialogue. However, Levinas strongly objects to the symmetry of I-Thou relation assumed by Buber and Marcel. See the remarks by Levinas in Maurice S. Friedman, "Interrogation of Martin Buber," in *Philosophical Interrogations*, ed. Sydney Rome and Beatrice Rome (New York: Holt, Rinehart and Winston, 1964), 23–29; also see Emmanuel Levinas, *Totality and Infinity*, trans. A. Lingus (Pittsburgh: Duquesne University Press, 1969); and *Otherwise than Being or Beyond Essence*, trans. A. Lingus (Boston: Kluwer, 1981).

10. I-Thou relation is the basis for an ethics encompassing both persons and nature. Maurice S. Friedman, "The Bases of Buber's Ethics," in *The Philosophy of Martin Buber*, ed. Paul A. Schilpp and Maurice Friedman (La Salle, IL: Open Court, 1967), 171–200.

11. Elements of Buber's political perspective can be traced back to the ideas of Gustav Landauer (1868–1919). As a socialist, Landauer accepts Marx's condemnation of capitalist society, but he rejects the assumption that the implementation of a new economic system would escape the vices of the past, such as corruption and avarice. According to Landauer, only if each individual works on changing the orientation of one's own soul, a step that is both mystical and revolutionary, could true "socialism" exist. His political outlook is markedly romantic and mystical, influenced by his studies of Meister Eckhart. Like Landauer, Buber believes that religious socialism requires the subject's openness to the divine Thou as its precondition. See the comments on Landauer in Buber's *Paths in Utopia* (PU 46–57).

12. Buber criticizes Marx for ignoring the "problematic of human decision" and existential freedom by theorizing only about historical agency on the level of class. Martin Buber, "What Is Man?" in *Between Man and Man* (New York: Collier Books, 1965), 137–145. Buber's negative comments on Marx are primarily based on his knowledge of cold stream Marxism, represented by Engel's mechanistic and determinist interpretation of Marx's ideas. It seems that Buber was unfamiliar with Marx's early writings that recognize the need for a change in human consciousness, as well as economics. Bernard Susser, *Existence and Utopia: The Social and Political Thought of Martin Buber* (Toronto: Associated University Presses, 1981), 81–94.

13. Laurence J. Silberstein, *Martin Buber's Social and Religious Thought: Alienation and the Quest for Meaning* (New York: New York University Press, 1989), 193–198.

14. Critic Gershom Scholem agrees that I-Thou relation and Buber's definition of revelation are both unmistakably mystical, seeking God as pervasive in all dimensions of reality. Gershom Scholem, *On Jews and Judaism in Crisis* (New York: Schocken Books, 1976), 157.

15. Buber admits that belief and trust are not mutually exclusive, for belief often leads to an I-Thou relation of trust in God, and, conversely, trust in God can lead one to accept certain things as true (TTF 8).

16. Buber enters a debate in the phenomenology of religion initiated by Friedrich Schleiermacher, *On Religion: Speeches to its Cultured Despisers* [1799], trans. Richard Crouter (Cambridge: Cambridge University Press, 1988), 96–140. Schleiermacher describes God-consciousness as "a feeling of absolute dependence" where the human subject is dependent to the point of being passive and unable to have any affect on God, whereas Otto thinks that the experience of God, or the Holy, exhibits absolute dependence as one of a number of possible feelings. In contrast, Buber differs in insisting that I-Thou relation with God is active dialogue and not passive reception. Rudolf Otto, *The Idea of the Holy*, trans. John W. Harvey (London: Oxford University Press, 1957), 1–30.

17. Existentialist theologian Rudolf Bultmann likewise claims that speech about God is derivative from speech to God. He claims that we can speak of God only insofar as we speak of God's words and acts in Scripture. Rudolf Bultmann, "What Does It Mean to Speak of God?" [1925] in *Faith and Understanding* (Minneapolis: Fortress Press, 1969), 53–65.

18. Even before its publication, Buber's colleague and closest collaborator, Franz Rosenzweig, criticized *I and Thou* for its "impoverished and sterile" portrayal of I-It language, which does not acknowledge nonpositivistic forms of I-It conceptual language to speak of God. For development of this criticism of Buber's I-Thou typology, see Walter Kaufmann's prologue to *I and Thou*, trans. Walter Kaufmann (New York: Simon and Schuster, 1970), 15–19.

19. Martin Buber, *Ecstatic Confessions* [1909], trans. Esther Cameron (San Francisco: Harper and Row, 1985).

20. The *via negativa* in Christian thought forbids positive knowledge of God's attributes. It limits statements about God's attributes to negative formulations—for example, God is not limited in time, or God does not have a body. Buber, however, is spartan in his use of negative as well as positive depictions of God. For the notion of negative theology, see *Pseudo-Dionysius: The Complete Works*, trans. Colm Luibheid (New York: Paulist Press, 1987), 32.

21. Against objections, Katz argues that Buber's I-Thou versus I-It distinction is Kantian, despite the fact that Buber considers the noumenal world accessible in I-Thou relation and Kant does not. Steven T. Katz, "Lawrence Perlman's 'Buber's Anti-Kantianism': A Reply," *AJS Review* 15 (Spring 1990): 109–118.

22. Pedro C. Sevilla, *God as Person in the Writings of Martin Buber* (Manila: Logos, 1970), 90.

23. Steven T. Katz, "A Critical Review of Martin Buber's Epistemology of I and Thou," in *Martin Buber: A Centenary Volume*, ed. Jochanan Bloch and Gordon Haim (New York: KTAV, 1984), 89–119.

24. Buber takes God's name "I am that I am" (Ex. 3:14) as God's pivotal words of revelation, indicating that God is both present and eternal (PF 28–30).

25. There is a tension between Buber's priority on language addressing God as Thou and his use of It-language to generalize about Thou-relations. As one scholar remarks cogently, Buber seems "to be torn between his conviction that to speak about the divine in positive terms is to reduce it to an It, and the need to correct misinterpretations that distort our understanding of religious faith". Silberstein, *Martin Buber's Social and Religious Thought*, 221.

26. According to my definition of theodicy as the refusal to explain or justify God's reasons for evil and suffering, Buber takes an anti-theodicy approach. However, Buber has been categorized by Zachary Braiterman as giving a theodicy because Buber affirms existential meaning in suffering through dialogue with God. Braiterman defines theodicy too broadly, in my opinion, as encompassing any and all attempts to give religious meaning to evil and suffering. See Zachary Braiterman, *(God) After Auschwitz* (Princeton: Princeton University Press, 1998), 62–67.

27. Confirming Buber's insights, Christian narrative theologian Stanley Hauerwas asserts that we know "who God is" through stories about God in the Bible, although "what God is" in God's nature is hidden. God is "a proper name" (or Thou) who engages persons. Stanley Hauerwas, "Story and Theology" in *Truthfulness and Tragedy* (Notre Dame: University of Notre Dame Press, 1977), 79.

28. For an analysis of Buber as a narrative theologian, see Stephen Kepnes, *The Text as Thou: Martin Buber's Dialogical Hermeneutics and Narrative Theology* (Bloomington: Indiana University Press, 1992), 144–148.

29. Silberstein, *Martin Buber's Social and Religious Thought*, 207.

30. Narratives of the Bible communicate I-Thou relation and create the renewal of I-Thou reality, according to Buber. S. Daniel Breslauer, *Martin Buber on Myth* (New York: Garland Publishing, 1990), 26–28.

31. Buber, "The Word That Is Spoken," trans. by Maurice Friedman in *The Knowledge of Man* (New York: Harper & Row, 1965), 110–118. For a comparison of Buber's hermeneutic theory with Hans-Georg Gadamer's hermeneutics of dialogue between reader and text developed in *Truth and Method*, 2d ed. (New York: Continuum, 1998), see Kepnes, *The Text as Thou*, 72–78.

32. Hasidism is a pietist branch of Judaism, founded by the Baal Shem Tov, that emerged in eighteenth-century Poland. Hasidism places importance on personal encounter with God and considers every being and every action as potentially holy. Buber promotes Hasidism as a classic example of faith in God that is rooted in I-Thou relation (HMM 13–35).

33. Buber's work on Hasidism has been criticized for its lack of historical accuracy. Buber's interpretive selectivity is deliberate, however, for his aim is to offer a portrayal of a personal, humanistic, and ethical faith to serve as a model for contemporary times, not to present an accurate historical account. For critique of Buber, see Walter Kaufmann, "Buber's Failures and Triumph" in *Martin Buber: A Centenary Volume*, 17. For a positive assessment, see S. Daniel Breslauer, *The Chrysalis of Religion* (Nashville: Abingdon, 1980), 54–67.

34. Scholem disputes Buber's reading of Hasidism, which minimizes or dismisses its gnostic and esoteric aspects. Scholem points out that Kabbalistic myths, central to Hasidism, offer esoteric knowledge of the cosmic struggle between good and evil, and these myths are adapted by some Hasidic thinkers. Gershom Scholem, *Major Trends in Jewish Mysticism* (New York: Schocken Books, 1961), 244–286. Against the view of Scholem, Joseph Dan supports Buber's moral-existential interpretation of

Hasidism when he points out that most Hasidic writings are edifying stories and not theoretical treatises of Kabbalism that develop complex concepts of God's being. Joseph Dan, *Jewish Mysticism and Jewish Ethics* (Seattle: University of Washington Press, 1986), 111–118.

35. Although Buber portrays redemption as dependent on human responsibility, he also affirms that human action is complemented by God's grace and God's turning to meet persons as Thou. Maurice Friedman, *Martin Buber: The Life of Dialogue*, 133.

36. The book of Job is part of the Wisdom literature in the Hebrew Bible, which focuses on individual righteousness and the injustice of the individual's suffering, rather than on the corporate or collective suffering of Israel. However, Buber interprets Job's speeches as also voicing the protest of Israel collectively against suffering in exile, in addition to Job's individual complaints.

37. The act/consequence principle of reward and punishment is applied in the Wisdom literature to the acts of individuals and in the Prophetic literature to the people of Israel who are said to be punished for their collective sins as a nation.

38. Buber criticizes the prophet Ezekiel's use of theodicy justifications for suffering, justifications that do not speak concretely from I-Thou relation with God. Like Job's friends and comforters, Ezekiel fails to speak truly of God (PF 187).

39. Buber's discussion of Job in his lecture "Between Heaven and Earth" concludes that Job is left in a state of agnosticism concerning God's justice (OJ 224). But in *Prophetic Faith*, Buber seemingly draws a conceptual conclusion from God's speeches, namely, that God's justice is not one of legal retribution but distribution, which means that God "gives each creature its being and its place" (PF 192). Jewish theologian Harold Schulweis takes this suggestion as Buber's "theodicy" affirming a supra-logical God. However, I disagree. Buber's interpretation of Job discusses how God appears in I-Thou dialogue and does not posit knowledge of God's nature to support a theodicy argument. Harold M. Schulweis, *Evil and the Morality of God* (Cincinnati: Hebrew Union College Press, 1984), 96–106.

40. Like Buber, Kant praises Job for his integrity, displayed in Job's confession that "he had spoken unwisely about things that were above his reach and which he did not understand," and for his persistence in worshipping God despite the inscrutability of divine justice given the apparent discrepancy between the natural and moral orders. Kant concludes that Job does not base his morality on faith, but his faith on morality. Immanuel Kant, "On the Miscarriage of All Philosophical Trials in Theodicy" [1791], in *Religion within the Boundaries of Mere Reason and Other Writings*, ed. Allen Wood and George DiGiovanni (London: Cambridge University Press, 1998), 25.

41. In discussing Jewish messianism, Buber accuses the apostle Paul of reversing the image, found in Isaiah, of the human being who suffers for God's sake, and perverting it into a gnostic belief in a God who suffers for the sake of humankind in order to remove humanity from bondage to the flesh and the law (TTF 149).

42. Kepnes, *The Text as Thou*, 135.

43. Irving Greenberg, "Cloud of Smoke, Pillar of Fire: Judaism, Christianity and Modernity after the Holocaust," in *Auschwitz: Beginning of a New Era?*, ed. Eva Fleischner (New York: KTAV, 1977), 26–40.

44. In Pharisaic Judaism, God is described as the "dynamic unity" of justice and mercy—dynamic in the sense that one side may be hidden to faith experience. However, this is not a gnostic ontological claim that posits contradictory attributes in God's nature. It is a statement describing the phenomenology of faith encounter (TTF 154).

45. Notable post-Holocaust Jewish thinkers claim that the Holocaust shatters faith in God's plan for history (Richard Rubenstein), that it demands a radically new kind of faith (Irving Greenberg), or that it requires creation of a new (613th) commandment for Jewish survival (Emil Fackenheim). Buber takes a less extreme position on the distinctive impact of the Holocaust on faith. For an overview of post-Holocaust Jewish thought, see Donald J. Dietrich, *God and Humanity in Auschwitz* (London: Transaction Publishers, 1995), 199–225.

46. As one contemporary critic sums up this line of objection, "What is missing from Buber's understanding of divine-human relation is the absence of absence, expressed in the Holocaust as human helplessness and as God's silence." Edith Wyschogrod, "Hasidism, Hellenism, Holocaust," in *Interpreting Judaism in a Postmodern Age*, ed. Steven Kepnes (New York: New York University Press, 1996), 308.

CHAPTER FOUR

1. David McLellan, *The Thought of Karl Marx*, 3d ed. (London: Macmillan, 1995), 252–254.

2. For example, Louis Althusser argues that there is a sharp break in Marx's thought in 1845 represented by *Theses on Feuerbach* [1845] and *The German Ideology* [1845–1846]. Louis Althusser, *For Marx* (New York: Pantheon Books, 1969). Other scholars accentuate the humanistic interests of Marx's mature work, reminiscent of his early work, such as Melvin Rader, *Marx's Interpretation of History* (New York: Oxford University Press, 1979).

3. It is remarkable that even before the publication of Marx's early works in the 1920s, Georg Lukacs and Ernst Bloch had already developed a humanist interpretation of Marx in opposition to Soviet apologists, reading the post–1845 Marx in tandem with Hegel. Georg Lukacs, *History and Class Consciousness* [1917], trans. R. Livingstone (Cambridge: Cambridge University Press, 1968); and Ernst Bloch, *Geist der Utopie* [1923] (Frankfurt: Suhrkamp Verlag, 1964).

4. Marx, *The German Ideology*, in *Karl Marx: Selected Writings*, ed. David McLellan (Oxford: Oxford University Press, 1977), 156.

5. Marx's emphasis on human productivity takes a technological I-It perspective toward other persons that Marcel and Buber would consider callous, dehumanizing, and even immoral.

6. Economic development from the Middle Ages to the industrial revolution is traced in Marx, *The German Ideology*, in *Karl Marx: Selected Writings*, 160–172.

7. Marx, preface to *A Contribution to the Critique of Political Economy* [1859], in *Karl Marx: Selected Writings*, 389.

8. Marx proposes this two-class model in the *Communist Manifesto* [1848] while in *Capital* vol. III [1864–1865] he paints a more complex picture, admitting, for example, that in England there is a third "landowner" class. Marx also points to a growing "middle class," intermediate between proletariat and bourgeois classes, whose work involves providing skilled services (e.g., doctors, lawyers, teachers, architects). McLellan, *The Thought of Karl Marx*, 183–184.

9. Marx, *The German Ideology*, in *Karl Marx: Selected Writings*, 176.

10. Marx, *Wage Labor and Capital* [1849], in *Karl Marx: Selected Writings*, 265. At times, Marx's analysis of the problems of capitalism resonates with the critique of technology and bureaucracy advanced by Marcel and Buber.

11. Marx's most extensive discussion of ideology is found in *The German Ideology*, in *Karl Marx: Selected Writings*, 160–179.

12. For a detailed introduction to Marx's notion of "ideology" and the critique of Hegel's idealism, see Bhikhu Parekh, *Marx's Theory of Ideology* (London: Croom Helm, 1982), 18–51.

13. Marx, *Contribution to the Critique of Hegel's Philosophy of Right: Introduction*, in *The Marx-Engels Reader*, ed. Robert C. Tucker (New York: W. W. Norton and Co., 1978), 54.

14. Some scholars, embarrassed by scientific Marxism, argue that Marx did not claim to predict the future, despite his occasional "arrogant remarks" about the advent of communism. Parekh, *Marx's Theory of Ideology*, 88.

15. Careful study of Marx's corpus reveals that Marx did not think that all aspects of the superstructure (such as art, philosophy, and religion) were slavish reflections of class interest, even though he maintained that economic factors were always of predominant influence. Rader, *Marx's Interpretation of History*, 53–55.

16. Hegel refers to the overcoming (*Aufhebung*) of contradictions in a given economic system as the dialectical "negation of the negation"—the negation of oppression—which creates new and improved conditions. Marx, *The Poverty of Philosophy*, in *Karl Marx: Selected Writings*, 200–201.

17. Marx, *Communist Manifesto*, in *Karl Marx: Selected Writings*, 230.

18. Cold stream Marxism's prediction of a future communist society presumes the rational development of history, which Hegel affirms. But since Marx rejects Hegel's idealistic definition of history as the history of Spirit or God, which is the only warrant for history's rationality, Marx is left with no grounds for asserting reason in history on a material level and no basis for predicting the *telos* of communism. Louis Dupré, *Marx's Social Critique of Culture* (New Haven: Yale University Press, 1983), 65–71.

19. For a concise definition of Western Marxism, see Martin Jay, *Marxism and Totality: The Adventures of a Concept from Lukacs to Habermas* (Berkeley: University of California Press, 1984), 3–13.

20. The later work of Jean Paul Sartre is Marxist, although Sartre worked in isolation from the warm stream Marxist movement based in Germany. Sartre attempts to graft an existentialist notion of the subject onto Marxist dialectical materialism by positing class-consciousness as both free and conditioned. His synthesis of existentialism and Marxism was never completed, and, in retrospect, scholars consider the project as a failure. Sartre's efforts show the need to balance consideration of the subject's existential freedom with acknowledgment of how material factors condition human choices and how group solidarity develops among individuals. Jean Paul Sartre, *Critique de la Raison Dialectique. I. Theorie des Ensembles Pratique* (Paris: Gallimard, 1960).

21. Marx, *Critique of Hegel's Philosophy of Right: Introduction*, in *The Marx-Engels Reader*, 51.

22. Marx's role as a pioneer in the sociology of knowledge is discussed in T. B. Bottomore and Maxmilien Rubel, *Karl Marx: Selected Writings in Sociology and Social Philosophy* (New York: Penguin Books, 1961), 17–63.

23. Marx makes certain comments to this effect, although at other times he expresses the cold stream view that all cultural products are determined by economic conditions. Rader, *Marx's Interpretation of History*, 53–55.

24. Bloch uses the term "utopian" hope in a Marxian context. Notably, Marx criticizes early nineteenth-century "utopianism," represented by French socialist

thinkers such as Saint-Simon and Fourier, as abstract imagining because it fails to recognize the revolutionary potential of poverty. This point is explored by theologian Nicholas Lash in *A Matter of Hope: A Theologian's Reflections on the Thought of Karl Marx* (Notre Dame: University of Notre Dame, 1982), 234–243.

25. Late capitalist culture is labeled "bourgeois" not because it is the culture of the very wealthy (factory owners and capitalists) but because it is shaped by, and its ideology condones, the "material conditions of production" of late capitalism. Bourgeois culture is uncritical of late capitalism and hence counterrevolutionary. George Friedman, *The Political Philosophy of the Frankfurt School* (Ithaca: Cornell University Press, 1981), 189–203.

26. Karl Marx, *Theses on Feuerbach*, in *The Marx-Engels Reader*, 143–145.

27. Marx, *Communist Manifesto*, in *Karl Marx: Selected Writings*, 228.

28. Most intellectuals do not turn against their class to take up the interests of the proletariat. Marx accuses the "intelligensia class" of earning its wages by acting as ideological representatives of the bourgeois class. Hegel is a chief culprit in this regard. Marx, *The German Ideology*, in *Karl Marx: Selected Writings*, 161.

29. Since Marx uses the terms "praxis" and "practice" interchangeably, and the use of the terms by Bloch, Moltmann, and Metz is not consistent, I prefer to use the word "practice" to refer to the political-religious postures of hope, resistance, memory, suffering, and solidarity. See the discussion of "praxis" in Marx, *The German Ideology*, in *Karl Marx: Selected Writings*, 156–173.

30. Adorno uses the Hegelian notion of dialectics, but he firmly rejects dialectics as a theory of progress in history. Theodor W. Adorno, *Negative Dialectics*, trans. E. B. Ashton (New York: Seabury Press, 1973), 362–381.

31. Marx's communist society enables free mutuality among persons that could be described in terms of I-Thou relation. Marx's ideal for human relations in communist society are explored in Melvin Rader, *Marx's Interpretation of History*, 228–230. In contrast, Buber takes I-Thou attitude as the moral basis for the establishment of socialism, rather than economic conditions as the prerequisite for I-Thou relation. Bernard Susser, *The Social and Political Thought of Martin Buber* (London: Associated University Presses, 1981), 46–53.

32. Marxian philosophers who embrace the determinist theory of dialectical materialism exhibit "optimism" about the future, while prophetic "hope" requires admitting that the future cannot be known and trusting in God's promises concerning future redemption. Neither warm stream Marxian thought nor eschatological hope qualify as optimism, as argued cogently by Christian theologian Nicholas Lash in *A Matter of Hope*, 269–280.

CHAPTER FIVE

1. Bloch's broad influence on Christian theology in Germany is demonstrated by contributions to the Festschrift for his seventieth birthday by Wolfhart Pannenberg, Jürgen Moltmann, Johann Baptist Metz, and Paul Tillich. Siegfried Unseld, ed., *Ernst Bloch zu ehren* (Frankfurt: Suhrkamp Verlag, 1965).

2. Bloch's uncritical acceptance of revolution as the means to overcome capitalism is troubling, for the violence of revolution itself leads to more suffering. From an existentialist viewpoint, Bloch's mistake is to assume that the establishment of the

economic conditions of communism, by whatever means necessary, will produce a society of freedom and justice. Buber counters that it is I-Thou relation that is the foundation for political justice and socialist government. Bernard Susser, *Existence and Utopia: The Social and Political Thought of Martin Buber* (London: Associated University Presses, 1981), 63–70.

3. Bloch would agree with Kant's definition of hope as the conviction that "evil will not have the last word either in one's own heart or in history," a conviction unsupported by a speculative teleology. Michael Despland, *Kant on History and Religion* (Montreal: McGill-Queens University Press, 1973), 280.

4. In comparison with Bloch, Marcel's portrait of hope is politically passive. Marcel claims that the goals of hope cannot be achieved by technical problem-solving analysis, such as Marxism offers, while Bloch insists that the religious person hopes and tries to achieve the realization of hope in history. For a comparison of Marcel and Bloch on religious hope, see Otto Friedrich Bollnow, "Marcel's Concept of Availability," in *The Philosophy of Gabriel Marcel*, ed. Paul A. Schilpp and Lewis E. Hahn (La Salle, IL: Open Court Press, 1984), 193–195.

5. Some scholars consider Bloch a metaphysician who, like Romantic philosopher F. W. J. Schelling, proposes an ontology of dynamic matter that is the ground of economic possibilities and anticipatory consciousness. For example, see Helmut Reinicke, *Materie und Revolution* (Kronberg: Scriptor Verlag, 1974); Alfred Jäger, *Reich ohne Gott* (Zurich: EVZ-Verlag, 1969); and Renate Damus, *Ernst Bloch* (Meisenheim: Verlag Anton Hain, 1971). However, I propose a Kantian, humanist reading of Bloch that focuses on the heuristic character of utopia as a critical ideal rather than a teleological metaphysics. My interpretation shares similarities with the postmodern reading of Bloch proposed by John Miller Jones in *Assembling (Post)modernism: The Utopian Philosophy of Ernst Bloch* (New York: Peter Lang, 1995), 176–183.

6. Bloch is unconcerned that the mature Marx rejected this absolute utopian possibility. Bloch, "Something's Missing: A Discussion between Ernst Bloch and Theodor W. Adorno on the Contradictions of Utopian Longing" [1964], in *The Utopian Function of Art and Literature*, trans. Jack Zipes and Frank Mecklenburg (Cambridge: MIT Press, 1988), 15.

7. In line with the humanism of the early Marx and warm stream Marxism, Bloch proclaims that "genuine Marxism in its impetus, its class struggle and its goal-content is, can be, will be nothing but the promotion of humanity" (PH III 1358). Within Marxist thought, Bloch is criticized for his general and undifferentiated concepts of both the proletariat and the means of liberation. Wayne Hudson, *The Marxist Philosophy of Ernst Bloch* (New York: St. Martin's Press, 1982), 55–67.

8. Given that utopian ideals are not fully comprehended but lie in latency, Bloch's commitment to the communist ideal appears insufficiently critical (PH III 1285). In conversation with Theodor Adorno, Bloch admits the negative status of utopian goals in "Something's Missing: A Discussion between Ernst Bloch and Theodor W. Adorno on the Contradictions of Utopian Longing," 12.

9. It is difficult to see how Bloch can maintain that the *Ultimum* is grounded in the real possibilities of the world process given that it is a "leap" beyond even a classless society. The *Ultimum* is more plausibly understood as a Kantian regulative ideal, a critical perspective to guide moral evaluation and political planning.

10. Richard J. Bernstein, *Praxis and Action: Contemporary Philosophies of Human Activity* (Philadelphia: University of Pennsylvania Press, 1971), 76–81.

11. Bloch's explicit target is existentialist theologian Rudolf Bultmann. Bultmann is accused of ahistoricizing and privatizing faith for two main reasons: he defines faith as the individual response of the subject to the Word of God, and he proposes a "realized eschatology" that posits the Kingdom of God as eternal and present to the believer. (AC 40; PH III 1285). Rudolf Bultmann, *History and Eschatology* (Edinburgh: University of Edinburgh Press, 1957), 150–55.

12. Bloch does not confront the dangers in the use of violence, driven by religious hope in political change, nor does he consider seriously the practical problem of deciding what is a real possibility in specific historical situations. Arno Munster, *Ernst Bloch: Messianisme et Utopie* (Paris: Presses Universitaires de France, 1989), 43.

13. The bravery and confidence of these heroes of faith is described in Nietzschean language, although these leaders are devoted to the liberation of the masses, whom Nietzsche scornfully dismisses (AC 239).

14. Gustavo Gutiérrez, *On Job: God-Talk and the Suffering of the Innocent*, trans. Matthew J. O'Connell (Maryknoll, NY: Orbis Books, 1995), 32–37. Dorothee Soelle, *Suffering*, trans. Everett R. Kalin (Minneapolis: Fortress Press, 1975), 110–119.

15. Terrence W. Tilley, *The Evils of Theodicy* (Washington, DC: Georgetown University Press, 1991), 106–110.

16. For her early view, see Soelle, *Suffering*, 116–119. For her later mystical reading of Job, see Soelle, *The Silent Cry* (Minneapolis: Fortress Press, 2001), 133–136. The idea of faith "without why" used to describe Job's faith can be traced back to the medieval German mystics Meister Eckhart and Angelus Silesius.

17. Similarly, Kant distinguishes justice in the moral order from lack of justice in the natural order. Both are under God's jurisdiction, but the connection between them is unfathomable to human understanding. Immanuel Kant, "On the Miscarriage of All Philosophical Trials in Theodicy," in *Religion within the Boundaries of Mere Reason and Other Writings*, ed. Allen Wood and George DiGiovanni (London: Cambridge University Press, 1998), 25.

18. Bloch's interpretation of Jesus is distinctively Jewish in his insistence that the Messiah comes to establish God's Kingdom in history. Bloch also interprets the eschatological significance of Jesus Christ in this light. Jürgen Moltmann, *The Coming of God*, trans. Margaret Kohl (Minneapolis: Fortress Press, 1996), 147–156.

19. Interestingly, Bloch's work had no comparable impact on Jewish thought. M. Douglas Meeks, *Origins of the Theology of Hope* (Philadelphia: Fortress Press, 1974), 1–9.

20. Jürgen Moltmann, *Hope and Planning*, trans. Margaret Clarkson (New York: Harper and Row, 1968), 50.

21. Jürgen Moltmann, *Theology of Hope*, trans. James W. Leitch (New York: SCM Press, 1967), 330.

22. See A. J. Conyers, *God, Hope and History* (Macon, GA: Mercer University Press, 1988), 91.

23. For a study of Moltmann's theology as a praxis theology, and critique of his Trinitarian speculation, see Rebecca S. Chopp, *The Praxis of Suffering: An Interpretation of Liberation and Political Theologies* (Maryknoll, NY: Orbis Books, 1992), 100–117.

24. Jürgen Moltmann, *The Crucified God*, trans. R. A. Wilson and John Bowden (Minneapolis: Fortress Press, 1993), 243–278.

25. Jürgen Moltmann, *The Trinity and the Kingdom*, trans. Margaret Kohl (Minneapolis: Fortress Press, 1993), 129–139.

26. Richard Bauckham, *The Theology of Jürgen Moltmann* (Edinburgh: T & T Clark, 1995), 88.

27. Jürgen Moltmann, "God and Resurrection: Resurrection Faith in the Forum of the Question of Theodicy," in *Hope and Planning*, 42–43.

28. Objections to Moltmann's theology of divine suffering are explored by Kenneth Surin in *Theology and the Problem of Evil* (Oxford: Basil Blackwell, 1986), 129–132. For Metz's critique of Moltmann, see ch. 6.

29. The incongruity between the Trinitarian and practical-political dimensions of Moltmann's response to suffering is analyzed by Chopp in *The Praxis of Suffering*, 115–117.

30. Delores Williams focuses on Jesus' "ministerial vision" as opposed to the cross. Delores Williams, "Black Women's Surrogacy Experience and the Christian Notion of Redemption," in *After Patriarchy: Feminist Transformations of the World Religions*, ed. Paula M. Cooey et al. (Maryknoll, NY: Orbis Books, 1998), 1–14.

31. Jesus chose love, not suffering. Suffering was accepted as a consequence of his mission, not its goal. This insight is elaborated in the context of a feminist reconstruction of the cross and redemption by Cynthia Crysdale, *Embracing Travail: Retrieving the Cross Today* (New York: Continuum, 1999), 144–150.

32. Weinandy effectively undercuts the practical advantages of Moltmann's position, although he agrees with Moltmann that "divine suffering" (of God's Son) should be a major part of any Christian response to human suffering. Thomas G. Weinandy, *Does God Suffer?* (Notre Dame: University of Notre Dame Press, 2000), 147–171.

33. Latin American liberation theologians are correct in their critique of political thinkers Bloch and Moltmann as offering a formal and abstract response to suffering because they do not examine concrete strategies for political resistance. In the view of liberation theologians, a political response must be applied to specific countries and social groups to be effective. Jose Miguez Bonino, *Doing Theology in a Revolutionary Situation* (Philadelphia: Fortress Press, 1975), 145–149.

CHAPTER SIX

1. Metz's Roman Catholic "fundamental" theology explores the questions that ground systematic theological reflection, such as the identity of the subject as situated in history, the importance of memory and narrative, the role of faith in society, and the praxis implications of theological discourse. By definition, fundamental theology focuses on theological anthropology and questions of method; however, not all fundamental theology is political. See J. Matthew Ashley, *Interruptions: Mysticism, Politics and Theology in the Work of Johann Baptist Metz* (Notre Dame: University of Notre Dame Press, 1998), 191–204.

2. These three "crises" are placed on par for biographical reasons; otherwise, there is vast difference between Marxian philosophy as an intellectual influence, the severe and lasting oppression that occurs in "Third World" countries, and the horrific event of the Holocaust. Johann Baptist Metz, "Communicating a Dangerous Memory," in *Communicating a Dangerous Memory: Soundings in Political Theology*, ed. Fred Lawrence (Atlanta: Scholars Press, 1987), 38.

3. Adorno's counter-proposal to Hegelian teleology, which asserts a positive resolution to the dialectics of history, is known as "negative dialectics"—philosophical

reflection that acknowledges the tensions between historical reality and political ideals as unresolvable. Massive suffering in history such as the Holocaust exposes the chronic nonfulfillment of political utopias. See Theodor W. Adorno, *Negative Dialectics* [1966], trans. E. B. Ashton (New York: Continuum, 1983). Objections to modern philosophy and theodicy are recounted in Theodor W. Adorno and Max Horkheimer, *Dialectic of Enlightenment* [1944], trans. John Cumming (New York: Seabury Press, 1972). For a study of the role of suffering in Adorno's negative dialectics see Susan Buck-Morss, *The Origin of Negative Dialectics* (New York: Free Press, 1977), 63–76.

4. Walter Benjamin, "Theses on the Philosophy of History," in *Illuminations*, ed. Hannah Arendt, trans. Harry Zohn (New York: Schocken Books, 1969), 253–264.

5. Metz recounts his trip to Mexico, Columbia, Peru, and Brazil in 1988 in *Augen für die Anderen: Latein Amerika, eine Theologische Erfahrung* (Munich: Kindler Verlag, 1991).

6. Metz found his childhood illusions of security and confidence shattered at age sixteen, when in 1944 as part of a Nazi unit he was sent alone on an overnight errand, from which he returned to find every soldier in his company dead, killed by a bombing attack. This traumatic event fuels his determination to write theology for people who have faced calamity, people who have no healing or intact visions of hope. Johann Baptist Metz, "Communicating a Dangerous Memory," 39.

7. For Metz and Wiesel, the shattering effect of the Holocaust on theistic explanations for suffering is immense and permanent. Ekkehard Schuster, *Hope against Hope: Johann Baptist Metz and Elie Wiesel Speak Out on the Holocaust*, trans. J. Matthew Ashley (New York: Paulist Press, 1999).

8. The German adjective *"bürgerlich"* may be translated literally as "bourgeois" or as "middle class" or "liberal." The term encompasses all persons "living in a [capitalist] market economy shaped by the bourgeois values of competition and exchange" (EC ix).

9. Metz observes that "values such as friendliness, thankfulness, attention to the dead, mourning, [also, religion] and so on for which there is no corresponding counter-value and for which one gets nothing in return" are on the decline in contemporary society (FHS 38). A critique of bourgeois culture influential for Metz's position is found in Adorno and Horkheimer, *Dialectic of Enlightenment*.

10. According to Metz, lack of respect for tradition is a result of the Enlightenment crusade for the autonomy of reason. The priority placed on the eternal truths of reason (mathematical, philosophical, and scientific) has displaced, in the modern era, respect given to the authority of the past. Metz argues that the decline of respect for tradition threatens the "identity of man [sic] and his state as a subject" (FHS 38).

11. Metz's criticism of bourgeois types of theology is directed toward the existentialist theology of Protestant thinker Rudolf Bultmann and also the "transcendental" theology of Catholic theologian Karl Rahner. Metz's academic training associates him closely with both theologians: he wrote his doctoral thesis on Aquinas under Karl Rahner, and he did a second doctorate in philosophy focusing on Martin Heidegger whose existentialist philosophy greatly influenced Bultmann's theology. Scholars agree that Metz underestimates the congruity of his political theology with the fundamental theology of Rahner. Titus F. Guenther, *Rahner and Metz: Transcendental Theology as Political Theology* (New York: University Press of America, 1994), ch. 1; Ashley, *Interruptions*, ch. 3.

12. Benjamin asserts that "there is no document of civilization which is not at the same time a document of barbarism" with its own sacrificial victims. Benjamin, "Theses on the Philosophy of History," 256–258.

13. Metz argues that suffering in history ruptures philosophical "systems" at large. He writes that "the least trace of meaningless suffering in the world we experience cancels all affirmative ontology and all teleology as untrue, and exposes them as a mythology of modern times." Johann Baptist Metz, "The Future in the Memory of Suffering," *Concilium* 76 (1972): 17.

14. The inappropriateness of claiming that God's suffering is representative of all human suffering—including Holocaust testimonies of suffering—is discussed with reference to Metz in Kenneth Surin, *Theology and the Problem of Evil* (Oxford: Basil Blackwell, 1986), 129–132.

15. Metz criticizes theological proposals that claim excessive knowledge of God's self as "gnostic," by which he means that they claim gnosis (knowledge or insight) of religious reality. Metz does not imply that they hold the views similar to the Gnostic religions of Roman times, combated as heresy by theologians of the early church, but that the tendency in ancient Gnosticism to propagate esoteric knowledge of the mysteries of God, good, and evil is reflected in theodicy (LS 95–96).

16. Elie Wiesel, *Night*, trans. Stella Rodway (New York: Bantam Books, 1960), 58–62. For theological commentary that rejects imposing redemptive meaning on the boy's suffering, but nevertheless interprets the passage as indicating God's nearness to those who suffer, see Dorothee Soelle, *Suffering*, trans. Everett R. Kalin (Philadelphia: Fortress Press, 1976), 145–150.

17. It is not Moltmann's *Theology of Hope* influenced by Bloch that Metz criticizes as much as Moltmann's later work in systematic theology following *The Crucified God* (TT 69–71).

18. Bloch does not accentuate the importance of memory. But since his development of the principle of hope is essentially a catalogue of hope narratives, it is clear that narrative memory is a major resource for examining the interplay between suffering and hope in Bloch's work. Metz accentuates the importance of narrative in Bloch's thought (SAN 103).

19. Metz's eschatological interpretation of the Bible is dependent on a particular hermeneutic of biblical exegesis represented emblematically in Gerhard von Rad's *Old Testament Theology*, vol. II, *The Theology of Israel's Prophetic Traditions* [1960], trans. D. M. G. Stalker (London: Oliver and Boyd, 1967), 114–124.

20. Metz's interpretation of the resurrection echoes Protestant theologian Wolfhart Pannenberg's insistence on its "proleptic" significance indicating the future fulfillment of God's Kingdom. Metz and Pannenberg are both representatives of the ecumenical "theology of hope" movement of the late 1960s. E. Frank Tupper, *The Theology of Wolfhart Pannenberg* (London: SCM Press, 1974), 241–259.

21. I have emphasized the role of biblical narrative as a dangerous memory, but, as a Roman Catholic thinker, Metz also considers church dogma as another source of dangerous memory (FHS 220).

22. While Adorno asserts that "the demand placed on thought" by redemption is crucial, he remarks that "the question of the reality or unreality of redemption itself hardly matters." Adorno secularizes the Jewish notion of hope for redemption and employs it as a critical idea that seems to lack real future possibility. Theodor W. Adorno, *Minima Moralia: Reflections from Damaged Life*, trans. E. F. N. Jephcott (London: NLB, 1974), 247.

23. The definition of freedom as conscious self-determination is not uniquely a Marxist concept. It is also authorized by thinkers who oppose Marxism, such as Isaiah

Berlin in his famous essay "Two Conceptions of Liberty," in *Four Essays on Liberty* [1958] (Oxford: Oxford University Press, 1979), 118–172.

24. Benjamin, "Theses on the Philosophy of History," 253–264. Benjamin combines Marxist and mystical meanings of redemption, equating the "messianic event" with revolution in history. He does not consider the anarchistic potential for violence of this expectation of joint political-religious redemption. On this issue see Rolf Tidemann, "Historical Materialism or Political Messianism?" *Telos* 15 (Fall–Winter 1983–1984): 71–104; and Richard Wolin, *Walter Benjamin: An Aesthetic of Redemption* (New York: Columbia University Press, 1982), 48–55.

25. Buber also stresses human participation in redemption (*tikkun*) where human beings restore creation to harmony with God by living lives guided by the I-Thou attitude.

26. Like Metz, Buber considers narratives as modeling faith postures. However, for Buber, biblical narratives recount and model I-Thou relation with the eternal Thou, while Metz prioritizes dangerous memories that provoke critical awareness. Interestingly, Metz explicitly agrees with Buber that religious narratives can have transformative power for individuals as well as collective import (SAN 103–105).

27. The ambiguity of the preposition "*aus*" is confirmed in the English translation of the phrase by J. Matthew Ashley in *A Passion for God: The Mystical-Political Dimension of Christianity* (New York: Paulist Press, 1997), 178.

28. In using the term "mystical," Metz is keen to dismantle the common assumption that mystical faith involves private religious experiences only and, moreover, that what is mystical is escapist and otherworldly in import (LS 84). His use of the term is a departure from its etymology based on the Greek verb "*muein*" ("to close one's eyes") that is associated with esoteric ancient Greek "mystery" religions. For discussion of definitions of mysticism, see Dorothee Soelle, *The Silent Cry* (Minneapolis: Fortress Press, 2001), 33–34. Soelle agrees with Metz that the mystical and political sides of faith are indispensable and complementary.

29. Metz uses the word "praxis" loosely as equivalent to "practice" with respect to the practices of memory, solidarity, hope, or prayer. For a discussion of "praxis" in political and liberation theology and the ambiguities of its definition, see Rebecca Chopp, *The Praxis of Suffering* (Maryknoll, NY: Orbis Books, 1992), 70.

30. In *The Crucified God*, Moltmann speaks of the "mysticism of the cross" where suffering (chosen and unchosen) can be made meaningful on the condition that persons consciously participate in Christ's mission. Jürgen Moltmann, *The Crucified God*, trans. R. A. Wilson and John Bowden (New York: Harper & Row, 1974), 45–53. Metz approves of Moltmann's presentation of Jesus' life as a paradigm for Christian praxis that includes both resistance and acceptance of suffering. What he objects to is Moltmann's approach to history in his Trinitarian systematic theology, as a form of theodicy.

CHAPTER SEVEN

1. Bloch's position on hope is preferred over Marcel's by liberation theologian Gustavo Gutiérrez, *A Theology of Liberation*, rev. ed. (Maryknoll, NY: Orbis Books, 1988), 123. In defense of Marcel, it must be noted that he does show some interest in improving society politically, most explicitly in his endorsement of the international peace movement known as the Moral Re-Armament movement, founded by Frank

Buchman of England and inspired by Gandhi's message of forgiveness and love. Nevertheless, Marcel clearly never abandons the existentialist position that individual change or conversion is the first step toward fixing social and political problems. See Marcel's introduction in Gabriel Marcel, ed., *Fresh Hope for the World: Moral Re-Armament in Action*, trans. Helen Hardinge (London: Longmans, 1960), 1–15.

2. Buber advocated creation of a binational Jewish and Palestinian state, and personally helped to build bridges of friendship with Palestinians. After the founding of the state of Israel in 1948, Buber defended the rights of Israel's Palestinian citizens. Bernard Susser, *Existence and Utopia: The Social and Political Thought of Martin Buber* (Toronto: Associated University Presses, 1981), 164–172.

3. For a critique of the shortcomings of political and liberation praxis in theology, see Rebecca Chopp, *The Praxis of Suffering* (Maryknoll, NY: Orbis Books, 1992), 144–148.

4. In tracing connections between existentialist and political continental approaches and Christian contextual theologies, I do not intend to deny or ignore the relevance of these approaches and authors for contemporary Jewish thought. Among the group of authors considered, Buber is the most prominent and influential, while Bloch is rarely discussed among recent Jewish thinkers. Regarding the relevance of the selected Christian authors on Jewish thought, Marcel is notable mainly due to the connections between his philosophy and that of Emmanuel Levinas, whereas Metz's post-Holocaust theology has been well received, but his methodology has not been influential on Jewish theologians.

5. The term "*Eingedenken*" used by Benjamin and Metz is not the common German word for "memory," which is "*Erinnerung.*" While *Erinnerung* refers to the factual repetition of stories of the past by rote, *Eingedenken* connotes a relationship of empathy that binds the subjects who remember in the present to the victims of the past. Helmut Peukert, *Science, Action and Fundamental Theology* (Cambridge: MIT Press, 1984), 207–208.

6. The intrinsic connection between reading and witnessing is developed using literary and psychoanalytic theory in Shoshana Felman and Dori Laub, *Testimony: Crises of Witnessing in Literature, Psychoanalysis, and History* (New York: Routledge, 1992), 108–113.

7. My critique of Metz's use of memory is indebted to the analysis of theological memory by post-Holocaust feminist theologian Flora A. Keshgegian, *Redeeming Memories: A Theology of Healing and Transformation* (Nashville: Abingdon Press, 2000), 135–143. Criticizing the insufficiency of Metz's position on memory and the feminist positions of Elizabeth Johnson, Elizabeth Schüssler Fiorenza, Sharon Welch, and Rita Nakashima Brock, Keshgegian argues convincingly that none of these theologians has dealt adequately with the role of memory in Christian faith responses to suffering.

8. The damaging effects of memory for Holocaust survivors have been extensively studied. For instance, see the psychological analysis of the impact of harmful memories on survivors in Lawrence L. Langer, *Holocaust Testimonies: The Ruins of Memory* (New Haven: Yale University Press, 1991), 204–205.

9. Keshgegian, *Redeeming Memories*, 121–125.

10. Sharon D. Welch, *A Feminist Ethic of Risk* (Minneapolis: Fortress Press, 1990), 139.

11. Sharon D. Welch, *Communities of Resistance and Solidarity: A Feminist Theology of Liberation* (Maryknoll, NY: Orbis Books, 1985), 35–42.

12. Welch finds a parallel between the aims of liberation theology and the political import of Foucault's philosophy. She points out that in his analysis of the penal system, Foucault uncovers the deceptions of institutional prison discourse where prisoners' voices are "subjugated knowledges" that are never heard, but that deserve attention. Michel Foucault, *Discipline and Punish: The Birth of the Prison* (New York: Vintage Books, 1979), cited in Welch, *Communities of Resistance and Solidarity*, 44.

13. Elie Wiesel, *A Jew Today*, trans. Marion Wiesel (New York: Random House, 1978), 14–19.

14. Dorothee Soelle, *Political Theology* (Philadelphia: Fortress Press, 1974), 87–88.

15. For a classic statement on theology as critical reflection on praxis, see Gutiérrez, *A Theology of Liberation*, 5–12.

16. Gustavo Gutiérrez, *We Drink from Our Own Wells: The Spiritual Journey of a People* (Maryknoll, NY: Orbis Books, 1995), 13–18.

17. Gutiérrez, *A Theology of Liberation*, 162–173.

18. The term "mujerista" theology was coined to indicate Hispanic feminist women's theology. Ada María Isasi-Díaz, "Solidarity: Love of Neighbor in the 1980s" in *Lift Every Voice: Constructing Christian Theologies from Underside*, ed. Susan Brooks Thistlethwaite and Mary Potter Engel (New York: Harper & Row, 1990), 31–39.

19. The resources of black women's literature are central to "womanist," or black feminist, responses to suffering in Katie Cannon, *Black Womanist Ethics* (Atlanta: Scholars Press, 1988); Emilie Townes, ed., *A Troubling in my Soul: Womanist Perspectives on Evil and Suffering* (Maryknoll, NY: Orbis Books, 1993); and Emilie Townes, *In a Blaze of Glory: Womanist Spirituality as Social Witness* (Nashville: Abingdon Press, 1995).

20. Welch, *A Feminist Ethic of Risk*, 15.

21. Darrell J. Fasching, *Narrative Theology After Auschwitz: From Alienation to Ethics* (Minneapolis: Fortress Press, 1992), 25.

22. James H. Cone, "An African-American Perspective on the Cross and Suffering," in *The Scandal of a Crucified World: Perspectives on the Cross and Suffering*, ed. Yacob Tesfai (Maryknoll, NY: Orbis Books, 1994), 59.

23. Kathleen M. Sands, *Escape from Paradise: Evil and Tragedy in Feminist Theology* (Minneapolis: Fortress Press, 1994), 138.

24. As Anthony Pinn has recently argued, based on black folklore, the novels of Richard Wright, rap lyrics, and other sources, "black humanism" is a persuasive alternative to black theological responses. Rejecting theodicy, his narrative nontheistic humanist response to suffering fosters empowerment by refusing to find anything positive in oppression. Anthony B. Pinn, *Why Lord? Suffering and Evil in Black Theology* (New York: Continuum, 1999), 139–158.

25. Ada María Isasi-Díaz, *En La Lucha, In the Struggle: A Hispanic Women's Liberation Theology* (Minneapolis: Fortress Press, 1993), 173–179.

26. Accounts of concentration camp life provide examples of immoral and selfish behavior warranted for the sake of survival. For example, see the works of Primo Levi, *The Drowned and the Saved* (New York: Summit Books, 1988); and *Survival in Auschwitz: The Nazi Assault on Humanity*, trans. Stuart Wolf (New York: Collier Books, 1958).

27. Welch, *A Feminist Ethic of Risk*, 138.

28. James Cone, *Black Theology and Black Power* (New York: Seabury Press, 1969), 38–49.

29. Cone, *Black Theology and Black Power*, 138. The multivalent meanings of the spirituals as texts of resistance and survival are analyzed positively by such writers as

Albert J. Raboteau, *Slave Religion* (New York: Oxford University Press, 1978), 243–266; and Cheryl Kirk-Duggan, *Exorcising Evil: A Womanist Perspective on the Spirituals* (Maryknoll, NY: Orbis Books, 1997), 57–77.

30. James H. Cone, *God of the Oppressed* (Maryknoll, NY: Orbis Books, 1977), 96.

31. Cone states that the debate between theoretical options of violence or nonviolence for Christians misplaces the primary issue, which is the recognition that violence is already institutionalized in American society against the oppressed. Cone, *God of the Oppressed*, 199–206.

32. For a comparison of King's nonviolence with James Cone's more militant black theology, see Noel Leo Erskine, *King Among the Theologians* (Cleveland: Pilgrim Press, 1994), 125–129.

33. Williams considers both "liberation" and "survival" types of religious hope as legitimate, but for womanist theologians survival hope seems most applicable to black women's suffering. Delores S. Williams, *Sisters in the Wilderness: The Challenge of Womanist God-Talk* (Maryknoll, NY: Orbis Books, 1996), 193–203.

34. Viktor Frankl, *Man's Search for Meaning*, trans. Ilse Lasch (New York: Simon and Schuster, 1984), 139–154.

35. David H. Hirsch and Eli Pfefferkorn, eds., *Justyna's Narrative*, trans. Roslyn Hirsch and David H. Hirsch (Amherst: University of Massachusetts Press, 1996).

36. Yehuda Bauer, *A History of the Holocaust* (Danbury, CT: Franklin Watts, 1982), 273–274.

37. For more extensive development of the idea of voluntary suffering, see Dorothee Soelle, *Suffering*, trans. Everett R. Kalin (Philadelphia: Fortress Press, 1975), 171–194.

38. Frankl writes, "Suffering had become a task on which we did not want to turn our backs. We had realized its hidden opportunities for achievement, the opportunities which caused the poet Rilke to write '*Wie viel ist aufzuleiden!*' [How much suffering there is to get through!]" He advises that individuals can create meaning in suffering by how they shape their lives and values, but this meaning does not necessarily involve reference to God. Frankl, *Man's Search for Meaning*, 82–87.

39. My definition of "mystical faith" is indebted to Soelle's portrayal of liberation mysticism, which democratizes the capacity for mysticism and exposes its political dimensions. Dorothee Soelle, *The Silent Cry: Mysticism and Resistance*, trans. Barbara and Martin Rumscheidt (Minneapolis: Fortress Press), 279–302.

40. Dorothee Soelle, *Thinking about God*, trans. John Bowden (Philadelphia: Trinity Press International, 1990), 171–186.

41. Martin Buber, *Ecstatic Confessions* [1909], ed. Paul Mendes-Flohr, trans. Esther Cameron (San Francisco: Harper and Row, 1985), 2. In *I and Thou* and his mature writings, Buber repudiates "mysticism" as antithetical to I-Thou faith that is rooted in everyday life (IT 130).

42. Soelle, *The Silent Cry*, 161–165.

43. Ibid., 11.

44. Ibid., 175–187.

45. In her embrace of everyday life as infused with the divine, Hillesum's mystical piety resembles Hasidic Jewish mysticism in the sense that both kinds of mysticism are resistance movements: either against the persecution and pogroms of Poland or against Nazi persecution during the Holocaust. This interesting comparison is explored, along

with the question of the "Jewishness" of Hillesum's faith, by Denise de Costa in *Anne Frank and Etty Hillesum: Inscribing Spirituality and Sexuality*, trans. Mischa F. C. Hoyinck and Robert E. Chesal (London: Rutgers University Press, 1998), 207–236.

46. Etty Hillesum, *An Interrupted Life: The Diaries of Etty Hillesum 1941–43*, ed. J. G. Gaarlandt (New York: Pocket Books, 1984), 238.

47. As Soelle puts it: "Human suffering can be endured in this oneness with the Father that Jesus put into words, in the indestructible certainty of the truth of a life lived for, and not against humanity." Soelle, *Suffering*, 140.

48. On this point, Soelle criticizes Moltmann, as well as mystic Simone Weil whose emphasis on the cross and affliction comes close to masochism. Soelle, *The Silent Cry*, 147–151. For Simone Weil's profound affirmation of nearness to God through suffering, see her essay "The Love of God and Affliction," in *Waiting for God* (New York: Harper and Row, 1951), 117–136.

49. This distinction between sympathetic "imitation" of Christ and mystical "participation" or identification with divine suffering is developed by Marilyn McCord Adams in "Horrendous Evils and the Goodness of God," *The Problem of Evil*, ed. Marilyn McCord Adams and Robert Merrihew Adams (Oxford: Oxford University Press, 1990), 219; and *Horrendous Evils and the Goodness of God* (Ithaca: Cornell University Press, 1999), 164–168.

50. Robert Gibbs, "Suspicions of Suffering," in *Christianity in Jewish Terms*, ed. Tikva Frymer-Kensky et al. (Boulder: Westview Press, 2000), 223–225.

51. Gustavo Gutiérrez, *On Job: God-Talk and the Suffering of the Innocent* (Maryknoll, NY: Orbis Books, 1995), 32–33 and 96–97.

52. The rejection of patriarchal images of deity and emphasis on divine immanence in response to evil are prevalent characteristics of feminist theology, including the writings of Soelle, *The Silent Cry*; Welch, *A Feminist Ethic of Risk*; Isabel Carter Heyward, *The Redemption of God* (New York: University Press of America, 1982); Marjorie Suchocki, *The End of Evil* (Albany: SUNY Press, 1988); and Sallie McFague, *Super, Natural Christians* (Minneapolis: Fortress Press, 1997).

CHAPTER EIGHT

1. For broad discussion of divine hiddenness, see Alexander Nava, "The Mystery of Evil and the Hiddenness of God," in *The Fascination of Evil*, ed. David Tracy and Herman Häring (Maryknoll, NY: Orbis Books, 1998), 74–84; James A. Keller, "The Hiddenness of God and the Problem of Evil," *International Journal for Philosophy of Religion* 37 (1995): 13–24; and Samuel Balentine, *The Hidden God* (New York: Oxford University Press, 1983).

2. There are strong parallels between Jewish and Christian understandings of God as infinite, mysterious, and transcendent. See the comparative essay by Jewish philosopher Peter Ochs, "The God of Jews and Christians," in *Christianity in Jewish Terms*, ed. Tikva Frymer-Kensky et al. (Boulder: Westview Press, 2000), 49–76.

3. Kant is contemptuous of emotional, charismatic, and mystical expressions of religious faith, which he terms, pejoratively, "*Schwärmerei*" (irrational fanaticism). Immanuel Kant, *Religion within the Boundaries of Mere Reason and Other Writings*, ed. and trans. Allen Wood and George DiGiovanni (London: Cambridge University Press, 1998), 166–170.

4. Kant holds that Job's faith is rooted solely in morality. Kant, "On the Miscarriage of All Philosophical Trials in Theodicy" [1791], in *Religion within the Boundaries of Mere Reason and Other Writings*, 26.

5. Emphasis on narrative provides an alternative to Enlightenment philosophical "illnesses" such as rationalism, objectivism, and foundationalism. Stanley Hauerwas and L. Gregory Jones, eds., *Why Narrative? Readings in Narrative Theology* (Grand Rapids: Eerdmans, 1989), 1–2.

6. The realist versus nonrealist debate occurs between Christian analytic philosophers, such as Kantian John Hick who holds that God is the ultimate *noumenon*, and nonrealist philosophers, such as D. Z. Phillips and Don Cupitt, who view God-language as describing human attitudes and not a superhuman divine being. John Hick, *An Interpretation of Religion* (New Haven: Yale University Press, 1989), 198–201; and D.Z. Phillips, "The Problem of Evil," in *Reason and Religion*, ed. Stuart C. Brown (Ithaca: Cornell University Press, 1977), 103–121. The practical continental thinkers studied do not enter into this debate, nor is debate over realism central in contemporary Jewish thought.

7. Dorothee Soelle, *Suffering*, trans. Everett R. Kalin (Minneapolis: Fortress Press, 1975), 121–150; and *Thinking about God*, trans. John Bowden (Philadelphia: Trinity Press International, 1990), 171–195.

8. There is a pronounced trend among Christian theologians to affirm divine suffering in response to the Holocaust, as catalogued by Thomas G. Weinandy in *Does God Suffer?* (Notre Dame: University of Notre Dame Press, 2000), ch. 1. Jewish post-Holocaust thinkers also employ the idea of divine suffering, sometimes with reference to Kabbalistic mysticism. For instance, see Abraham J. Heschel, *The Prophets*, vol. 2 (New York: Harper Torchbooks, 1962), 1–26; Elie Wiesel, "God's Suffering: A Commentary, in *All Rivers Run to the Sea* (London: HarperCollins, 1996), 103–105; Hans Jonas, "The Concept of God after Auschwitz: A Jewish Voice," in *Mortality and Morality: A Search for the Good After Auschwitz* (Evanston: Northwestern University Press, 1996), 131–143; and Eliezer Berkovits, "In the Beginning Was the Cry: A Midrash for Our Times," in *Holocaust: Religious and Philosophical Implications*, ed. John K. Roth and Michael Berenbaum (St. Paul: Paragon House, 1989), 296–301.

9. Kant, "On the Miscarriage of All Philosophical Trials in Theodicy," 18–23.

10. For instance, Plantinga explicitly states that philosophical attempts to mount a theodicy or a defense of God's goodness do not aim to be of help to those who suffer, to enable them to find peace, or to preserve faith in God. Alvin Plantinga, *God, Freedom and Evil* (Grand Rapids: Eerdmans, 1991), 29.

11. An analytic philosopher who affirms this insight has recently argued that religious belief should be held as "tentative" and open to revision. Robert McKim, *Religious Ambiguity and Religious Diversity* (Oxford: Oxford University Press, 2001).

12. Paul Ricoeur, "Towards a Narrative Theology," and "Evil, a Challenge to Philosophy and Theology," in *Figuring the Sacred*, ed. Mark I. Wallace (Minneapolis: Fortress Press, 1995), 236–248 and 258–266.

13. Clifford Geertz, "Religion as Cultural System," in *The Interpretation of Cultures* (New York: Basic Books, 1973), 87–125. Influenced by Geertz and the later writings of Ludwig Wittgenstein, various narrative schools of theology have developed since the 1970s among Jewish and Christian thinkers, alternately known as "cultural-linguistic," "postliberal," "postmodern," or "scriptural reasoning" approaches. Among numerous representatives, here is a brief list of thinkers who advocate a narrative orientation for

religious thought: Hans Frei, George Lindbeck, Stanley Hauerwas, Paul Ricoeur, David Burrell, Terrence Tilley, Michael Goldberg, Stephen Kepnes, Robert Gibbs, and Peter Ochs. Such narrative approaches open up nontheodicy modes for responding to evil and suffering.

14. The separation of theodicy from existential-practical issues in the work of prominent analytic philosophers Alvin Plantinga, John Hick, and Richard Swinburne is inconsistent and self-deceptive, as Michael Scott argues in "The Morality of Theodicies," *Religious Studies* 32 (1996): 1–13.

15. Marilyn McCord Adams, *Horrendous Evils and the Goodness of God* (Ithaca: Cornell University Press, 1999), 181–202.

16. Irving Greenberg, "Cloud of Smoke, Pillar of Fire," in *Auschwitz: Beginning of a New Era?*, ed. Eva Fleischner (New York: KTAV, 1977), 9–10.

17. If God permits suffering, then God is an "abuser," as argued convincingly using analogies between Holocaust survivors and child abuse victims, by Jewish thinker David Blumenthal in *Facing the Abusing God* (Louisville, KY: Westminster/John Knox Press, 1993).

18. Among the many Jewish and Christian responses to the Holocaust where theodicy is conspicuously rejected, here are two works that offer a helpful overview of objections and alternatives: Zachary Braiterman, *(God) After Auschwitz: Tradition and Change in Post-Holocaust Jewish Thought* (Princeton: Princeton University Press, 1998); and Kenneth Surin, *Theology and the Problem of Evil* (Oxford: Blackwell Publishers, 1986).

19. Viktor Frankl, *Man's Search for Meaning*, trans. Ilse Lasch (Boston: Beacon Press, 1959), 126–142.

20. My rejection of theodicy has been influenced by the thought of Jewish post-Holocaust philosopher Emmanuel Levinas, who insists that I must view the suffering of the other as "meaningless" and "useless" suffering. I agree with Levinas's conclusion that the suffering of the "Other" entails an asymmetrical responsibility on the part of the "I," and that this ethical responsibility "makes waiting for the saving actions of an all-powerful God impossible without degredation." Emmanuel Levinas, "Useless Suffering," in *The Provocation of Levinas*, ed. Robert Bernasconi and David Wood (New York: Routledge, 1988), 159.

21. Leora Batnitzky, "On the Suffering of God's Chosen," in *Christianity in Jewish Terms*, ed. Tikva Frymer-Kensky et al. (Boulder: Westview Press, 2000), 215–220.

22. James E. Young, "Against Redemption" in *Humanity at the Limit: The Impact of the Holocaust Experience on Jews and Christians*, ed. Michael A. Signer (Bloomington: Indiana University Press, 2000), 44–59.

23. Surin, *Theology and the Problem of Evil*, 142–151.

24. In using the term "declarative power" I am drawing on the speech act theory of J. L. Austin, which is applied by Terrence Tilley to analysis of the "evils" of theodicy. Tilley argues that theodicy is a declarative discourse operating with a dichotomy between moral and natural evil that construes structural social evils mistakenly as natural ones; hence, social evils are assumed to be beyond human control and resistance is neglected. Terrence W. Tilley, *The Evils of Theodicy* (Washington, DC: Georgetown University Press, 1991), 221–251.

25. Examples of attention to practice in liberation and feminist spiritualities of suffering are found in Dorothee Soelle, *Suffering* (Philadelphia: Fortress Press, 1975); Gustavo Gutiérrez, *We Drink from our own Wells: The Spiritual Journey of a People*

(Maryknoll, NY: Orbis, 1984); Robert McAfee Brown, *Spirituality and Liberation* (Philadelphia: Westminster Press, 1988); and Kristine M. Rankka, *Women and the Value of Suffering* (Collegeville, MN: Liturgical Press, 1998).

26. There is a convergence between Jewish theology and Christian liberation theologies in that both prioritize "orthopraxis" rather than prepositional "orthodoxy." Dan Cohn-Sherbok, *On Earth as it is in Heaven: Jews, Christians and Liberation Theology* (Maryknoll, NY: Orbis Books, 1987), 92–111. The most prolific Jewish liberation theologian is Marc H. Ellis, author of *Towards a Jewish Theology of Liberation* (Maryknoll, NY: Orbis, 1987); and *Ending Auschwitz: The Future of Jewish and Christian Life* (Louisville, KY: Westminster/John Knox Press, 1994). For a collection representing Jewish and Christian liberation thought, see Otto Maduro, ed., *Judaism, Christianity and Liberation: An Agenda for Dialogue* (Maryknoll, NY: Orbis Books, 1991).

27. Of the many books on Jewish post-Holocaust theology, I have found the following helpful in comparing different approaches to the memory of Auschwitz: Donald J. Dietrich, *God and Humanity in Auschwitz* (London: Transaction Publishers, 1995); Zachary Braiterman, *(God) After Auschwitz;* and Steven Kepnes, Peter Ochs, and Robert Gibbs, eds., *Reasoning After Revelation: Dialogues in Postmodern Jewish Philosophy* (Boulder: Westview Press, 1998).

28. Some authors who emphasize the importance of narrative for post-Holocaust theology are Michael Goldberg, *Jews and Christians: Getting our Stories Straight* (Nashville: Abingdon Press, 1985); Darrell J. Fasching, *Narrative Theology After Auschwitz* (Minneapolis: Fortress Press, 1992); Eliezer Berkovits, *With God in Hell* (New York: Sanhedrin, 1979); Steven Kepnes, *The Text as Thou: Martin Buber's Dialogical Hermeneutics and Narrative Theology* (Bloomington: Indiana University Press, 1992); and Henry F. Knight, *Confessing Christ in a Post-Holocaust World: A Midrashic Experiment* (Westport, CT: Greenwood Press, 2000).

29. Cheryl Kirk-Duggan, *Exorcising Evil: A Womanist Perspective on the Spirituals* (Maryknoll, NY: Orbis Books, 1997), 325–336.

30. Nicholas Wolterstorff, *Lament for a Son* (Grand Rapids: Eerdmans, 1987), 90. Interestingly, narrative thelogian Stanley Hauerwas quotes *Lament for a Son* in order to argue "on theological grounds against the very idea of theodicy as a theoretical enterprise." Stanley Hauerwas, *God Medicine and Suffering* (Grand Rapids: Eerdmans, 1990), xii.

31. Alison Owings, *Frauen: German Women Recall the Third Reich* (London: Rutgers University Press, 1993).

Selected Bibliography

Adams, Marilyn McCord. *Horrendous Evils and the Goodness of God.* Ithaca: Cornell University Press, 1999.

Adams, Marilyn McCord, and Robert Merrihew Adams, eds. *The Problem of Evil.* Oxford: Oxford University Press, 1990.

Adams, Pedro. "Marcel: Metaphysician or Moralist." *Philosophy Today* 10 (Fall 1966): 182–189.

Adorno, Theodor W., and Max Horkheimer. *Dialectic of Enlightenment.* Translated by John Cumming. New York: Continuum, 1982.

———. *Minima Moralia: Reflections from Damaged Life.* [1971] Translated by E. F. N. Jephcott. London: NLB, 1974.

———. *Negative Dialectics.* Translated by E. B. Ashton. New York: Seabury Press, 1973.

———. "Something's Missing: A Discussion between Ernst Bloch and Theodor W. Adorno on the Contradictions of Utopian Longing." In *The Utopian Function of Art and Literature,* edited and translated by Jack Zipes and Frank Mecklenburg. Cambridge: MIT Press, 1988.

Ancic, Nedjeljko. *Die 'Politische Theologie' von Johann Baptist Metz als Antwort auf die Herausforderung des Marxismus.* Frankfurt: Peter Lang, 1981.

Anderson, Thomas. "Gabriel Marcel's Notions of Being." *Philosophy Today* 19 (Spring 1975): 29–49.

Ashley, J. Matthew, ed. *A Passion for God: The Mystical-Political Dimension of Christianity.* New York: Paulist Press, 1997.

———. *Interruptions: Mysticism, Politics and Theology in the Work of Johann Baptist Metz.* Notre Dame: University of Notre Dame Press, 1998.

Bauckham, Richard J. *Moltmann: Messianic Theology in the Making.* Basingstoke, England: Marshall Morgan and Scott, 1987.

Bauer, Gerhard. *Christliche Hoffnung und menschlicher Fortschritt: Die Politische Theologie von J.G. Metz als theologische Begründung gesellschaftlicher Verantwortung des Christen.* Mainz: Matthias-Grünewald Verlag, 1976.

Belay, Marcel. *La Mort dans le Théâtre de Gabriel Marcel.* Paris: Librairie Philosophique J. Vrin, 1980.

Benjamin, Walter. "Theses on the Philosophy of History." [1940] In *Illuminations,* edited by Hannah Arendt and translated by Harry Zohn. New York: Schocken Books, 1969.

Berkovits, Eliezer. *Faith After the Holocaust.* New York: KTAV, 1973.

———. *A Jewish Critique of the Philosophy of Martin Buber.* Brooklyn: Balshon Printing and Offset, 1962.

————. *With God in Hell*. New York and London: Sanhedrin, 1979.

Bernasconi, Robert. "Failure of Communication as Surplus: Dialogue and Lack of Dialogue between Buber and Levinas." In *The Provocation of Levinas: Rethinking the Other*, edited by Robert Bernasconi and David Wood. London: Routledge, 1988.

Bielander, Raphael. *Martin Bubers Rede von Gott*. Bern: Herbert Lang, 1975.

Birnbaum, David. *God and Evil*. Hoboken, NJ: KTAV, 1989.

Bloch, Ernst. *Atheism in Christianity: Religion of Exodus and the Kingdom*. Translated by J. T. Swann. New York: Herder and Herder, 1972.

————. *Gesamtausgabe der Werke Ernst Bloch in sechzehn Bänden*. Frankfurt: Suhrkamp Verlag, 1959–1985.

————. *Man on His Own: Essays in the Philosophy of Religion*. Translated by E. B. Ashton. New York: Herder and Herder, 1970.

————. *On Karl Marx*. Translated by John Maxwell. New York: Herder and Herder, 1971.

————. *A Philosophy of the Future*. Translated by John Cumming. New York: Herder and Herder, 1970.

————. *The Principle of Hope*. Translated by N. and S. Plaice and P. Knight. Cambridge: MIT Press, 1986.

————. *Religion im Erbe: Eine Auswahl aus seinen religionsphilosophischen Schriften*. Hamburg: Siebenstern Taschenbuch Verlag, 1967.

————. *Thomas Münzer als Theologe der Revolution*. Frankfurt: Suhrkamp Verlag, 1962.

————. *The Utopian Function of Art and Literature*. Edited by Jack Zipes and Frank Mecklenburg. Cambridge: MIT Press, 1988.

Bloch, Jochanan, and Gordon Haim, eds. *Martin Buber: A Centenary Volume*. New York: KTAV, 1984.

Bollnow, Otto Friedrich. "Marcel's Concept of Availability." In *The Philosophy of Gabriel Marcel*, edited by Paul A. Schilpp and Lewis E. Hahn. La Salle, IL: Open Court Press, 1984.

Bonhoeffer, Dietrich. *Letters and Papers from Prison*. Edited by Eberhard Bethge. New York: Macmillan Publishing, 1971.

Boni, Sylvain. *The Self and the Other in the Ontologies of Sartre and Buber*. Washington, DC: University Press of America, 1982.

Bonino, Jose Miguez. *Doing Theology in a Revolutionary Situation*. Philadelphia: Fortress Press, 1975.

Borne, Gerhard F. *Christlicher Atheismus und Radikales Christentum*. Munich: Kaiser Verlag, 1979.

Braiterman, Zachary. *(God) After Auschwitz: Tradition and Change in Post-Holocaust Jewish Thought*. Princeton: Princeton University Press, 1998.

Breisach, Ernst. *Introduction to Modern Existentialism*. New York: Grove Press, 1962.

Breslauer, S. Daniel. *The Chrysalis of Religion: A Guide to the Jewishness of Buber's I and Thou*. Nashville: Abingdon Press, 1980.

————. *Martin Buber on Myth*. New York: Garland Publishing, 1990.

Brown, James. *Kierkegaard, Heidegger, Buber and Barth*. New York: Collier Books, 1955.

Brown, Robert McAfee. *Spirituality and Liberation*. Philadelphia: The Westminster Press, 1988.

Brown, Stuart C., ed. *Reason and Religion*. Ithaca: Cornell University Press, 1977.

Buber, Martin. *A Believing Humanism: My Testament, 1902–1965*. Translated by Maurice Friedman. New York: Simon and Schuster, 1965.

————. *Between Man and Man.* Translated by Ronald Gregor Smith. New York: Macmillan Publishing, 1965.

————. *For the Sake of Heaven.* Translated by Ludwig Lewisohn. New York: Meridian Books, 1958.

————. *Eclipse of God: Studies in the Relation between Religion and Philosophy.* New York: Harper and Brothers, 1952.

————. *Ecstatic Confessions.* Translated by Esther Cameron. New York: Harper and Row, 1985.

————. *Good and Evil.* New York: Charles Scribner's Sons, 1952.

————. *Hasidism and Modern Man.* Translated by Maurice Friedman. New York: Horizon Press, 1958.

————. *I and Thou.* Translated by Ronald Gregor Smith. New York: Macmillan Publishing, 1987.

————. *Israel and the World: Essays in a Time of Crisis.* New York: Schocken Books, 1948.

————. *Jewish Mysticism and the Legends of the Baal Shem.* Translated by Lucy Cohen. London: J. M. Dent and Sons, 1931.

————. *The Knowledge of Man: Selected Essays.* Edited and translated by Maurice Friedman and Ronald Gregor Smith. New York: Harper and Row, 1965.

————. *The Legend of the Baal Shem.* Translated by Maurice Friedman. New York: Harper and Brothers, 1955.

————. *Mamre: Essays in Religion.* Translated by Greta Hort. Melbourne: Melbourne University Press, 1946.

————. *On Judaism.* Edited by Nahum N. Glatzer. New York: Schocken Books, 1967.

————. *The Origin and Meaning of Hasidism.* Edited and translated by Maurice Friedman. New York: Horizon Press, 1960.

————. *Paths in Utopia.* Translated by R. F. C. Hull. Boston: Beacon Press, 1958.

————. *Pointing the Way: Collected Essays.* Edited and translated by Maurice Friedman. New York: Harper and Brothers, 1957.

————. *The Prophetic Faith.* Translated by Carlyle Witton-Davies. New York: Macmillan Publishing, 1949.

————. *The Tales of Rabbi Nachman.* Translated by Maurice Friedman. Atlantic Highlands, NJ: Humanities Press International, 1988.

————. *Two Types of Faith.* Translated by Norman P. Goldhawk. New York: Macmillan Publishing, 1951.

————. *The Way of Response: Martin Buber.* Edited by N. N. Glatzer. New York: Schocken Books, 1966.

Buck-Morss, Susan. *The Origin of Negative Dialectics: Theodor W. Adorno, Walter Benjamin and the Frankfurt Institute.* New York: The Free Press, 1977.

Busch, Thomas. "Gabriel Marcel: An Overview and Assessment." *Philosophy Today* 19 (Spring 1975): 4–11.

Cain, Seymour. *Gabriel Marcel.* South Bend: Regnery/Gateway, 1979.

————. *Gabriel Marcel's Theory of Religious Experience.* New York: Peter Lang, 1995.

Camus, Albert. *The Myth of Sisyphus and Other Essays.* Translated by Justin O'Brien. New York: Vintage Books, 1955.

Cannon, Katie. *Black Womanist Ethics.* Atlanta: Scholars Press, 1988.

Capps, Walter. *Time Invades the Cathedral.* Philadelphia: Fortress Press, 1972.

————, ed. *The Future of Hope*. Philadelphia: Fortress Press, 1970.

Cassell. Eric. J. *The Nature of Suffering and the Goals of Medicine*. New York: Oxford University Press, 1991.

Chopp, Rebecca. *The Praxis of Suffering: An Interpretation of Liberation and Political Theologies*. Maryknoll, NY: Orbis Books, 1986.

Clark, Gary. "God and Experience: Rejuvenation, Hope, Participation." *Philosophy Today* 19 (Spring 1975): 68–75.

Cohen, Arthur. *Martin Buber*. New York: Hillary House, 1957.

Cohn-Sherbok, Daniel. *Holocaust Theology*. London, Lamp, 1989.

————. *On Earth as it is in Heaven: Jews, Christians and Liberation Theology*. Maryknoll, NY: Orbis Books, 1987.

Collins, James. *The Existentialists*. Chicago: Henry Regnery Company, 1968.

Columbo, J. A. *An Essay on Theology and History: Studies in Pannenberg, Metz and the Frankfurt School*. Atlanta: Scholars Press, 1990.

Cone, James H. *Black Theology and Black Power*. New York: Seabury Press, 1969.

————. *God of the Oppressed*. San Francisco: Harper, 1975.

Conyers, A. J. *God, Hope, and History: Jürgen Moltmann and the Christian Concept of History*. Macon, GA: Mercer University Press, 1988.

Cooey, Paula M. et al., eds. *After Patriarchy: Feminist Transformations of the World Religions*. Maryknoll, NY: Orbis Books, 1998.

Cooney, William, ed. *Contributions of Gabriel Marcel to Philosophy*. Lewiston, ME: Edwin Mellen Press, 1989.

Cooper, David E. *Existentialism: A Reconstruction*. Oxford: Basil Blackwell, 1990.

Cousins, E. H., ed. *Hope and the Future of Man*. Philadelphia: Fortress Press, 1972.

Crysdale, Cynthia S. W. *Embracing Travail: Retrieving the Cross Today*. New York: Continuum, 1999.

Damus, Renate. *Ernst Bloch: Hoffnung als Prinzip—Prinzip ohne Hoffnung*. Meisenheim am Glan: Verlag Anton Hein, 1971.

Davignon, René. *Le Mal chez Gabriel Marcel: Comment Affronter la Souffrance et la Mort?* Montréal: Éditions Bellarmin, 1985.

Desan, Willfrid. *The Marxism of Jean Paul Sartre*. New York: Anchor Books, 1966.

Deuser, Hermann, ed. *Ernst Blochs Vermittlungen zur Theologie*. Mainz: Matthias-Grünewald Verlag, 1983.

Diamond, Malcolm. *Martin Buber, Jewish Existentialist*. New York: Harper and Row, 1968.

Dietrich, Donald J. *God and Humanity in Auschwitz*. London: Transaction Publishers, 1995.

Draenger, Gusta Davidson. *Justyna's Narrative*. Edited by Eli Pfefferkorn and David H. Hirsch. Translated by Roslyn Hirsch and David H. Hirsch. Amherst: University of Massachusetts Press, 1996.

Eckert, Michael. *Transzendieren und immanente Transzendenz*. Vienna: Herder, 1981.

Edwards, Paul. *Buber and Buberism: A Critical Evaluation*. Kansas City: University of Kansas, 1970.

Ellis, Marc. *Ending Auschwitz: The Future of Jewish and Christian Life*. Louisville, KY: Westminster/John Knox Press, 1994.

Fackenheim, Emil. *God's Presence in History*. New York: Harper Torchbooks, 1972.

————. *To Mend the World: Foundations of Future Jewish Thought*. New York: Schocken Books, 1978.

Fahrenbach, Helmut, et al. *Laboratorium salutis*. Stuttgart: Dieter Gross, 1985.

Farley, Margaret. *Personal Commitments*. New York: Harper and Row, 1986.

Farley, Wendy. *Tragic Vision and Divine Compassion: A Contemporary Theodicy*. Louisville: Westminster/John Knox Press, 1990.

Fasching, Darrell J. *Narrative Theology After Auschwitz: From Ethics to Alienation*. Minneapolis: Fortress Press, 1992.

Felman, Shoshana, and Dori Laub. *Testimony: Crises of Witnessing in Literature, Psychoanalysis, and History*. New York: Routledge, 1992.

Feuerbach, Ludwig. *The Essence of Christianity*. Translated by George Eliot. New York: Harper and Row, 1957.

Fiorenza, Francis. "Dialectical Theology and Hope." *Heythrop Journal of Theology* 9 (1968): 142–163 and 384–399; 10 (1969): 26–42.

Fleischner, Eva, ed. *Auschwitz: Beginning of a New Era?* New York: KTAV, 1977.

Frankl, Viktor E. *Man's Search for Meaning: An Introduction to Logotherapy*. Third edition. Translated by Ilse Lasch. New York: Simon and Schuster, 1984.

Friedman, George. *The Political Philosophy of the Frankfurt School*. Ithaca: Cornell University Press, 1981.

Friedman, Maurice. *Abraham Joshua Heschel and Elie Wiesel: You Are My Witnesses*. New York: Farrar, Straus and Giroux, 1987.

———. "The Human Dimension of Evil." *Journal of Pastoral Counselling* 25 (1990): 26–36.

———. *Martin Buber: The Life of Dialogue*. New York: Harper and Brothers, 1960.

———. *Martin Buber and the Eternal*. New York: Human Sciences Press, Inc., 1986.

———. *Martin Buber's Life and Work*. Vol. I, *The Early Years, 1878–1923*. Vol II, *The Middle Years, 1923–1945*. Vol III, *The Later Years, 1945–1965*. New York: Dutton, 1981–1983.

Fromm, Erich. *To Have or to Be?* New York: Harper and Row, 1976.

Frymer-Kensky, Tikva et al., eds. *Christianity in Jewish Terms*. Boulder: Westview Press, 2000.

Gallagher, Kenneth T. *The Philosophy of Gabriel Marcel*. New York: Fordham University Press, 1962.

Geertz, Clifford. *The Interpretation of Cultures*. New York: Basic Books, 1973.

Geoghegan, Vincent. *Ernst Bloch*. London: Routledge, 1996.

Gerber, Rudolph J. "Marcel and the Experiential Road to Metaphysics." *Philosophy Today* 12 (Winter 1968): 262–281.

Gibbs, Robert. "Substitution: Marcel and Levinas." In *Correlations in Rosenzweig and Levinas*. Princeton: Princeton University Press, 1992.

Gillman, Neil. *Gabriel Marcel on Religious Knowledge*. Washington, DC: University Press of America, 1980.

Gilson, Étienne. *Existentialisme Chrétien: Gabriel Marcel*. Paris: Librairie Plon, 1947.

Glatzer, Nahum N. *Baeck-Buber-Rosenzweig: Reading the Book of Job*. New York: Leo Baeck Institute, 1966.

Gollwitzer, Helmut. *Die marxistische Religionskritik und der christliche Glaube*. Frankfurt: Siebenstern Taschenbuch, 1974.

Gouhier, Henri, ed. *Gabriel Marcel et la Pensée Allemande*. Paris: Presence de Gabriel Marcel, 1979.

Greenberg, Irving. "Cloud of Smoke, Pillar of Fire: Judaism, Christianity and Modernity after the Holocaust." In *Auschwitz: Beginning of a New Era*. Edited by Eva Fleischner. New York: KTAV, 1977.

Grimsley, Ronald. *Existentialist Thought*. Cardiff: University of Wales Press, 1967.

Guenther, Titus F. *Rahner and Metz: Transcendental Theology as Political Theology*. New York: Lanham, 1994.

Gutiérrez, Gustavo. *A Theology of Liberation: History, Politics and Salvation*. Translated by Caridad Inda and John Eagleson. Maryknoll, NY: Orbis Books, 1988.

———. *On Job: God-Talk and the Suffering of the Innocent*. Translated by Matthew J. O'Connell. Maryknoll, NY: Orbis Books, 1987.

———. *We Drink from Our Own Wells: The Spiritual Journey of a People*. Translated by Matthew J. O'Connell. Maryknoll, NY: Orbis Books, 1995.

Häring, Hermann. *Das Problem des Bösen in der Theologie*. Darmstadt: Wissenschaftliche Buchgesellschaft, 1985.

Hanley, Katharine Rose. *Dramatic Approaches to Creative Fidelity*. Boston: University Press of America, 1987.

Hauerwas, Stanley. *God, Medicine and Suffering*. Grand Rapids: Eerdmans, 1990.

———. "Story and Theology." In *Truthfulness and Tragedy*. Notre Dame: University of Notre Dame Press, 1977.

Hazelton, R. "Marcel on Mystery." *Journal of Religion* 38 (July 1958): 52–78.

Hegel, G. W. F. *Lectures on the Philosophy of History*. Translated by J. Sibree. New York: Dover Publications, 1956.

Heschel, Abraham Joshua. *Man Is Not Alone: A Philosophy of Religion*. Philadelphia: Jewish Publication Society, 1951.

———. *The Prophets*. Philadelphia: Jewish Publication Society, 1962.

Hewitt, Marsha Aileen. *Critical Theory of Religion: A Feminist Analysis*. Minneapolis: Fortress Press, 1995.

Heyward, Isabel Carter. *The Redemption of God: A Theology of Mutual Relation*. Landham, MD: University Press of America, 1982.

Hick, John. *Evil and the God of Love*. London: Fontana, 1968.

———. *An Interpretation of Religion: Human Responses to the Transcendent*. New Haven: Yale University Press, 1989.

Hillesum, Etty. *An Interrupted Life: The Diaries of Etty Hillesum, 1941–43*. Edited by J. G. Gaarlandt. New York: Pocket Books, 1984.

Holz, Heinz Hans. *Logos Spermatikos: Ernst Blochs Philosophie der unfertigen Welt*. Darmstadt: Herman Luchterhand, 1975.

Horkheimer, Max, and Theodor W. Adorno. *Dialectic of Enlightenment*. Translated by John Cumming. New York: Seabury Press, 1972.

Hudson, Wayne. *The Marxist Philosophy of Ernst Bloch*. New York: St. Martin's Press, 1982.

Inbody, Tyron L. *The Transforming God: An Interpretation of Suffering and Evil*. Louisville, KY: Westminster/John Knox Press, 1997.

Isasi-Díaz, Ada María. *En La Lucha/In the Struggle: A Hispanic Women's Liberation Theology*. Minneapolis: Fortress Press, 1993.

———. "Solidarity: Love of Neighbor in the 1980s." In *Lift Every Voice: Constructing Christian Theologies from Underside*, edited by Susan Brooks Thistlethwaite and Mary Potter Engel. New York: Harper and Row, 1990.

Jäger, Alfred. *Reich ohne Gott*. Zurich: EVZ-Verlag, 1969.

Janssen, Hans-Gerd. *Das Theodizee-Problem der Neuzeit: Ein Beitrag zur historisch-systematischen Grundlegung politischer Theologie*. Frankfurt: Peter Lang, 1982.

Jay, Martin. *Marxism and Totality*. Berkeley: University of California Press, 1984.

Jones, Paul Miller. *Assembling (Post)modernism: The Utopian Philosophy of Ernst Bloch.* New York: Peter Lang, 1995.

Joseph, Dominic Anton. *Self-Realization and Intersubjectivity in Gabriel Marcel.* Rome: Tipografica Armellini, 1988.

Kant, Immanuel. *Critique of Practical Reason.* Translated by Lewis White Beck. New York: Macmillan Publishing, 1993.

———. *Critique of Pure Reason.* Translated by Norman Kemp Smith. London: Macmillan Publishing, 1956.

———. *Religion within the Boundaries of Mere Reason and Other Writings.* Translated and edited by Allen Wood and George DiGiovanni. London: Cambridge University Press, 1998.

Katz, Steven T. *Post-Holocaust Dialogues: Critical Studies in Modern Jewish Thought.* New York: New York University Press, 1983.

Kelly, Andrew. "Reciprocity and the Height of God: A Defence of Buber against Levinas." *Sophia* 34 (March–April, 1995): 65–73.

Kepnes, Steven. *The Text as Thou: Martin Buber's Dialogical Hermeneutics and Narrative Theology.* Bloomington: Indiana University Press, 1992.

Kepnes, Steven, Peter Ochs, and Robert Gibbs. *Reasoning After Revelation: Dialogues in Postmodern Jewish Philosophy.* Boulder: Westview Press, 1998.

Kerstiens, Ferdinand. *Die Hoffnungsstruktur des Glaubens.* Mainz: Matthias-Grünewald Verlag, 1969.

Keshgegian, Flora A. *Redeeming Memories: A Theology of Healing and Transformation.* Nashville: Abingdon Press, 2000.

Kimmerle, Heinz. *Die Zukunftsbedeutung der Hoffnung.* Bonn: Bouvier Verlag, 1966.

Kirk-Duggan, Cheryl A. *Exorcizing Evil: A Womanist Perspective on the Spirituals.* Maryknoll, NY: Orbis Books, 1997.

Kleinman, Arthur. "Everything that Really Matters: Social Suffering, Subjectivity, and the Remaking of Human Experience in a Disordering World." *Harvard Theological Review* 90 (July 1997): 315–335.

Koselleck, R., and W. D. Stempel, eds. *Geschichte, Ereignis und Erzählung.* Munich: Kaiser Verlag, 1972.

Kruttschnitt, Elke. *Ernst Bloch und das Christentum: Der geschichtliche Prozeß und der philosophische Begriff der 'Religion des Exodus und des Reiches'.* Mainz: Matthias-Grünewald Verlag, 1993.

Lakeland, Paul. *Theology and Critical Theory.* Nashville: Abingdon Press, 1990.

Langer, Lawrence L. *Holocaust Testimonies: The Ruins of Memory.* New Haven: Yale University Press, 1991.

Lapointe, François H., and Claire C. Lapointe. *Gabriel Marcel and His Critics: An International Bibliography (1928–1976).* New York: Garland Publishing, 1977.

Lash, Nicholas. *A Matter of Hope: A Theologian's Reflections on the Thought of Karl Marx.* Notre Dame: University of Notre Dame Press, 1982.

Lazaron, Hilda. *Gabriel Marcel the Dramatist.* Gerrards Cross, England: Colin Smythe, 1978.

Leibniz, Gottfried Wilhelm. *Essais de Theodicée sur la bonté de Dieu, la liberté de l'homme et l'origine du mal.* Paris: Erdmann, 1946.

Lenhardt, Christian. "Anamnestic Solidarity: The Proletariat and Its Manes." *Telos* 25 (Fall 1975): 133–154.

Levi, Primo. *Survival in Auschwitz: The Nazi Assault on Humanity.* Translated by Stuart Woolf. New York: Collier, 1993.

Levinas, Emmanuel. "La Pensée de Martin Buber et le Judaisme Contemporain." In *Martin Buber: L'Homme et le Philosophe*, edited by Gabriel Marcel. Brussels: Editions de l'Institut de Sociologie de l'Université Libre de Bruxelles, 1968.

―――. "Martin Buber, Gabriel Marcel and Philosophy." In *Martin Buber: A Centenary Volume*, edited by Haim Gordon and Joachanan Bloch. New York: KTAV, 1984.

―――. "Useless Suffering." In *The Provocation of Levinas: Rethinking the Other*, edited by Robert Bernasconi and David Wood. London: Routledge, 1988.

Löwith, Karl. *Weltgeschichte und Heilsgeschehen*. Stuttgart: Metzler, 1953.

Mackie, J. L. "Evil and Omnipotence," In *The Problem of Evil*, edited by Marilyn McCord Adams and Robert Merrihew Adams. Oxford: Oxford University Press, 1990.

Marcel, Gabriel. "L'Anthropologie Philosophique de Martin Buber." In *Martin Buber: L'Homme et le Philosophe*. Brussels: Editions de l'Institut de Sociologie de L'Université Libre de Bruxelles, 1968.

―――. "An Autobiographical Essay." In *The Philosophy of Gabriel Marcel*, edited by Paul A. Schilpp and Lewis E. Hahn. La Salle, IL: Open Court Press, 1983.

―――. *Being and Having: An Existentialist Diary*. Translated by Katherine Farrer. New York: Harper and Row Publishers, 1965.

―――. *Cinq Pièces Majeures*. Paris: Plon, 1973.

―――. "Contemporary Atheism and the Religious Mind." *Philosophy Today* 4 (Winter 1960): 252–262.

―――. *Creative Fidelity*. Translated by Robert Rosthal. New York: Farrar, Straus and Co., 1964.

―――. *The Decline of Wisdom*. New York: Philosophical Library, 1955.

―――. *The Existential Background of Human Dignity: The William James Lectures*. Cambridge: Harvard University Press, 1963.

―――. *Homo Viator: Introduction to a Metaphysic of Hope*. Translated by Emma Crawfurd. Chicago: Henry Regnery Co., 1951.

―――. *The Influence of Psychic Phenomena on my Philosophy*. London: Society for Psychical Research, 1955.

―――. *Man Against Humanity*. Translated by G. S. Fraser. London: Harvill Press Ltd., 1952.

―――. *Metaphysical Journal*. Translated by Bernard Wall. Chicago: Henry Regnery Co., 1952.

―――. *The Mystery of Being*. Vol. I, *Reflection and Mystery*. Vol. II, *Faith and Reality*. South Bend: Gateway Editions, 1950.

―――. *The Philosophy of Existentialism*. Translated by Manya Harari. New York: Citadel Press, 1956.

―――. *Presence and Immortality*. Translated by Michael A. Machado. Pittsburgh: Duquesne University Press, 1967.

―――. *Problematic Man*. Translated by Brian Thompson. New York: Herder and Herder, 1967.

―――. *Three Plays: A Man of God, Ariadne, The Funeral Pyre*. New York: Hill and Wang, 1958.

―――. *Tragic Wisdom and Beyond, including Conversations between Paul Ricoeur and Gabriel Marcel*. Translated by Stephen Jolin and Peter McCormick. Evanston: Northwestern University Press, 1973.

————, ed. *Fresh Hope for the World: Moral Re-Armament in Action.* Translated by Helen Harding. London: Longmans, 1960.

Marsch, Wolf-Dieter, ed. *Diskussion über die 'Theologie der Hoffnung' von Jürgen Moltmann.* Munich: Kaiser Verlag, 1967.

Matic, Marko. *Jürgen Moltmanns Theologie in Auseinandersetzung mit Ernst Bloch.* Frankfurt: Peter Lang, 1983.

McCarthy, Donald. "Marcel's Absolute Thou." *Philosophy Today* 10 (Fall 1966): 175–181.

McCown, Joe. *Availability: Gabriel Marcel and the Phenomenology of Human Openness.* Missoula, MT: Scholars Press, 1978.

McLellan, David, ed. *Karl Marx: Selected Writings.* Oxford: Oxford University Press, 1977.

————. *The Thought of Karl Marx: An Introduction.* Third Edition. London: Macmillan, 1995.

Meeks, M. Douglas. *Origins of the Theology of Hope.* Philadelphia: Fortress Press, 1974.

Mendes-Flohr, Paul. *From Mysticism to Dialogue: Martin Buber's Transformation of German Social Thought.* Detroit: Wayne State University Press, 1989.

Metz, Johann Baptist, "Communicating a Dangerous Memory." In *Communicating a Dangerous Memory: Soundings in Political Theology,* edited by Fred Lawrence. Atlanta: Scholars Press, 1987.

————. *The Emergent Church: The Future of Christianity in a Postbourgeois World.* New York: Crossroad, 1981.

————. *Faith in History and Society.* Translated by David Smith. New York: Seabury Press, 1980.

————. *Followers of Christ: The Religious Life and the Church.* Translated by Thomas Linton. New York: Paulist Press, 1978.

————. "Gott vor uns: Statt eines theologischen Arguments." In *Ernst Bloch zu ehren,* edited by Siegfried Unseld. Frankfurt: Suhrkamp, 1965.

————. "Plädoyer für mehr Theodizee-Emfindlichkeit in der Theologie." In *Worüber man nicht schweigen kann: Neue Diskussionen zur Theodizeefrage,* edited by Willi Oelmüller. Munich: Wilhelm Fink Verlag, 1992.

————. *Poverty in Spirit.* New York: Paulist Press, 1968.

————. "A Short Apology of Narrative." In *Love's Strategy: The Political Theology of Johann Baptist Metz,* edited by John K. Downey. Harrisburg, PA: Trinity Press International, 1999.

————. "Theodizee-empfindliche Gottesrede." In *Landschaft aus Schreien: Zur Dramatik der Theodizeefrage,* edited by Johann Baptist Metz. Mainz: Matthias-Grünewald Verlag, 1995.

————. *Theology of the World.* Translated by William Glen-Doepel. New York: Herder and Herder, 1969.

————. "Theology as Theodicy?" In *A Passion for God: The Mystical-Political Dimension of Christianity,* edited and translated by J. Matthew Ashley. New York: Paulist Press, 1998.

————. "Theologie versus Polymythie oder Apologie der Einfalt." In *Einheit und Vielheit,* edited by Odo Marquard. Hamburg: Feliz Meiner Verlag, 1987.

————. *Unterbrechungen: Theologisch-politische Perspektiven und Profile.* Gütersloh: Gütersloher Verlagshaus, 1981.

————. *Zum Begriff der neuen Politischen Theologie 1967–1997*. Mainz: Matthias-Grünewald Verlag, 1997.

————, ed. *Christianity and the Bourgeoisie*. New York: The Seabury Press, 1979.

————, ed. *Die Theologie der Befreiung: Hoffnung oder Gefahr für die Kirche?* Düsseldorf: Patmos Verlag, 1986.

Metz, Johann Baptist, and Hans-Eckehard Bahr. *Augen für die Anderen: Latainamerika—eine theologische Erfahrung*. Munich: Kindler Verlag, 1991.

Metz, Johann Baptist, and Jürgen Moltmann. *Faith and the Future: Essays on Theology, Solidarity and Modernity*. Maryknoll, NY: Orbis Books, 1995.

————, *Meditations on the Passion*. New York: Paulist Press, 1979.

Metz, Johann Baptist, Jürgen Moltmann, and Willi Oelmüller. *Kirche im Prozeß der Aufklärung: Aspekte einer neuen politischen Theologie*. Mainz: Kaiser-Grünewald Verlag, 1970.

Metz, Johann Baptist, and Tiemo Rainer Peters. *Gottespassion: Zur Ordensexistenz heute*. Freiburg: Herder, 1991.

Miceli, Vincent P. *Ascent to Being: Gabriel Marcel's Philosophy of Communion*. New York: Desclee Company, 1965.

Michalson, Carl, ed. *Christianity and the Existentialists*. New York: Charles Scribner's Sons, 1956.

Miranda, Juan Peter. *Wider die Gotzen—für das utopische Potential der Religion: zur Religionskritik Ernst Blochs*. Frankfurt: Peter Lang, 1987.

Moltmann, Jürgen. *The Coming of God*. Translated by Margaret Kohl. Minneapolis: Fortress Press, 1996.

————. *The Crucified God*. Translated by R. A. Wilson and John Bowden. Minneapolis: Fortress Press, 1993.

————. *The Experiment Hope*. Translated by M. Douglas Meeks. Philadelphia: Fortress Press, 1975.

————. *Hope and Planning*. Translated by Margaret Clarkson. New York: Harper and Row, 1968.

————. *Im Gespräch mit Ernst Bloch*. Munich: Kaiser Verlag, 1976.

————. *Religion, Revolution and the Future*. Translated by M. Douglas Meeks. New York: Charles Scribner's Sons, 1969.

————. *Theology of Hope*. Translated by James W. Leitch. New York: Harper and Row, 1967.

————. *Umkehr zur Zukunft*. Munich: Kaiser Verlag, 1970.

Moran, Denis P. *Gabriel Marcel: Existentialist Philosopher, Dramatist, Educator*. New York: University Press of America, 1992.

Morse, Christopher. *The Logic of Promise in Moltmann's Theology*. Philadelphia: Fortress Press, 1979.

Münster, Arno. *Ernst Bloch: Messianisme et Utopie*. Paris: Presses Universitaires de France, 1989.

————. *Figures de l'Utopie dans la Pensee d'Ernst Bloch*. Paris: Aubier, 1984.

————, ed. *Tagträume vom aufrechten Gang: Sechs Interviews mit Ernst Bloch*. Frankfurt: Suhrkamp Verlag, 1977.

Noddings, Nel. *Caring: A Feminine Approach to Ethics and Moral Education*. Berkeley: University of California Press, 1984.

————. *Women and Evil*. Berkeley: University of California Press, 1989.

Oelmüller, Willi, ed. *Theodizee—Gott vor Gericht?* Munich: Wilhelm Fink Verlag, 1990.

————, ed. *Worüber man nicht schweigen kann: neue Diskussionen zur Theodizeefrage.* Munich: Fink Verlag, 1994.

Oesterreicher, John M. *The Unfinished Dialogue: Martin Buber and the Christian Way.* New York: Philosophical Library, 1986.

O'Malley, John B. *The Fellowship of Being.* The Hague: Martinus Nijhoff, 1966.

O'Regan, Cyril. *The Heterodox Hegel.* Albany: State University of New York Press, 1994.

Owings, Alison. *Frauen: German Women Recall the Third Reich.* London: Rutgers University Press, 1993.

Pannenberg, Wolfhart. *Theology and the Kingdom of God.* Philadelphia: Westminster Press, 1969.

Parain-Vial, Jeanne. "Notes on the Ontology of Gabriel Marcel." *Philosophy Today* 12 (Winter 1960): 271–277.

Pax, Clyde. *An Existential Approach to God: A Study of Gabriel Marcel.* The Hague: Martinus Nijhoff, 1972.

Peukert, Helmut. *Science, Action and Fundamental Theology: Toward a Theology of Communicative Action.* Translated by James Bohman. Cambridge: MIT Press, 1984.

————, ed. *Diskussion zur 'Politischen Theologie'.* Mainz: Matthaias-Grünewald Verlag, 1969.

Pinn, Anthony B. *Why Lord? Suffering and Evil in Black Theology.* New York: Continuum, 1995.

Place, Jean Michel. *Gabriel Marcel - interrogé par Pierre Boutang.* Paris: Archives du XXe Siècle, 1977.

Plantinga, Alvin C. *God, Freedom and Evil.* Grand Rapids: Eerdmans, 1974.

Plattel, Martin G. *Utopian and Critical Thinking.* Pittsburgh: Duquesne University Press, 1972.

Plourde, Simonne. *Gabriel Marcel: Philosophe et Témoin de L'Espérance.* Montréal: Les Presses de l'Université du Québec, 1975.

————. *Vocabulaire Philosophique de Gabriel Marcel.* Montréal: Éditions Bellarmin, 1985.

Prini, Pietro. *Gabriel Marcel.* Paris: Economica, 1984.

Rankka, Kristine M. *Women and the Value of Suffering: An Aw(e)ful Rowing Toward God.* Collegeville, MN: Liturgical Press, 1998.

Reinicke, Helmut. *Materie und Revolution.* Kronberg: Scriptor Verlag, 1974.

Richard, Lucien. *What Are They Saying about the Theology of Suffering?* New York: Paulist Press, 1992.

Ricoeur, Paul. "Evil, a Challenge to Philosophy and Theology." In *Figuring the Sacred,* edited by Mark I. Wallace. Minneapolis: Fortress Press, 1995.

————. *Gabriel Marcel and Karl Jaspers.* Paris: Éditions du Temps Présent, 1947.

————. "Gabriel Marcel and Phenomenology." In *The Philosophy of Gabriel Marcel,* edited by Paul A. Schilpp and Lewis E. Hahn. La Salle, IL: Open Court Press, 1984.

————. "Ideology and Utopia as Cultural Imagination." In *Being Human in a Technological Age,* edited by Donald M. Borchert and David Stewart. Athens: Ohio University Press, 1979.

Roberts, David E. *Existentialism and Religious Belief.* New York: Oxford University Press, 1959.

Roberts, Richard H. *Hope and Its Hieroglyph: A Critical Decipherment of Ernst Bloch's Principle of Hope.* Atlanta: Scholars Press, 1990.

Rome, Sydney, and Beatrice Rome. *Philosophical Interrogations*. New York: Holt, Rinehart and Winston, 1964.

Rottländer, Peter, ed. "Politische Theologie und die Herausforderung des Marxismus. Ein Gespräch des Herausgebers mit Johann Baptist Metz." In *Theologie der Befreiung und Marxismus*. Münster: Edition Liberación, 1986.

Rubenstein, Richard L. *After Auschwitz: Response to Catastrophe in Modern Jewish Culture*. Indianapolis: Bobbs-Merrill, 1966.

———. *The Cunning of History*. New York: Harper and Row, 1975.

Sacquin, Michèle, ed. *Gabriel Marcel: Colloque*. Paris: Bibliotheque Nationale, 1989.

Samuelson, Norbert M. *An Introduction to Modern Jewish Philosophy*. Albany: State University of New York Press, 1989.

Sands, Kathleen M. *Escape from Paradise: Evil and Tragedy in Feminist Theology*. Minneapolis: Fortress Press, 1994.

Sartre, Jean Paul. *Critique de la Raison Dialectique: Theorie des Ensembles Pratique*. Paris: Gallimard, 1960.

Scarry, Elaine. *The Body in Pain: The Making and Unmaking of the World*. New York: Oxford University Press, 1985.

Schaeder, Grete. *The Hebrew Humanism of Martin Buber*. Translated by Noah J. Jacobs. Detroit: Wayne State University Press, 1973.

Schaeffler, Richard. *Was Dürfen Wir Hoffen?* Darmstadt: Wissenschaftliche Buchgesellschaft, 1979.

Schillebeeckx, Edward, ed. *Mystik und Politik: Theologie im Ringen um Geschichte und Gesellschaft, Johann Baptist Metz zu Ehren*. Mainz: Matthias-Grünewald Verlag, 1988.

Schiwy, Günther. *Abschied vom allmächtigen Gott*. Munich: Kösel Verlag, 1995.

Schilpp, Paul A., and Lewis E. Hahn, eds. *The Philosophy of Gabriel Marcel*. La Salle, IL: Open Court Press, 1984.

Schilpp, Paul A., and Maurice Friedman, eds. *The Philosophy of Martin Buber*. La Salle, IL: Open Court Press, 1967.

Schmidt, Burghart. *Ernst Bloch*. Stuttgart: Metzler, 1985.

———. *Ernst Blochs Wirkung: Ein Arbeitsbuch zum 90. Geburtstag*. Frankfurt: Suhrkamp Verlag, 1975.

———, ed. *Materialien zu Ernst Blochs Prinzip Hoffnung*. Frankfurt: Suhrkamp Verlag, 1978.

Scholem, Gershom G. *Major Trends in Jewish Mysticism*. New York: Schocken Books, 1961.

Schrader, George Alfred, Jr. *Existential Philosophers: Kierkegaard to Merleau-Ponty*. New York: McGraw-Hill, 1967.

Schulte, Christoph. "Jüdische Theodizee? Überlegungen zum Theodizee-Problem bei Immanuel Kant, Hermann Cohen und Max Weber." *Zeitschrift für Religions- und Geistesgeschichte* 49 (1997): 127–162.

Schulweis, Harold M. *Evil and the Morality of God*. Cincinnati: Hebrew Union College Press, 1984.

Schüssler-Fiorenza, Elizabeth, and David Tracy, eds. *The Holocaust as Interruption*. Edinburgh: T. and T. Clark, 1984.

Schuster, Ekkehard. *Hope against Hope: Johann Baptist Metz and Elie Wiesel Speak out on the Holocaust*. Translated by J. Matthew Ashley. New York: Paulist Press, 1999.

Scott, Nathan A., Jr. *The Unquiet Vision: Mirrors of Man in Existentialism*. New York: World Publishing Co., 1969.

Sheldon, Mark. "Job, Human Suffering and Knowledge: Some Contemporary Jewish Perspectives." *Encounter* 41 (Summer 1980): 229–235.

Signer, Michael A. *Humanity at the Limit: The Impact of the Holocaust Experience on Jews and Christians.* Bloomington: Indiana University Press, 2000.

Silberstein, Laurence J. *Martin Buber's Social and Religious Thought: Alienation and the Quest for Meaning.* New York: New York University Press, 1989.

Slater, Christopher Peter R. L. "The Question of Evil in Marcel, Some Philosophical Analysts and Saint Augustine." Ph.D. dissertation, Harvard University, 1964.

Smith, Roy Steinhoff. "Mourning Becomes Existence: Martin Buber's Melancholy Ontology." *Journal of Religion* 69 (July 1989): 326–343.

Soelle, Dorothee. *Celebrating Resistance: The Way of the Cross in Latin America.* Translated by Joyce Irwin. London: Mowbray, 1993.

———. *On Earth as in Heaven: A Liberation Spirituality of Sharing.* Translated by Marc Batko. Louisville: Westminster/John Knox Press, 1993.

———. *Political Theology.* Translated by John Shelley. Philadelphia: Fortress Press, 1974.

———. *The Silent Cry: Mysticism and Resistance.* Translated by Barbara and Martin Rumscheidt. Minneapolis: Fortress Press, 2001.

———. *Suffering.* Translated by Everett R. Kalin. Minneapolis: Fortress Press, 1975.

———. *Thinking about God: An Introduction to Theology.* Translated by John Bowden. Philadelphia: Trinity Press International, 1990.

———. *The Window of Vulnerability: A Political Spirituality.* Translated by Linda M. Maloney. Minneapolis: Fortress Press, 1990.

Sonnemans, Heino. *Hoffnung ohne Gott?* Freiburg: Herder, 1973.

Sottiaux, Edgard. *Gabriel Marcel: Philosophe et Dramaturge.* Louvain: E. Nauwelaerts, 1956.

Spelman, Elizabeth V. *Fruits of Sorrow: Framing Our Attention to Suffering.* Boston: Beacon Press, 1997.

Steele, Michael R. *Christianity, Tragedy and Holocaust Literature.* Westport, CT: Greenwood Publishing, 1995.

Suchocki, Marjorie Hewitt. *The End of Evil: Process Eschatology in Historical Context.* Albany: State University of New York Press, 1988.

Surin, Kenneth. *Theology and the Problem of Evil.* Oxford: Basil Blackwell, 1986.

Susser, Bernard. *Existence and Utopia: The Social and Political Thought of Martin Buber.* London: Associated University Presses, 1981.

Tidemann, Rolf. "Historical Materialism or Political Messianism? An Interpretation of the Theses 'On the Concept of History.'" *Telos* 15 (Fall–Winter 1983–1984): 71–104.

Tilley, Terrence W. *The Evils of Theodicy.* Washington, DC: Georgetown University Press, 1991.

———. *Postmodern Theologies: The Challenge of Religious Diversity.* Maryknoll, NY: Orbis Books, 1995.

———. *Story Theology.* Wilmington: Michael Glazier, 1985.

Tracy, David, and Hermann Häring, eds. *The Fascination of Evil.* Maryknoll, NY: Orbis Books, 1998.

Troisfontaines, Roger. *De L'Existence à L'Être: La Philosophie de Gabriel Marcel.* Louvain: Nauwelaerts, 1953.

Tucker, Robert C. *The Marx-Engels Reader.* Second Edition. New York: W. W. Norton and Co., 1978.

Unseld, Sigrid. *Ernst Bloch zu ehren*. Frankfurt: Suhrkamp Verlag, 1968.

van Ewijk, Thomas J.M. *Gabriel Marcel: An Introduction*. Translated by Matthew J. van Velzen. New York: Paulist Press, 1965.

Warnock, Mary. *Existentialism*. Oxford: Oxford University Press, 1970.

Waschenfelder, Jacob L.C. "J. B. Metz's Critique of Religious Apathy" Ph.D. dissertation, McMaster University, 1989.

Weil, Simone. "The Love of God and Affliction." In *Waiting for God*, translated by Emma Craufurd. New York: Harper and Row, 1951.

Weinandy, Thomas G. *Does God Suffer?* Notre Dame: University of Notre Dame Press, 2000.

Welch, Sharon D. *Communities of Resistance and Solidarity: A Feminist Theology of Liberation*. Maryknoll, NY: Orbis Books, 1985.

———. *A Feminist Ethic of Risk*. Minneapolis: Fortress Press, 1990.

———. *Sweet Dreams in America: Making Ethics and Spirituality Work*. New York: Routledge, 1999.

West, Thomas H. *Ultimate Hope Without God: The Atheistic Eschatology of Ernst Bloch*. New York: Peter Lang, 1991.

Widmer, Charles. *Gabriel Marcel et le Théisme Existential*. Paris: Les Éditions du Cerf, 1971.

Widmer, Peter. *Die Anthropologie Ernst Blochs*. Frankfurt: Akademische Verlagsgesellschaft, 1974.

Wiegmann, Hermann. *Ernst Blochs ästhetische Kriterien und ihre interpretative Funktion in seinen Literarischen Aufsätzen*. Bonn: Bouvier Verlag, 1976.

Wiesel, Elie. *All Rivers Run to the Sea: Memoirs*. Translated by Jon Rothschild. New York: Knopf, 1995.

———. *A Jew Today*. Translated by Marion Wiesel. New York: Random House, 1978.

———. *Night*. Translated by Stella Rodway. New York: Bantam Books, 1960.

Williams, Delores S. *Sisters in the Wilderness: The Challenge of Womanist God-Talk*. Maryknoll, NY: Orbis Books, 1996.

Wolin, Richard. *Walter Benjamin: An Aesthetic of Redemption*. New York: Columbia University Press, 1982.

Wolterstorff, Nicholas. *Lament for a Son*. Grand Rapids: Eerdmans, 1987.

Wood, Allen W. *Kant's Rational Theology*. Ithaca: Cornell University Press, 1978.

Wood, Robert E. *Martin Buber's Ontology*. Evanston: Northwestern University Press, 1969.

Wyschogrod, Edith. *Spirit in Ashes: Hegel, Heidegger and Man-Made Mass Death*. New Haven: Yale University Press, 1985.

Zudeick, Peter. *Die Welt als Wirklichkeit und Möglichkeit*. Bonn: Bouvier Verlag, 1980.

Index

Abraham, 46, 119

acceptance: Buber on, 52, 54; Marcel on, 35; Metz on, 95; Moltmann on, 76; and resistance, 97, 129

Adams, Marilyn McCord, 4, 136, 139

Adorno, Theodor W., 61, 64, 80, 82, 91–92, 103, 160n. 30, 163n. 3, 165n. 22

African-American experience (*see also* spirituals, African-American; theology: womanist), 2, 92, 108, 115, 116–117, 142, 168n. 24

agency, moral, 112, 115, 116, 118, 125, 133

Anselm, Saint, 3

anti-Semitism, 8, 10

apathy, 85, 87, 103, 127

apocalyptic interruption, 85, 87, 90–92

Aquinas, Thomas, 3

atheism, 70, 104

Augustine, Saint, 3, 140

Auschwitz, 1, 9, 10, 32, 37, 51, 53, 79, 82–83, 87–88, 120, 121, 133, 137, 140

Baal Shem, 49

being (*see also* philosophy of existence): as opposite of having, 25

belief: as opposite of trust, 42

Benjamin, Walter, 61, 80, 82, 86, 91–93, 103, 109, 164n. 12, 167n. 5

Berger, Peter, 11, 147n. 25

Bible. *See* Scripture

Bloch, Ernst, 7, 21, 82, 86, 92, 103, 108, 133–134; atheistic faith, 70; and Buber, 8; and Christian theology, 65, 75–76,

81–82, 108; and existentialist thought, 70–71; and German Romanticism, 68; and Hegel, 66–67, 70; Holocaust, 66; hope, philosophy of, 70–76, 124; Job, 72–73; Kingdom of God, 74–75; leap, utopian, 69; and liberation theology, 73–74; and Marcel, 152n. 19, 161n. 4; as Marxist, warm stream, 65, 68; and Metz, 81–82; as middle-class, 118; and Moltmann, 75–76, 79–80; Moses, 71–72; political faith, 70–71, 75; praxis, 70; solidarity, 113; theodicy objections of, 65–67; *Ultimum*, 69, 72, 75

bourgeois subject: Marx, 57; Metz, 83, 84, 87, 164n. 8; Welch, 111

bourgeois thought: existentialist, 98–99, 102, 124, 133–134; middle-class, 83, 105, 114

Buber, Martin, 7, 21, 108; and Bloch, 8, 70, 72, 74; as bourgeois, 98–99; eclipse of God, 51–53; as existentialist, 39, 48, 54; God-language of, 42–46; and Hasidism, 39, 42, 45–49; Holocaust response, 53–54; I-It, 40–42; I-Thou, 40–42, 99, 105–107; Jewishness of, 8, 153n. 1; and Job, 49–51; and Kant, 40, 43–44, 157n. 40; and Marcel, 39, 47, 52, 54, 99–101; and Metz, 81, 83, 95, 141; mysticism, 44, 49, 50; narrative, 46–47, 156n. 27; prayer, 48, 54, 123; revelation, 8, 43, 45; Scripture, 44–47, 50–52; sin, 48, 153n. 3; socialism of, 41, 102, 154n. 12; theodicy objections of, 42–46, 48, 156n. 26, 157n. 39

Bultmann, Rudolph, 24, 39, 74, 86, 155n. 17, 162n. 11

189

16007216R00116

Printed in Great Britain
by Amazon